外国语言学及应用语言学研究丛书

本书获中央高校基本科研业务费专项资金资助（E1E41702X2）

Conceptual Variations of Chinese Break Verbs:
A Diachronic Semantic Perspective

汉语"破"类动词的概念变异：

历时语义学视角

杜 静 著

ZHEJIANG UNIVERSITY PRESS
浙江大学出版社
·杭州·

图书在版编目 (CIP) 数据

汉语"破"类动词的概念变异：历时语义学视角：
英文 / 杜静著. — 杭州：浙江大学出版社，2022.6
ISBN 978-7-308-22630-1

Ⅰ. ①汉… Ⅱ. ①杜… Ⅲ. ①现代汉语—动词—研究
—英文 Ⅳ. ①H146.2

中国版本图书馆CIP数据核字（2022）第083563号

汉语"破"类动词的概念变异：历时语义学视角
杜　静　著

策　　划	包灵灵
责任编辑	田　慧
责任校对	徐　旸
封面设计	项梦怡
出版发行	浙江大学出版社
	（杭州市天目山路 148 号　邮政编码 310007）
	（网址:http:// www. zjupress. com）
排　　版	杭州朝曦图文设计有限公司
印　　刷	广东虎彩云印刷有限公司绍兴分公司
开　　本	710mm×1000mm　1/16
印　　张	19.25
字　　数	410 千
版 印 次	2022 年 6 月第 1 版　2022 年 6 月第 1 次印刷
书　　号	ISBN 978-7-308-22630-1
定　　价	68.00 元

前　言

　　本书以历时原型语义学为研究框架,探索汉语"破"类动词的历时概念变异。

　　历时原型语义学整合了原型理论、历时语义学以及词汇范畴化,基于原型概念结构,从外延和内涵两个层面探讨词汇的历时概念变异。"破"类动词属于表征分离状态变化事件,即物体由完整状态进入不完整状态的词汇范畴。既往研究基于不同理论视角从共时层面论述了"破"类动词的句法和概念结构,但是对该类动词的概念边界仍存在争议。基于历时原型语义学,本书将"破"类动词的概念结构研究由共时层面扩展到历时层面,由句法层面扩展到多维概念层面,旨在揭示这一词汇范畴的概念变异路径及深层认知机制。

　　本书力图回答以下研究问题:(1)汉语动词"破"的外延所指呈现何种历时概念变异路径? 受到什么认知机制的驱动? (2)汉语动词"破""切"和"开"的概念边界呈现何种历时概念变异路径? 受到什么认知机制的驱动? (3)汉语动词"破"的内涵语义呈现何种概念变异路径? 受到什么认知机制的驱动?

　　为回答上述研究问题,本书基于CCL(Center for Chinese Linguistics PKU)语料库,采用多维变量统计方法分别探讨了动词"破"的外延所指历时变异,"破""切"和"开"的概念边界变异以及"破"的内涵语义历时变异,最终尝试性构建了多维变量模型。

　　第四章(案例研究一)考察了动词"破"在四个汉语历史时期(早期中古汉语时期、近期中古汉语时期、早期普通话时期和现代普通话时期)的原型概念结构,主要发现如下:

（1）"破"的原型范畴成员并非一成不变，而呈现出"损坏性分离偏向"和"身体相关倾向"，即由不同物体的分离状态变化演变为身体部位损伤以及衣物破损等分离状态变化。"破"的边缘范畴成员在原型范畴成员的基础上灵活变化，新范畴成员不断被吸纳，旧范畴成员不断被剔除。

（2）"破"的所指范围呈现由外向内缩小的变异路径，由表征新功能性分离、消除障碍性分离和损坏性分离等多种分离状态变化事件演变为仅表征损坏性分离。

（3）"破"的所指范围变异主要受到深层概念化方式调整的驱动，表现为概念重组。"破"的所指范围由多重特征维度相互交织构成，由于特征维度值的重新调整，"破"所表征的分离状态变化事件的类型范围也逐渐缩小。另外，社会文化的发展变化也是驱动"破"外延所指变异的重要因素。随着新工具的发明以及技术的提高，只有粗糙性分离状变化事件概念化为"破"。

第五章（案例研究二）探索了"破""切"和"开"概念边界的变异，证明三个动词的概念边界变异受到概念重组机制的驱动。主要发现如下：

（1）古汉语时期（即早期中古汉语时期和近期中古汉语时期），"切"和"开"的所指范围被"破"的所指范围涵盖，"破"的外延所指与"切"和"开"部分重合。但是进入普通话时期（即早期普通话时期和现代普通话时期）后，三个动词的所指范围演变为并行的连续统分布趋势，与不同概念变量水平关联密切。

（2）就概念边界而言，古汉语时期这三个动词的概念边界相互重叠，同一分离状态变化事件可由不同的动词交替表征。普通话时期，这三个动词的概念边界更为明晰，它们分别用于表征不同的分离状态变化事件类型。

（3）究其原因，这三个动词的概念范围在概念重组机制的驱动下不断调整，对分离状态变化事件的概念化分工逐渐明确。"破"主要负责表征损坏性分离，"切"表征新功能性分离，而"开"则表征消除障碍性分离。

第六章（案例研究三）追溯了"破"的内涵语义变异，指出"破"处于语法化初期阶段。

（1）"破"的内涵语义由物理状态变化逐渐向关系状态变化、认知状态变化、所有状态变化、遵循状态变化、情感状态变化以及时间状态变化扩展。

（2）"破"的内涵语义并非凭空而生，而是对应于其外延所指。"破"的内涵语义共呈现三条历时概念变异路径，包括由新功能性分离演化为所有状态变化,由损坏性分离演化为情感和时间状态变化,以及由消除障碍性分离演化为认知状态变化。内涵语义既对应于外延所指,又相对独立于外延所指。

(3)"破"的语义变异主要受到隐喻以及转喻的驱动。在这两种认知机制的驱动下,"破"的语义核心逐渐图式化,由分离状态变化图式化为状态变化。但是"破"并没有完全语法化,而是尚处于语法化初期。

基于上述实证研究,本书修正了历时原型语义学,并尝试性构建了多维变量模型。概念原型在历时变异中也会发生相对演变,概念边界的动态变化呈现为同一概念场中不同词语间边界的变异。多维变量模型为双轨模型,整合了外延所指变异和内涵语义变异。

List of abbreviations

BA: dispositive marker, "把"

CL: classifier

Ctree: conditional inference tree

DE: possessive marker, "的"

DEIXIS: deixis like "这" (this), "那" (that)

DPS: diachronic prototype semantics

EMand: Early Mandarin

EMC: Early Middle Chinese

ES: endstate

FC: functional change

JIANG: causative marker, "将"

LE: perspective aspect marker, "了"

LCS: lexical conceptual structure

LMC: Late Middle Chinese

LOC: location

MC: material composition

MCA: multiple correspondence analysis

MdMand: Modern Mandarin

MDS: multidimensional scaling

SC: spatial configuration

ZHE: aspectual marker, "着"

ZHI: possessive marker, "之"

Contents

CHAPTER 3 Research methodology and design / 78

CHAPTER 1

Introduction

This introductory chapter first introduces the background and pinpoints the necessity for undertaking this research in section 1.1; then articulates the research objectives and research questions in section 1.2, and points out the research significance in section 1.3. Finally, section 1.4 outlines the organization of this book.

1.1 Research background

Break verbs, exemplified by English verbs like *break*, *snap* and *tear*, refer to actions that bring about complete or incomplete separation in the material integrity of entities, as exemplified in (1.1) (Guerssel et al. 1985; Hale and Keyser 1987; Levin 1993: 241-242; Pye 1996). Such breaking events, or alternatively termed as events of separation state change, are recorded to have been central to hominid cognition for more than 2.5 million years (Toth and Schick 1993: 349), thus they are generally identified as decipherer of human cognitive evolution, especially in disciplines like biological anthropology, socio-cultural anthropology, developmental psychology, archeology and primatology (Gibson and Ingold 1993). Consistent with this pursuit, break verbs, particularly the conceptual categorization of break verbs, have also evoked long and animate discussions in the field of linguistics.

(1.1)

a. She ***broke*** the window.

b. He ***snapped*** the stick.

c. The lady ***tore*** the cloth with her hands.

Straightforwardly speaking, the categorization of break verbs has been widely addressed from perspectives of generative semantics, developmental psycholinguistics as well as cognitive linguistics. But whatever perspectives have been taken, since breaking events are universally accessible to everyone and require no specialized knowledge (Majid et al. 2004), these studies are broadly motivated with an objective to examine whether the conceptual boundary of break verbs is equally universal. And in this regard, there remain controversial arguments.

To be specific, generative semantic studies (Fillmore 1967; Guerssel et al. 1985; Levin 1993; Levin and Rappaport Hovav 1995, 2008) probe into break verbs through their participation in causative alternation (e.g. breaktr - breakintr) [1] and propose that the identification of break verbs as a verb class is innate and universal. But even so, different generative semantic approaches have reached different conclusions on the boundary between break verbs and cut verbs. Generative derivational studies (Guerssel et al. 1985; Hale and Keyser 1987) tell break verbs apart from cut verbs based on their syntactic behaviors across typologically different languages. They find that break verbs but not cut verbs (*cut*, *slash*, *chop*, *grind*, *hit*, *shoot*, *strike*) participate in causative alternation, cut verbs but not break verbs appear in conative constructions. Both cut verbs and break verbs show up in middle constructions. Guerssel et al. (1985) argue that such syntactic difference reflects different lexical conceptual structures (LCSs). The basic structure of *break* is monadic while the basic structure of *cut* is dyadic. Different from this view, Hale and Keyser (1987) propose that the basic LCS of break verbs is composite and complex, consisting of an "event of causation" and

---

[1] Breaktr for transitive use of "break", breakintr for intransitive use of "break".

a "central event". Nonetheless, the basic LCS of cut verbs is only a simple "central event". In contrast to these binary divisions of break verbs and cut verbs, Levin and Rappaport Hovav (2008) and Rappaport Hovav and Levin (2010) support that both break verbs and cut verbs are subtypes of result verbs. And they hold that the basic LCSs of both break verbs and cut verbs are dyadic and causative. The reason why cut verbs do not allow causative alternation is they "require an animate intentional and volitional agent as subject". But this is not the case for break verbs. Such diverse arguments in generative semantics indicate that the seemingly clear-cut syntactic diagnostic is far from uncontroversial to locate the boundary of break verbs.

Developmental psycholinguistic studies (Shaefer 1979, 1980; Pye et al. 1995; Bowerman et al. 2004; Bowerman 2005, 2012), with evidence from children's first language acquisition of break verbs, prove that the conceptual boundaries between break verbs, cut verbs, and open verbs are not sharp but indiscrete, language-specific and determined by multiple conceptual variables in a matrix-like combination. Different conceptual variables assume different weights in accounting for the conceptual boundary between break verbs and other verb classes. Since young children have not mastered the weight combination among different conceptual variables, they have difficulty in correctly categorizing breaking events, cutting events, and opening events. Pye et al. (1995) further demonstrate that linguistic specificity is also an important factor that influences semantic categorization. Children's overextension in event categorization displays language-specific patterns. This indicates that specific linguistic input rather than nonlinguistic cognition influences semantic categorization (Bowerman and Choir 2001, 2003). Generally speaking, developmental psycholinguistic studies have pointed out the importance of variable combination and linguistic specificity in determining verb and event categorization. But they fail to show the specific internal structure and the specific weight hierarchy demonstrated by different conceptual variables in differentiating break verbs from other verb classes.

Cognitive linguistic studies are characterized by their attention to languages of diverse typologies and cultural backgrounds. They address the conceptual boundary of break verbs through cross-linguistic comparison and aim to arrive at universal patterns or typological distributions. Such cognitive typological studies include cognitive extensionalist studies (Majid et al. 2007a), natural semantic metalanguage (NSM) studies (Goddard and Wierzbicka 2009), Frame Semantic studies (Fujii et al. 2013a) as well as Causal Chain studies (Croft 2015). Cognitive extensionalist studies (Majid et al. 2007a, 2007b; Enfield 2007; Essegbey 2007; Narasimhan 2007) compare event categorizations by utilizing elicitation tools of video clips. Based on event descriptions produced by participants speaking diverse languages, these studies try to explore typological universals in the linguistic categorization of these events of separation state change and meanwhile try to reveal the underlying dimensions that motivate such typological universals. Majid et al. (2007a) build an MCA (multiple correspondence analysis) plot based on a dataset of 28 languages and reveal that three conceptual variables (predictability of locus of separation, rigidity, and spatial configuration) are accountable for demarcating breaking events from other event types. But despite such universal distributions, they also show that there are always exceptions in event categorization in languages like Yélî Dnye, Sranan, and Mandarin (Chen 2007; Levinson 2007).

NSM studies (Wierzbicka 1996, 2006; Goddard and Wierzbicka 1994, 2002, 2009; Goddard 1998, 2005; Otomo and Torii 2005) approach the conceptual structure of lexical items by means of extended explanatory paraphrases. NSM argues against the view that the non-durative structure is basic (as in the case of Guerssel et al. 1985 and Levin and Rappaport Hovav 2008) and supports that imperfective structure is basic because imperfective denotes only the action in progress. In this way, break verbs and cut verbs are distinguished from each other because break verbs appear in perfective structures while cut verbs show up in imperfective structures. Frame Semantics treats lexical items in terms of the frames they evoke (Fillmore 1982, 1985; Fillmore and Atkins 1992). Those evoked frames demonstrate the variable combinations that differentiate break verbs from other verb classes. And the element profiled in the frame indicates a higher proportion of weight accorded to certain conceptual variables. Moreover, since Frame Semantics follows a gestalt principle, it puts forward more variables that cannot be neglected, like <functionality>[1], <intentionality> and <focus> etc. (Bouveret 2009; Bouveret and Sweetser 2009; Fujii et al. 2013b) But despite this, Frame Semantics remains an interpretative approach. It fails to uncover the weight assumed by different variables within a frame. Causal Chain studies (Croft 2009, 2012, 2015) address the categorization of break verbs by employing a three-dimensional event structure, which is composed of qualitative, aspectual, and causal dimensions. With such an event structure, they support the conclusion that cut verbs encode both manner and result (Goldberg 2010: 46-50; Beavers and Koontz-Garboden 2012) and state that cut verbs are akin to break verbs when they are particularly used to denote result.

In terms of Chinese break verbs, the majority of previous studies on break verbs are concerned with the transitivity of break verb *pò*. For instance, Li (1994) holds that *pò* is a pseudo autonomous verb. Jiang (1999) states that *pò* was originally a transitive verb. Wu (1999: 330) insists that *pò* was initially an autonomous verb. Wei (2000: 821) proves that *pò* can be used either as a causative verb or as a resultative verb. Xu (2005, 2006: 174) conducts a diachronic study and shows that *pò* has evolved from a monosyllabic transitive verb to an intransitive verbal complement as well as an adjective. In addition, a limited number of studies have investigated the categorization of break verbs based on causative alternation. For instance, Bohnemeyer (2007) insists that there are neither break verbs nor cut verbs in Mandarin because Mandarin verbs appear in compound forms and do not allow causative alternation. In contrast, Chen (2007) states that Mandarin does not support the binary division of break and cut verbs but supports a three-way division of break verbs, cut verbs, and resultative compounds. To conclude, previous studies have paid much attention to the syntactic structure of Chinese break verbs, but little attention has been

---

[1] In this study, angel brackets (< >) are used to mark conceptual variables, while *italics* are used for variable levels.

shifted to the conceptual variation of Chinese break verbs. In view of this, it is necessary to further explore Chinese break verbs, particularly from a perspective of conceptual variation.

Above all, break verbs have aroused a wide range of discussion and have been examined from a great number of theoretical perspectives. But even so, some problems remain unresolved.

First of all, previous studies address the linguistic categorization of break verbs primarily based on the causative alternation structures where they appear and the conceptual variables relevant to the events of separation state change they represent. But the syntactic variable of causative alternation gives rise to controversial arguments and the numerous conceptual variables are addressed in a piecemeal fashion. More importantly, historical corpora reveal that causative alternation was not a sensitive issue at all in ancient Chinese as it is claimed in Mandarin. In examples (1.2a–1.2c), *pò*, *qiē*, and *kāi* all appeared in causative structures in EMC. It is the evolving conceptual range of break verbs that remains a catching but underestimated question. Comparing examples (1.2a–1.2c) with examples (1.2d–1.2f), we can find these three verbs vary in their conceptual ranges. In this sense, there is a necessity to revisit the conceptual range of break verbs by giving up causative alternation and by taking into consideration those conceptual variables systematically through corpus-based multivariate methods.

(1.2)[①]

  a. EMCpoe34: 内白滑， 四**破**去之。

                  nèi báihuá,   sì pò qù zhī

                  inside white smooth, four break remove it

                  "The fruit is white and smooth inside. Break it into four parts and remove its seeds."

  b. EMCqie32: 猪肉一斤， 合煮令熟， 细**切**之。

---

① This book adopts a glossing form where the Chinese sentences are glossed with both Chinese spellings and word to word translations.

zhūròu yījīn,   hézhǔ   lìng shú,   xì qiè zhī

pork one-kilo, together-boil make cooked, fine cut it

"Take a kilo of pork, boil it cooked and cut it finely."

c. EMCkai23: 开匣得书，见公之功。

kāi guì dé shū, jiàn gōng zhī gōng

open case get book, see him DE contribution

"Opened the case, got the book and found his contribution."

d. MdMandpoe1153: 一个不小心，把手指划破了。

yī gè bùxiǎoxīn, bǎ shǒuzhǐ   huápò le

one-CL not careful, BA finger scratch-wound-LE

"Uncarefully, he scratched wound his finger."

e. MdMandqie79: 铁三爷拿起刀来……"唰"就切下一块肉来。

Tiě Sānyé náqǐ   dāo lái … "shuā" jiù qiēxià   yīkuài
ròu lái

Tie Sanye hold-up knife DEIXIS …'shua' and cut-down a

piece meat DEIXIS

"Tie Sanye held up the knife …and cut down a piece of
meat."

f. MdMandkai73: 等到了跟前一瞧，把虎儿小子的衣裳撕开了。

děng dào le gēnqián yī qiáo, bǎ Hǔér xiǎozi de yīshang

sīkāi le

wait reach LE front a look, BA Huer boy DE clothes tear-
open-LE

"When came closer, they found Huer's clothes was torn
apart."

Secondly, most previous studies attend to break verbs from a synchronic
perspective. Since synchronic data only constitute a snapshot of the history of
a language, this study decides to trace the diachronic evolution of break verbs.
Only with a diachronic track can we tell a full story of the conceptual boundary
variation of break verbs. As shown in example (1.2), although *qiē* behaved

exactly in the same way as *pò* did both syntactically and conceptually in ancient Chinese, they are claimed to be rather different in Mandarin [compare (1.2a) with (1.2b) and (1.2d) with (1.2e)].

Finally, it is the extensional reference of break verbs that has been emphasized while their intensional readings are seldom discussed. Thus, this study also diachronically traces the arising of the intensional readings of break verbs.

In view of these research gaps, this study intends to attend to the extensional and intensional usages of Chinese break verbs from both a diachronic and a multivariate conceptual perspective.

1.2 Research objectives and research questions

Given the above research gaps, we aspire to achieve the following research objectives:

Firstly, this study intends to verify that event categorization is dynamic and the lexical items utilized for event categorization are variant in their conceptual ranges. Specifically, lexical items keep adjusting themselves in their peripheral edge and their prototypical core in accordance with cognitive evolution and social-cultural development. Within-category conceptual fine-tuning leads first to conceptual variation and further to cross-category conceptual reorganization. Meanwhile, conceptual boundaries between semantically related lexical items are dynamically evolving through time. Such reorganization is reflected in the different segmentation patterns employed in the categorization of the same event categories across different chronological stages.

Secondly, through investigating the conceptual variation of break verbs from a diachronic perspective, this study aspires to establish a multivariate model of diachronic conceptual variation. For one thing, this model reflects the cognitive mechanisms that drive and contribute to conceptual variation. Further, it also displays the multiple pathways of conceptual variation. Most importantly, this model not only reveals the conceptual variation within the extensional domain, but also uncovers the conceptual variation across the extensional and intensional domains.

Finally, methodologically speaking, this study aims to make a bold attempt to employ multivariate statistical methods in a diachronic semantic investigation. Although corpus-based methods are increasingly employed in diachronic semantics, the feasibility of multivariate statistical methods like MCA, Ctree (Conditional Inference Tree), and random forest call for more attention, especially in diachronic studies of Chinese.

This study addresses the conceptual boundary of break verbs from a diachronic point view and a multivariate conceptual one. Our research target involves three break verbs, namely *pò, qiē* and *kāi*. It should be noted that these three verbs are explored in terms of their collocational context. It makes no sense to focus on a single verb without taking into consideration its context. These three verbs are dynamic in their syntactic forms. They were more frequently used in their monomorphemic forms in ancient Chinese but are more pervasively used in their compound or phrasal forms in Mandarin Chinese. Despite this, these three lexical items are consistent in their conceptual ranges all through the development of Chinese, though their syntactic forms have changed. Given this, we set their syntactic changes in this background, and focus on their conceptual variations. Since *pò, qiē,* and *kāi* behaved the same in ancient Chinese, we subsume them under the node break verbs for the time being and observe how they gradually diverge into different verb classes in Mandarin.

This study sets Chinese *pò, qiē,* and *kāi* as the research target for two reasons. For one thing, the categorization of their English counterparts *break, cut,* and *open* constitutes a controversial issue in previous studies. A Chinese story of these three lexical items will contribute to previous arguments on their categorization. For another, these three lexical items are all along frequently used to describe events of separation state change in the development of Chinese. This makes a diachronic Chinese story of these three lexical items possible. It should be noted that this does not mean Chinese *pò, qiē,* and *kāi* can be completely equalized with English *break*, *cut* and *open*. Historical corpora reveal that these three lexical items were used similarly as English *break*, *cut*, and *open* in ancient Chinese but have gradually changed in their syntactic patterns in the development of Mandarin Chinese (compare 1.2a and 1.2d, 1.2b and 1.2e, 1.2c and 1.2f). Although such a syntactic change is backgrounded in this study, it is not ignored in our analysis of conceptual variation. Although they have changed in their syntactic patterns, the conceptual ranges of their new syntactic forms are in line with those of their older syntactic forms. In this sense, it is still feasible to explore the diachronic variation of break verbs by targeting at *pò*, *qiē*, and *kāi*.

The specific research questions to be explored can be presented from two aspects. The first aspect focuses on the specific conceptual variation pathways displayed by break verbs. The second aspect delves into the cognitive mechanisms that drive and contribute to these conceptual variations. The corresponding research questions to be answered are as follows:

1) What diachronic conceptual variation pathways do Chinese break verbs display?
   a. What diachronic conceptual variation pathway is exhibited in the extensional reference of *pò*?
   b. What diachronic conceptual variation pathways are displayed in the conceptual boundaries between *pò*, *qiē*, and *kāi*?
   c. What diachronic conceptual variation pathways are exhibited in the intensional readings of *pò*?

2) What cognitive mechanisms motivate break verbs' diachronic conceptual variation?
   a. What cognitive mechanisms drive the referential range variation of *pò?*
   b. What cognitive mechanisms motivate the conceptual boundary adjustment of *pò*, *qiē*, and *kāi*?
   c. How did the multiple intensional readings of *pò* arise from its extensional references?

A number of theoretical frameworks have been put forward in cognitive linguistics to explore diachronic semantic change, including Invited Inference

Theory of Semantic Change (Traugott 1985, 1989; Traugott and Dasher 2002), Diachronic Prototype Semantics (DPS) (Geeraerts 1997) as well as theories of grammaticalization (Traugott 1982, 1988). This study gears toward DPS because this theoretical approach is essentially a usage-based approach and it argues for the prototypically-organized conceptual structures of lexical items. Moreover, DPS does not exclusively focus on extensional usages or intensional readings but integrates these two domains into a united whole. With this approach, this study tracks the semantic change of break verbs based on their usage variations recorded in historical corpora and represents their conceptual patterns in a prototypical conceptual structure. And in doing so, diachronic conceptual variation of break verbs is displayed through cross-stage prototypical structure comparison. Diachronic boundary variation among break verbs is concluded based on their segmentation of events of separation state change across different chronological stages. Meanwhile, not only literal usages of break verbs are analyzed in detail but also the semantic parallels between extensional usages and intensional readings are extensively mapped out.

To reach these ends, multivariate statistical methods, such as MCA, Ctree, as well as random forest, are employed to analyze the historical dataset of break verbs and their near-synonymous verb classes. Among these methods, MCA maps the conceptual structure of lexical items out in a prototypical structure, with a conceptual centroid and a conceptual boundary. The distribution of numerous individual usages reflects the conceptual ranges of lexical items. The distribution of differential variable levels indicates the underlying variables that drive the conceptual ranges of lexical items. Ctree and random forest demonstrate the weight hierarchy of different conceptual variables in a more fine-grained fashion.

1.3 Research significance

Given those unresolved problems in the synchronic investigation on break verbs, our proposed diachronic study is significant in the following four aspects.

First of all, since "diachrony within synchrony equals variation" (Geeraerts 1997: 6), a diachronic semantic study on conceptual variation will display the traces and principles of language and cognitive development. Although it might be uneasy to predict language's future developing trend, a closer look at the evolutionary trajectory of polysemous break verbs affords a key to understanding how the human mind continually adapts and extends its conceptual apparatus (Evans 2010). Moreover, the integration of synchronic and diachronic perspectives refutes Saussure's underestimation of the diachronic perspective. For Saussure, the relations between elements of a language are located in the consciousness of speakers. The psychological unreality of diachronic relations leads Saussure to assign historical phenomena to a totally different domain of investigation (Weinreich et al. 1968: 120). This study demonstrates that a diachronic investigation shows the psychological reality of conscious speakers across different time periods. A comparison of linguistic categories across historical stages reveals the cognitive development of a community on the one hand and indicates social-cultural advancement on the other hand.

Secondly, Mel'čuk (1981: 51) notes that "Not only every language, but every lexeme of a language, is an entire world in itself". In this sense, the significance of this diachronic study resides in its revelation of the world of Chinese verbs of separation like *pò, qiē*, and *kāi* across different historical stages. On the one hand, the diachronic trajectories of these verbs in their conceptual ranges are dated and visualized in terms of their prototypical conceptual structures. On the other hand, the interaction among these verbs is explored and how their conceptual boundaries vary diachronically is reported. Such diachronic conceptual variation demonstrates that human categorization of their external experience of separation is not invariant but dynamic.

Thirdly, theoretically, a lack of theoretical innovation and theoretical application characterizes the research status quo of diachronic studies, particularly in Chinese (Wu 2015). The empirical employment of DPS in Chinese break verbs introduces an applicable and analytical theoretical framework for future diachronic studies. Specifically speaking, DPS affords a prototype-based analysis of the conceptual structure of lexical items. Lexical items are not simply summarized in terms of their extensional and intensional readings but structurally analyzed in terms of their prototypical and peripheral usages as well as their prototypical and peripheral readings. In addition, DPS offers an interpretive apparatus for explaining diachronic conceptual variation. Two extensional hypotheses and two intensional ones have been put forward to explain and predict conceptual variation. Two characterizing features of prototypical structure evolution, namely structural stability and flexible adaptability, are also brought forth.

Finally, this study brings together diachronic semantics, cognitive linguistics, corpus-based methods as well as empirical methods like MCA and Ctree. In this sense, it is not only significant in providing empirical evidence for diachronic variation but also significant in contributing quantitative methods to the diachronic semantic investigation. It is not expected that this bold attempt will completely change the research status quo of example enumeration in diachronic studies. But it is expected that statistical methods and linguistic evidence will play an increasingly important role in demonstrating language change and predicting language development.

1.4 Structure of the book

This book is structured into seven chapters altogether.

Chapter 1 introduces the research background, research gaps, research methodology, research objectives, and research questions, defines some important terms, and concludes the research significance.

Chapter 2 is a literature review of previous studies on break verbs. These previous studies are reviewed from perspectives of classical linguistics, generative semantics, developmental psycholinguistics as well as cognitive linguistics. Classical linguistics refers to minimal pair comparisons conducted by Jespersen, Fillmore, and some Chinese linguists. Generative semantic studies include Guerssel et al.'s generative derivational studies, Jackendoff's generative decompositional studies as well as Levin's generative decomposition studies. Developmental psycholinguistic studies are captured based on adult-child variations in the categorization of break verbs and cross-linguistic variations in children's categorization of break verbs. Cognitive linguistic studies are reviewed in terms of theoretical approaches, including cognitive semantic extensionalist studies, NSM studies, Frame Semantic studies, Causal Chain studies as well as Talmy's cognitive semantic study. In addition, a limited number of diachronic syntactic and constructional studies on break verbs and diachronic linguistic studies on other lexical items are also reviewed.

Chapter 3 introduces the research methodology adopted in this book, including both the theoretical framework and the statistical methods. The theoretical framework is DPS. As mentioned, this approach accounts for lexical conceptual structure in terms of a prototypical structure. Two extensional and two intensional hypotheses are put forward under this framework. With regard to statistical methods, compatible with DPS, the MCA is made use of to map out prototypical structures. Ctree and random forest are utilized to uncover the weight assumed by different conceptual variables.

Chapter 4 attends to diachronic conceptual variation of extensional *pò* and answers research questions (1a) and (2a). In this chapter, the extensional usages of *pò* across four historical stages are collected and coded. Both the frequency measure and association measure are employed to plot the prototypical structure of extensional *pò*. It is found that extensional *pò* is undergoing a specialization trajectory. Its prototypical core gradually narrows down from denoting all kinds of separation to only denoting disruptive separation. Its peripheral members appear and disappear flexibly and thus its extensional range expands and narrows all through its development.

Chapter 5 addresses the conceptual boundary variation of extensional *pò*, *qiē*, and *kāi* and answers research questions (1b) and (2b). Extensional usages of *pò*, *qiē*, and *kāi* are mapped into prototypically-organized conceptual structures with the statistical method of MCA. By comparing their conceptual structures across four historical stages, it is found that their conceptual boundaries vary as their conceptual ranges fluctuate. From ancient Chinese to Mandarin Chinese, the conceptual boundaries among these three verb classes have changed from conceptual overlapping to conceptual discreteness. As for the reason, segmentation and categorization of events of separation state change are reorganized both at the variable level and the structural level. The variable level reorganization shows value adjustment and the structural level reorganization demonstrates prototypical range adjustment.

Chapter 6 explores the diachronic conceptual variation of intensional *pò* and answers research questions (1c) and (2c). Apart from the intensional reading of physical object separation, another fifteen intensional readings across six domains are captured, including relational, cognitive, possessive, observance, emotional, and temporal domains. On the one hand, it is concluded that intensional readings emanate from extensional usages. We can always find extensional sources of intensional readings. Altogether three diachronic lineages of the conceptual development of *pò* are revealed. On the other hand, intensional readings may also be further semantic extensions from those intensional readings that already exist. With the evolution of intensional readings, intensional *pò* becomes increasingly impoverished in its semantic content.

Chapter 7 concludes this book by first summarizing the research findings from perspectives of diachronic conceptual variation pathways, the motivating cognitive mechanisms as well as the proposed revisions of DPS. Then a tentative multivariate model of diachronic conceptual variation is put forward. It is a twin-track model integrating both extensional and intensional levels. The extensional range of lexical items is mapped out in a prototypical structure. In addition, implications, limitations as well as directions for future studies are also pointed out.

CHAPTER 2

Literature review

This chapter reviews what previous linguistic studies have done in categorizing break verbs. Section 2.1 elaborates how classical linguistics makes use of grammatical minimal pairs in differentiating break verbs from other verb classes. Section 2.2 reveals how generative semantic studies argue for the categorization of break verbs based on causative alternation. Section 2.3 summarizes how developmental psycholinguistics utilizes children's language acquisition as evidence to prove that knowledge of break verbs is not universal. Section 2.4 accounts for how five cognitive approaches argue for the identification of break verbs, including cognitive extensionalist studies, NSM, Frame Semantics, Causal Chain as well as Talmy's Macro-event. Section 2.5 elaborates the limited number of diachronic syntactic and constructional studies on break verbs. Section 2.6 reviews diachronic Chinese linguistic studies on lexical semantic change. Section 2.7 concludes these previous studies and points out the necessity for a diachronic study on conceptual variation.

2.1 Break verbs in classical linguistics

Classical linguistics places heavy emphasis on break verbs' syntactic function. In English, break verbs are pervasively identified as a subtype of change of state verbs. Their participation in both inchoative (e.g. *The vase* *broke.*) and causative constructions (e.g. *She broke the vase.*) and their illicitness in conative constructions (e.g. **She broke at the vase.*) have been central concerns in English classical linguistics (Jespersen 1928 [1927]; Fillmore 1967). For instance, Jespersen (1928 [1927]: 332-333) might be one of the first few linguists who have noticed that "move and change" verbs involve two meanings: "(1) to produce a change or movement in something; (2) to perform the same movement or undergo the same change". But he doesn't go any further to explore the relationship between these two variant readings. Fillmore (1967) compares the syntactic behaviors of break verbs and hit verbs and attributes break verbs' constructional bias toward causative alternations to the fact that they are a particular type of change of state verbs. Different from the English tradition, Chinese grammarians (Jiang 1999; Wu 1999; Sun 1999) show more interest in break verbs' transition from predicate verbs (e.g. 伯牙破琴。 *Boya broke the lute.*) to subordinate complements in resultative compounds (e.g. 他打破鼓。 *He hit-break the drum.*). There are controversial arguments concerning the original transitivity of break verbs. For instance, Li (1994) classifies *pò* as a pseudo autonomous verb. Jiang (1999), citing evidence from *Records of Historian*(《史记》), insists that break verbs are initially attested to be transitive in Early Middle Chinese (200BC-AD600) but later develops to be intransitive. On the contrary, Wu (1999: 330) keeps a systematic record of how *pò* changes from intransitive to transitive and later to intransitive again.

In later studies, causative alternation stands out as an important criterion in demarcating break verbs from other verb classes, particularly in generative studies.

2.2 Generative studies on break verbs

In generative semantics, verbs with flexible ways of argument realization are called "variable behavior verbs" (Borer 1994). Verbs' syntactic behavior is a typical diagnostic variable that generative semantic studies make use of in their categorization of verb classes. These studies usually probe into verb classes by way of interpreting the correlation between verb meanings and the syntactic structures where the verb can appear (Levin and Pinker 1991). In terms of break verbs, generative studies resort to causative alternations and take advantage of this syntactic behavior as a key to distinguishing break verbs from other verb classes. As exemplified in (2.1), *break* can be used either transitively or intransitively. In the causative construction, *break* denotes how the agent causes the breaking of an affected object. In the inchoative construction, *break* describes the autonomous breaking of an affected object. These alternating ways of argument realization displayed by verbs like *break* are called "causative alternation"[①] (Yang 2015).

(2.1)

a. Janet **broke** the cup.

b. The cup **broke**.

But despite this common categorization criterion, different generative semantic approaches are divergent on the specific verb classes they intend to distinguish break verbs from as well as the specific predicate decomposition patterns (distinctive LCS patterns) they adopt to represent break verbs' semantic structure (Jackendoff 1990; Levin and Rappaport Hovav 1995).

2.2.1 Generative derivational studies on break verbs

Guerssel et al. (1985) tell break verbs (*break, shatter, crumble, open, close*) apart from cut verbs (*cut, slash, chop, grind, hit, shoot, strike*) based on their syntactic behaviors across four typologically diverse languages, including English, Berber, Warlpiri, and Winnebago. Their insightful finding is that break verbs but not cut verbs participate in causative/inchoative alternations [(2.1) and

---

① Break in (2.1a) is termed "causative verb" while in (2.1b) is termed "inchoative verb" or "anticausative verb", thus causative alternation is also alternatively termed "inchoative alternation" or "anticausative alternation" (Levin and Rappaport Hovav 1995).

(2.2)]. Cut verbs but not break verbs appear in conative constructions (2.3). Both of the two verb classes show up in middle constructions (2.4).

(2.2)
a. Margaret *cut* the bread.
b. *The bread *cut*.

(2.3)
a. *Janet *broke* at the vase.
b. Margaret *cut* at the bread.

(2.4)
a. The vase *breaks* easily.
b. The bread *cuts* easily.

In their account for the divergence between the two verb classes, Guerssel et al. (1985) claim that different syntactic behaviors reflect the differences in the underlying LCS. As shown in example (2.5), they argue that the basic LCS of *break* is monadic while that of *cut* is dyadic. Since break verbs are basically monadic, they allow the addition of an AGENT argument to derive a causative counterpart, but this is not the case for cut verbs. Cut verbs appear in conative constructions because conative constructions only occur with verbs whose LCS includes both the "EFFECT" clause and the "CONTACT" clause. Both verb classes participate in middle constructions, because their LCSs denote an action involving an agent, thus they satisfy the condition of middle constructions. As Hale and Keyser (1987) have noted, both break verbs and cut verbs (but not verbs like *see, consider, hit* and *believe*) appear in middle constructions, because cut verbs and break verbs (in their derived causative structure) both denote an event in which some entity causes another entity to undergo change [as represented in (2.6)].

(2.5)

a. cut LCS: x produce CUT on y, by sharp edge coming into contact
with y

b. break LCS: x cause (y come to be BROKEN)

(2.6)

[x cause [y, "undergo change"], by (…)]

Hale and Keyser (1987) further Guerssel et al.'s (1985) derivational proposal through analyzing the event structure involved in the LCS of break verbs and cut verbs. They state that break verbs' participation in causative alternations amounts to direct evidence that their LCS is composite or complex. This complex LCS consists of an "event of causation" and a "central event". As represented in (2.7a), the "event of causation" refers to the "actor" or "agent" (x) that does something and causes some effect. The "central event" refers to the "theme" (y) that undergoes a change of some sort. In this sense, the causative construction of break verbs corresponds to the complex event and their inchoative construction represents the central event. Although implicitly stated, Hale and Keyser (1987) explain that cut verbs do not appear in inchoative constructions because the central events in the LCS of cut verbs cannot be realized "autonomously", i.e., without the participation of an external agent (2.7b). But since the complex events of break verbs and cut verbs are analogous, they both appear in causative constructions and middle constructions.

(2.7)

a. LCS of "break"

[x cause [y, rigid or taut entity, develop separation in material integrity], (by …)]

b. LCS of "cut"

[x cause [y, develop linear separation in material integrity], by sharp edge coming into contact with the latter]

Divergent from the above argument, Levin and Rappaport Hovav (1995: 102-103) reveal that break verbs and cut verbs are subsets of externally caused change of state verbs, which constitute the prototypical verb class that participates in causative constructions. Furthermore, departing from Guerssel et al. (1985) and Hale and Keyser's (1987) holding that the basic LCS of break verbs is monadic, Levin and Rappaport Hovav (1995: 94) and Rappaport Hovav and Levin (2005) argue that externally caused change of state verbs, including break verbs and cut verbs, are basically dyadic and causative. All externally caused change of state verbs have transitive causative uses, but not all have intransitive uses[①]. The reason why cut verbs do not alternate is that such verbs "require an animate intentional and volitional agent as subject" (2.8a). But in the case of break verbs, the change can occur without the intervention of a volitional agent (2.8b). Thus, the inchoative variant of *break* can be derived from its causative variant. In other words, verbs' syntactic structures are actually determined by their LCS. Since cut verbs and break verbs display the same LCS, they are identified as belonging to the same verb class. Although this categorization has not been empirically substantiated, some studies prove the effectiveness of LCS. For instance, Mckoon and Love (2011) propose that break verbs are more complex than hit verbs in terms of LCS and successfully verify this hypothesis through three time-measurement experiments.

(2.8)

a. [[x ACT <*MANNER*>] CAUSE [y BECOME *STATE*]]

b. [x CAUSE [BECOME [y <*STATE*>]]]

In addition, consistent with Hale and Keyser (1987), Rappaport Hovav and Levin (2001) propose that externally caused change of state verbs, like *break*, *cut*, *open*, *melt*, are associated with complex event structures. But different

---

① The intransitive uses have the same LCS as the transitive uses, though the causer is lexically bound and receives no direct syntactic expression (Levin and Rappaport Hovav 1995: 108; Rappaport Hovav and Levin 1998: 117-118).

from Hale and Keyser (1987), they hold that the complex structure is the basic structure and underlies the flexible syntactic behaviors of externally caused change of state verbs. The complex event structure is composed of a causing subevent and a result subevent. Both the causative uses and intransitive uses of externally caused change of state verbs have this complex event structure. In their causative uses, externally caused change of state verbs display a complex event structure, but in their intransitive uses, only the result event is represented. This is because the causing event is lexically bound in the mapping from event structure to the argument realization (2.9). Meanwhile, it should be noted that the lexical binding does not apply to *cut* because the execution of cutting requires an external causer.

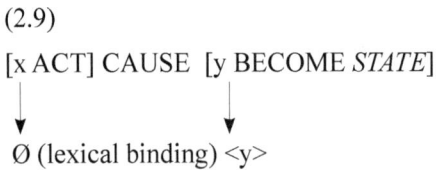

(2.9)

[x ACT] CAUSE [y BECOME *STATE*]

Ø (lexical binding) <y>

2.2.2 Jackendoff's generative decompositional study on break verbs

Apart from the above categorization of break verbs as change of state verbs based on causative alternations, some studies (Hale and Keyser 1987; Jackendoff 1990: 121) also further specify that break verbs denote a separation or decomposition in the material integrity of a certain entity. For instance, Hale and Keyser (1987: 8), in differentiating break verbs from cut verbs, implicitly point out that both of the two verb classes denote the separation in material integrity. As shown in the LCSs of *break* and *cut* in (2.7a) and (2.7b), the intricate difference is that cut verbs indicate the specific activities performed by the agent but break verbs encode pure integrity separation. Along a different research path, Jackendoff (1990: 121) also argues for the categorization of break verbs as a subclass of decomposition verbs. Although both composition verbs and decomposition verbs participate in resultative constructions, they are distinct in terms of LCS. As exemplified in (2.10), although both *build* and *assemble* are composition verbs, they are distinct from break verbs in different ways. *Build* differs from *break* in its Path-function (FROM vs. TO) whereas *assemble* and *break* are opposite in their composition encoding (comp+ vs. comp–). That is, verbs of composition and decomposition are distinguished from each other. The prepositions *out of* and *into* correspond to Path-function FROM and TO [compare (2.10a) with (2.10b) and (2.10c)]. The composition encoding further clarifies the mapping of whole and parts to thematic relations. Verbs of composition with Goal-expression have the parts as the theme and are therefore comp– (2.10b). On the contrary, verbs of decomposition with Goal-expression have the whole complete unit as the theme and are therefore comp+ (2.10c).

(2.10)

a. Sam ***built*** the house out of bricks.

　　[CAUSE ([SAM], GO$_{comp+}$[1] ([HOUSE], [FROM [BRICKS]])])]

b. Sam ***assembled*** the bricks into a house.

　　[CAUSE ([SAM], GO$_{comp-}$ ([BRICKS], [TO [HOUSE]])])]

c. Sam ***broke*** the bowl into pieces.

　　[CAUSE([SAM], [GO$_{comp+}$([BOWL], [TO[PIECES]])])]

2.2.3 Levin's generative decompositional study on break verbs

Drawing insights from prior discussions, Levin (1993: 29-30) conducts a closer inspection on the syntactic behavior of hit verbs, touch verbs, cut verbs, and break verbs. Along the line of Hale and Keyser (1987), she proposes that syntactic patterns are sensitive to particular components of verb meanings. In other words, verbs' syntactic behavior is attributable to their meaning components. To be specific, all the four verb classes are transitive and thus show up in causative constructions (2.11). But among them *hit, touch* and *cut*

---

[1] "comp+" stands for WHOLE as the theme, PART as the reference point while "comp-" represents the reverse (Jackendoff 1990: 121).

encode *CONTACT*, thus also appearing in ascension constructions (2.12)[①]. Furthermore, both *hit* and *cut* encode *MOTION* and *CONTACT*, thus they participate in conative constructions (2.13). On the other hand, both *cut* and *break* involve the meaning component *CHANGE OF STATE*, thus both allowing middle constructions (2.14). Finally, break verbs encode *PURE CHANGE OF STATE*, thus they are the only verb class appearing in inchoative constructions [example (2.11)]. That is to say, through isolating verbs' grammatically relevant components, it is possible to predict these verbs' syntactic behaviors. This assumed prediction operation is termed "the grammatically relevant semantic subsystem hypothesis" (Pinker 1989; Mohanan and Wee 1999). More significantly, some neuropsychological studies have already verified that grammatically relevant and irrelevant meaning components have "at least partially distinct neural substrates" (Kemmerer 2003).

(2.11)

a. Margaret *cut* the bread. b. Janet *broke* the vase.

c. Terry *touched* the cat.   d. Carla *hit* the door.

(2.12)

a. Margaret *cut* Bill on the arm. b. *Janet *broke* Bill on the finger.

c. Terry *touched* Bill on the shoulder. d. Carla *hit* Bill on the back.

(2.13)

a. Margaret *cut* at the bread. b. * Janet *broke* at the vase.

c. *Terry *touched* at the cat.   d. Carla *hit* at the door.

(2.14)

a. The bread *cuts* easily. b. Crystal vase *break* easily.

---

① The interaction between the semantic component of *contact* and the ascension construction is later verified in neurological studies (Kemmerer 2003).

c. * Cats *touch* easily. d. * Door frames *hit* easily.

Based on Levin and Rappaport Hovav's (1995) identification of *cut* and *break* as externally change of state verbs, Levin and Rappaport Hovav (2008) and Rappaport Hovav and Levin (2010) further propose that *cut* is a prototypical type of result verbs, the same as break verbs. More straightforwardly, same as *break*, *cut* prototypically denotes the separation involved in material integrity. In order to demonstrate why *cut* should be categorized the same as *break*, Levin and Rappaport Hovav (2008) first clarify why *cut* constitutes a special case and then put forward evidence to elucidate that *cut* is basically or prototypically a result verb, akin to *break*. For one thing, *cut* stands out as a special case because there is evidence showing that it is a result verb and evidence suggesting it is a manner verb. To be specific, its zero-related nominal *a cut$_N$* suggests it is a result verb because manner verbs lack a result interpretation. But on the other hand, it appears in conative constructions, a syntactic behavior shared with manner verbs but not result verbs. Meanwhile, *cut* is incompatible with the inchoative construction. This is a typical syntactic property of result verbs.

In view of the contradictory evidence, Levin and Rappaport Hovav, on account of their manner/result complementary hypothesis[1] (Levin and Rappaport Hovav 1991, 2008; Rappaport Hovav and Levin 1998, 2010), argue that *cut* in its basic use is a result verb for two main reasons. Firstly, *cut* only encodes a result of clean separation, thus does not count as a counterexample to the manner/result complementarity. The reason why *cut* is usually understood as brought about by a sharp-edged instrument is an issue of conventionality. Since cutting events are conventionally conducted with a sharp-edged instrument, the verb *cut* is conceptualized as denoting a corresponding action and manner. But this is not necessarily the case, because cutting events are flexible about the action performed and the instrument used (Bohnemeyer 2007). In addition,

---

[1] Manner and result are often in complementary distribution: that is a given verb tends to be classified as a manner verb or a result verb, but not both (Rappaport Hovav and Levin 2010).

cut also appears in inchoative constructions in particular contexts (2.15a). Such inchoative uses of *cut* are overlooked because in most cases *cut* is used to describe the separation of food which requires the agent's continued intervention (Haspelmath 1993; Levin and Rappaport Hovav 1995). But in cases where the agent's intervention is not necessary, *cut* is licit in the inchoative constructions. This further supports the proposal that *cut* should be categorized as a result verb, akin to *break*. Despite the categorization of *cut* as a result verb, in some limited cases as in (2.15b), *cut* simply denotes the handling of a sharp-edged instrument for intended use but does not entail any result. In such cases, *cut* is categorized as manner verbs. Overall, in terms of the categorization of *cut*, Levin and Rappaport Hovav hold that in most uses *cut* is a result verb akin to *break*, but in some uses, *cut* is a manner verb the same as *climb*, *hit*, *kick*, *splash*, and *pull*.

(2.15)

a. ... the rope **cut** on the rock releasing Rod on down the mountain.

b. Finally, she got the blade pulled out and started **cutting** at the tape on Alex...

2.2.4 Interim summary

In sum, the categorization of break verbs in generative semantic studies is to a large extent attributed to their syntactic behaviors and their grammatically relevant meaning components, especially to their idiosyncratic ability to participate in causative alternations. Table 2.1 is a contingency table of the various constructions that break verbs and related verb classes appear in or do not appear in.

This table suggests that the seemingly clear-cut syntactic diagnostic is far from being uncontroversial to locate the boundary of break verbs. For one thing, one view (Guerssel et al. 1985; Hale and Keyser 1987; Levin 1993) holds that although hit verbs and touch verbs share semantic components with break verbs, due to their constraint in causative alternation, they are identified as different verb classes. But verbs like *open*, *split*, *shatter* and *smash*, which allow causative alternation, are accepted as class members of break verbs. The other view (Levin and Rappaport Hovav 2008; Rappaport Hovav and Levin 2010) argues that cut verbs also belong to break verbs because cut verbs simply denote clean separation and in particular contexts also appear in causative alternations. On the other way around, Jackendoff (1990) emphasizes that break verbs are decomposition verbs and share semantic components of PATH and COMP with composition verbs like *assemble* and *build*. Both decomposition and composition verbs allow causative alternation.

Table 2.1   Syntactic behaviors of different verbs

Syntactic construction	Verb						
	break	*open*	*cut*	*touch*	*hit*	*assemble*	*build*
Conative	No	No	Yes	No	Yes	No	No
Ascension	No	No	Yes	Yes	Yes	No	No
Middle	Yes	Yes	Yes	No	No	No	No
Causative	Yes	Yes	Yes	No	No	Yes	Yes
Inchoative	Yes	Yes	No	No	No	No	No
Decomposition	Yes	No	Yes	No	No	Yes	Yes

Furthermore, categorizing verb classes merely in terms of their syntactic behaviors is overly coarse. For instance, although *open* is more similar to break verbs in terms of syntactic properties, the specific types of change of state encoded by *open* and *break* are different, one denoting reversal separation while the other depicting irreversible separation (Clark et al. 1995). On the other hand, although *cut* and *break* in most cases are different in causative alternation, they both denote separation in material integrity (Hale and Keyser 1987; Levin and Rappaport Hovav 2008). In this sense, the categorization criteria of break verbs should neither be confined to their participation in causative alternation nor be restricted to their encoding of grammatically relevant components like CHANGE OF STATE or RESULT, but should be further refined from a conceptual point of view. As mentioned in Hale and Keyser (1987), what specific kinds of change of state are denoted by these verbs call for further research.

In view of these downsides, the universal claim reached in generative approaches needs further verification beyond the syntactic range. The succeeding sections show how developmental psycholinguistic and cognitive linguistic studies address the categorization of break verbs in terms of more fine-grained conceptual variables.

2.3 Developmental psycholinguistic studies on break verbs

Different from generative semantic studies' heavy emphasis on the syntactic diagnostic of causative alternation, psychological and cognitive approaches are more concerned with the categorization of break verbs in terms of conceptual variables. Moreover, their categorization does not depend on one particular variable, but takes into consideration multiple variables and endeavors to pinpoint the differential proportion assumed by these distinct variables. This section reviews how developmental psycholinguistic studies attend to the semantic categorization of break verbs from the perspective of children's semantic overextension.

Developmental psycholinguistic studies have been engaged in the semantic categorization of break verbs since researchers find that *open*, one of the earliest (as early as 17 months) words acquired by children (Bowerman 1978), is frequently overextended to depict separations like *tearing the paper*, *peeling a tangerine*, and *breaking a roll* (Shaefer 1979; Clark et al. 1995; Bowerman 2005). Such overextension reflects that children tend to amalgamate different variables in their early category construction stage (Clark 1978, 1979). But with the development of their cognitive ability, they gradually master the matrix-like relations between relatively uncorrelated variables[①] (Huttenlocher and Lui 1979). In tracing children's category construction process of separation verbs, developmental psycholinguistic studies uncover how nonlinguistic variables and linguistic specific variables are utilized in children's acquisition of the verb category of separation.

2.3.1 Adult-child variations in the categorization of break verbs

To begin with, Shaefer (1979) explores how three perceptional variables, namely <affected object>, <instrument>, and <action>, are resorted to in the categorization of separation verbs. He finds that although these three variables are all employed in adults' and children's categorization, they are used in different proportions by adults and children. Specifically speaking, following Rosch and Mervis' (1975) research methodology in object categorization, Shaefer conducted a sorting experiment by eliciting 30 subjects (20 children, 10 adults) to classify 33 photographs on the basis of five verbal stimuli (*cut*, *tear*, *open*, *peel* and *break*). In doing so, he came up with five apparently different sorting patterns. And a closer inspection of these sorting patterns revealed that children and adults' classifications were non-identical and such classification differences result from their different views on the internal structure of the three category variables. In other words, the three categorial variables were weighted differentially by children and adults in their categorization process. For instance, in the dominant response pattern, all the adults showed an inclination to categorize "peeling an apple with a knife" under one category (*peel*) but children classified the same stimuli under three categories (*peel*, *tear* and *break*). This suggested that adults weigh the variable of <action> much heavier than children do. But in spite of this insightful finding, Shaefer did not take any further steps

---

① Uncorrelated variables counter with correlated variables (Huttenlockher and Lui 1979). For instance, "bird" is usually categorized based on variables like <wing>, <feather>, <egg> and <beak> etc. Such variables are regarded as correlated variables. In contrast, the separation verbs are defined in terms of variables like instrument, action, affected object, and endstate. Such variables are however not correlated.

to figure out the specific variable hierarchy differentially utilized by children and adults.

In light of Shaefer (1979), Shaefer (1980) fine-tunes the division of subject groups and broadens the combination of variables to <instrument>, <affected object>, <endstate> and <action>. Briefly speaking, six subject groups, including toddlers, preschool children, kindergarten children, second-grade children, deaf children, and adults, were administered to complete a matching task. The matching task was simply to choose which of the 24 experiment videos match the 6 sample videos. These 24 videos included 12 expected videos and 12 unexpected videos. By "expected", it refers to the expected combination of different variables. For instance, using a hand to cut melon is unexpected while using a knife to cut melon is expected. The matching results showed that toddlers matched the videos arbitrarily because they had not mastered the mature knowledge of the boundaries of separation verbs. Kindergarten and second-grade children displayed a significant preference for unexpected situations because they lacked the knowledge regarding the variable weight that could be related to individual boundary features. Both deaf children and preschool children produced fewer criterion level responses, but due to different reasons. Preschool children uttered fewer criterion level responses because their cognitive system was less developed. But deaf children, despite their developed cognitive system, were constrained by their limited exposure to language, thus failing to perform at the same level as hearing kindergarten children did. In contrast to children groups, adults produced more vacillating response patterns. Their preference for expected and unexpected videos was not significantly different. The most convincing account for such a response pattern is that adults' knowledge consists of the indeterminate and interdependent nature of category boundaries (Labov 1978). The indeterminate quality of boundary refers to the difficulty to determine the boundary between videos of separation. For instance, matching experimental videos of cutting melon with a knife and tearing cloth with a scissor to the sample video of cutting cloth with a knife is somewhat a dilemma. The interdependent quality stresses the matrix-like relations between different variables. For instance, the categorial boundary of *cut* is more often than not delimited by variables like <instrument> and <motion> in a crosscut fashion.

In order to further examine how children categorize cut verbs and break verbs, Bowerman et al. (2004) and Bowerman (2012) investigate how children describe the video clips employed in MPI studies. To make the description task more challenging, they replace some clips with more non-typical event clips, like cutting a banana with scissors. They reveal that Chinese children master cut and break verbs more exactly. As shown in Figure 2.1, the very first observation finds that children of 6, 4, 3, and 2 years old come to grips with verbs like *qiē*, *sī*, *kāi*, and *jiǎn* as good as adults do. But a closer inspection reveals that children's use of cut verbs like *jiǎn* is closer to *qiē* because these two verbs both describe separation with bladed-instruments. Moreover, children's mastering of break verbs is poorer than their mastering of cut verbs. For instance, children of the four ages have difficulty distinguishing break verbs like *duàn*, *làn*, and *kāi*. Children's use of *duàn* is closer to their use of *qiē* and *làn*. Children's use of *làn* is more mixed with their use of *bāi*. But clearly, as they grow older, their understanding of these break verbs moves closer to the adults'. In this sense, children are not born with a native categorization system. It takes time for them to completely acquire the categorization in their native language.

In view of this, a further question worth considering is whether children of different cultural backgrounds are born with a universal categorization system. If there is a universal categorization system, then children should start with the same event categories and diverge from each other as they learn more about their mother tongue. Then it should be expected that same-age children of different languages should behave more similarly than with the adults of their language. To answer this question, Bowerman (2012) compares children's categorization of break and cut verbs across Mandarin, Dutch, and Tamil (Figure 2.2).

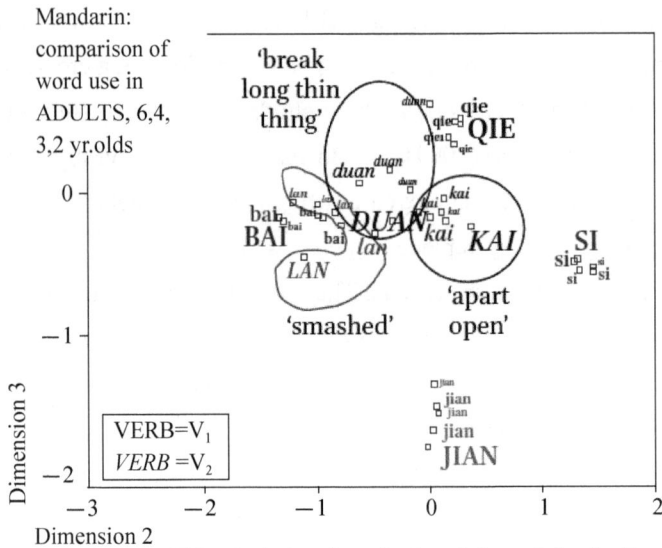

Figure 2.1 The acquisition of Mandarin break verbs by adults and 6–, 4–, 3–, and 2–year–old children

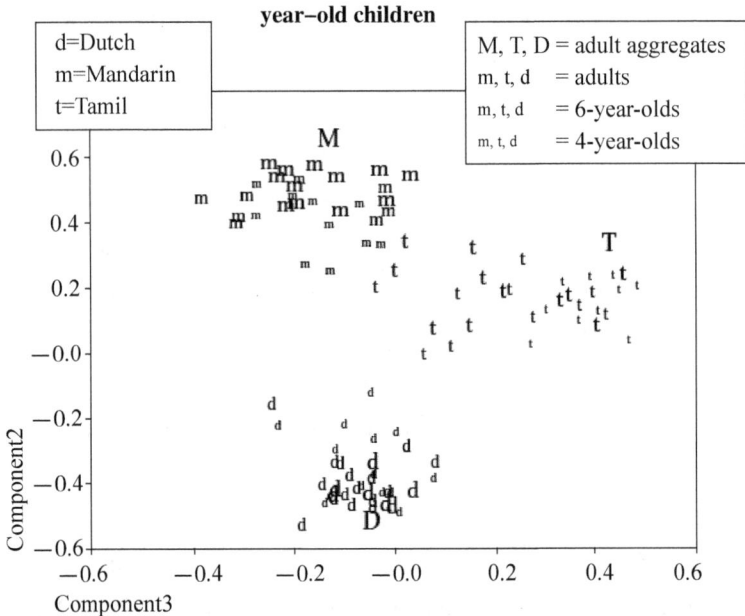

Figure 2.2 The acquisition of break verbs by Dutch, Mandarin and Tamil adults and 6– and 4–year–old children[①]

① Tamil is better represented with a fourth dimension, so more attention should be paid on Mandarin and Tamil.

Contrary to our expectation, as the three clusters in Figure 2.2 demonstrate, children categorize events in the same way as the adults of their mother tongue. Children of different ages float around their adults rather than cluster with their counterparts in other languages. Moreover, older children move even closer to their adults. In this view, there seems to be no evidence for a universal event categorization. Although children of younger ages do not categorize verbs exactly as adults do, they increasingly fine-tune their categorization as they understand more of their native languages. In other words, children are not born with a binary division of cut and break verbs. They pick up the categorial boundaries between cut and break verbs in the acquisition of their mother tongue. In this sense, more attention should be paid to the potential variables that give rise to the different categorization structures.

2.3.2 Cross-linguistic variations in children's categorization of *break* verbs

Pye et al. (1995) further the adult-child comparison to a cross-linguistic context. They show that linguistic specificity is another key factor that influences semantic categorization. The variables they are concerned with are <action>, <instrument> and <endstate>. With cross-linguistic elicited data from English, K'iche', and Mandarin, they not only verify that children's categorization is different from that of adults but also show that children's overextension displays language-specific patterns. For instance, English children tend to overextend the verb *break* more often than Mandarin and K'iche' children do, like "breaking a stick", "breaking dough" and "breaking the paper". This indicates that specific linguistic input rather than nonlinguistic cognition has an influence on semantic categorization (Bowerman and Choir 2001, 2003). As shown in Table 2.2, English *break* depicts the separation of all hard objects, Mandarin *duàn* describes long objects, Thai *kneet* is used for flexible objects while K'iche' *t'oqopinik* is applicable to long and flexible objects. Clearly, it is the wide application range of *break* specifically in English that triggers English children to overextend *break*.

Table 2.2 Crosslinguistic comparison of break verbs (adapted from Pye et al. 1995; Bowerman 2005)

	Plates	Sticks	Ropes	Clothes
English	break	break	break	tear/rip
Mandarin	pò	duàn	duàn	pò
Thai	taeaek	hak	kheet	kheet
K'iche'	paxik	q'upinik	t'oqopinik	rach'aqij

On the basis of the foregoing studies demonstrated above, Bowerman (2005) further delves into the overextension of break verbs and other separation verbs across English, K'iche', Mandarin, and Thai, but her focal spot shifts exclusively to the variable <affected object>. She proposes that verbs like *break* "encompass a vast range of perceptually and functionally diverse objects" (Bowerman 2005: 230-231), and in different languages break verbs are applicable to objects of diverse variables and variable combinations. The reason why children are more likely to overextend break verbs is that children pay more attention to the overall similarity between affected objects but adults keep an eye on specific variables as well as the variable combinations. For instance, as shown in Table 2.2, Mandarin *duàn* highlights the variable <shape>, Thai *kneet* emphasizes the variable <dimensionality> while K'iche' *t'oqopinik* shows the combination of <shape> and <dimensionality>. In view of this, children can successfully master the distinction between break verbs only if they come to grips with the implicit categorization principle that adults make use of. Put it in another way, the correct semantic categorization of break verbs requires the accurate grasp of varying variables and variable combinations underspecified in adult speech.

Apart from the explicit variables mentioned above, <reversal> is another important variable proposed by Clark et al. (1995). By <reversal>, Clark and his colleagues mean the move from one state to some prior state of affairs, for instance, shoes from tied to untied, parcels from wrapped to unwrapped, and dishes from covered to uncovered. Although explained implicitly, this <reversal> variable distinguishes break verbs from open verbs. That is, in terms of reversibility, *open* denotes a reversible separation like a door's separation from the doorframe, while *break* denotes an irreversible separation like a vase's separation into pieces. In this sense, this variable also indicates that children overextend *open* to describe breaking events at an early age (Bowerman 1978), simply because they have not come to grips with this subtle variable. Some other variables that have been simply mentioned or inferred in developmental studies include <material integrity>, <being unitary>, <predetermined line>, and <access to something> (Bowerman and Choi 2003; Bowerman 2005).

2.3.3 Interim summary

In sum, developmental studies, drawing insights from children's category construction, bring to light some important variables that play major roles in the categorization of break verbs. These variables on the one hand show that children are different from adults in categorization and on the other hand further prove that such a child-adult difference results from children's feebleness in understanding subtle variables and complicated variable combinations. Moreover, the crosslinguistic variances in children's overextension demonstrate that verb categorization is language-specific rather than nonlinguistic. In this sense, both children's feebleness and overextension variances form strong counter-evidence against generative studies' hypotheses that speakers are born with universal lexical knowledge which includes both meaning components and the syntactic behaviors of verbs (Levin 1993: 11). But be this as it may, the developmental psycholinguistic studies are limited in some aspects.

For one thing, the variables, in developmental psycholinguistic studies, are interpreted in a piecemeal fashion. Although the above-reviewed studies have selected certain categorial variables as their research focus, few of them have systematically investigated all possible variables that might account for the categorization of break verbs. The majority of variables attended to in these studies are perceptual variables, while interactive variables like <function>, <agent>, and <intentionality> are greatly overlooked.

Moreover, the interrelations, as well as the internal structures of variables are to a great extent unexplored. For instance, despite the fact that Shaefer (1979, 1980) reveals that children have not mastered the categorization principles that adults have, he fails to specify how adults weigh different categorial variables in their categorization of break verbs. In view of these limitations, we will recap in the next part the systematic multivariate investigations carried out in cognitive linguistic studies.

2.4 Cognitive linguistic studies on break verbs

Cognitive linguistic studies, characterized by their attention to languages of diverse typologies and cultural backgrounds, attend to crosslinguistic variations in the categorization of break verbs. In doing so, they not only bring to light more subtle categorization variables but also have craftily integrated some applicable theoretical frameworks. In what follows, we will review how these cognitive typological studies observe and interpret break verbs' categorization from perspectives of cognitive semantics extensionalist in section 2.4.1, NSM in section 2.4.2, Frame Semantics in section 2.4.3, Causal Chain in section 2.4.4, and Talmy's cognitive semantic study in section 2.4.5.

Before proceeding to the details, it is worth mentioning at this stage that cognitive linguistic studies, framed under whatever specific theories, generally agree to integrating the extensional and the intensional perspectives (Taylor 2007). The extensional perspective, similar to what psycholinguistic studies do, examines the semantic extension of break verbs by observing the events or experiences they are used to designate. In distinction, the intensional semantic perspective is more concerned with break verbs' argument structure as generative semantic studies do. But different from both psycholinguistic and generative studies, cognitive linguistic studies argue for the interdependent relationship between the two perspectives and emphasize more on how these two perspectives illuminate each other.

2.4.1 Cognitive semantic extensionalist studies on break verbs

Pye (1996) is one of the few researchers who first caught sight of crosslinguistic variations in the semantic extension of break verbs. His central focus is on the differences between English and K'iche' cut and break verbs. For one thing, with the method of illustration and example elicitation, he reveals that K'iche' speakers categorize break verbs in much more specific ways than English speakers do. In English, *break* is a cover term for around 27 subtypes of breaking events, ranging from breaking crackers, breaking a leg, breaking water, breaking the skin to breaking the law. In stark contrast, K'iche' has as many as 47 specific break verbs, which respectively depict breaking a banana, breaking clay, breaking something hollow and squashing bugs. Besides, Pye also finds that K'iche' break verbs, either encoding *cut* or *break*, all allow causative alternation. In his explanation for such crosslinguistic variations, Pye holds that although both English and K'iche' have break verbs, K'iche' break verbs are more difficult to define because they are captured by a different set of conceptual variables. In the same vein, K'iche' cut verbs appear in causative alternations simply because they are not the exact cut-type verbs equivalent to those in English. To further generalize his conclusion, Pye claims that the concepts denoted by verbs might be captured with an n-dimensional semantic space. The corresponding dimensions include <degree of force>, <direction of force>, <instrument>, <type of object>, <spatial configuration of the object> and the <object's material>.

Influenced by Pye's (1996) preliminary crosslinguistic work, and also inspired by relevant findings in generative semantics and developmental psycholinguistic studies, research members at Max Plank Institute (MPI for short) for Psycholinguistics carried out an Event Representation Project (Majid et al. 2007a). On the basis of previous investigations, this project took one step further both in the utilization of elicitation tools and the selection of language samples. Specifically speaking, with an elicitation tool, 61 video clips depicting the separation of various kinds were recorded (Bohnemeyer et al. 2001), involving actions like cutting, breaking, opening, tearing as well as splitting. As for language samples, altogether 28 languages from 13 distinct language families were selected (Majid et al. 2007a). With such a research methodology implemented, successive fieldwork studies are conducted and some significant findings concerning break verbs' extensional range and argument structure are uncovered.

2.4.1.1 Crosslinguistic variations in the conceptual categorization of break verbs

To begin with, although most languages distinguish breaking events from opening events, some other languages show unexpected variations. To be specific, Majid et al. (2007a), in analyzing the dataset of the 28 languages, employ a large-scale correspondence analysis (Greenacre 1984) and reveal that the first few dimensions distinguish separation events like opening and peeling from cutting and breaking events. Although they do not state explicitly what these first few dimensions are, this finding indicates that there exists an underlying fault line between separation events of material integrity and simple separation events like opening. But in spite of this, languages like Tidore, Kuuk Thaayorre, Tamil, and Mandarin show some exceptions. In Tidore, the verb *hoi* both describes opening doors, opening jars, and gutting fish or events of dismemberment (van Staden 2007). This is because *hoi* is indifferent to the material of the affected object, but sensitive to the separation of a distinguishable part from a certain object. Similarly, the Kuuk Thaayorre verb *thuuth* denotes both the removal of container lids and the snapping of a string (Gaby 2007). The Tamil verb *pirii* describes both tearing cloth and opening books or scissors (Narasimhan 2007). The Mandarin verb *kai* denotes both snapping sticks and opening doors and opening books (Chen 2007). In view of this, the categorial boundary between opening events and breaking events is not necessarily definite and universal. It seems that the extensional range of verbs denoting *open* encompasses that of some break verbs.

Secondly, as for the categorization of breaking and cutting events, although Majid et al. (2007a) uncover some general universal categorization variables, closer inspections of specific languages display variations. Majid et al. (2007a) show that primarily three dimensions are accountable for the categorization of breaking events, namely predictability of the locus of separation (dimension 1), two-dimensional flexible objects (dimension 2) and rigid objects (dimension 3). As can be seen from Figure 2.3, the first-dimension divides clips describing cutting and slicing (high degree of predictability) to the left while smashing and breaking events (low degree of predictability) to the right. The second dimension categorizes tearing events as an independent group while the third-dimension singles snapping and smashing events out. Admittedly, these three variables capture the three most prominent variables in the categorization of breaking events, but even so, some languages display variations, especially in cases of the clips falling in the middle part.

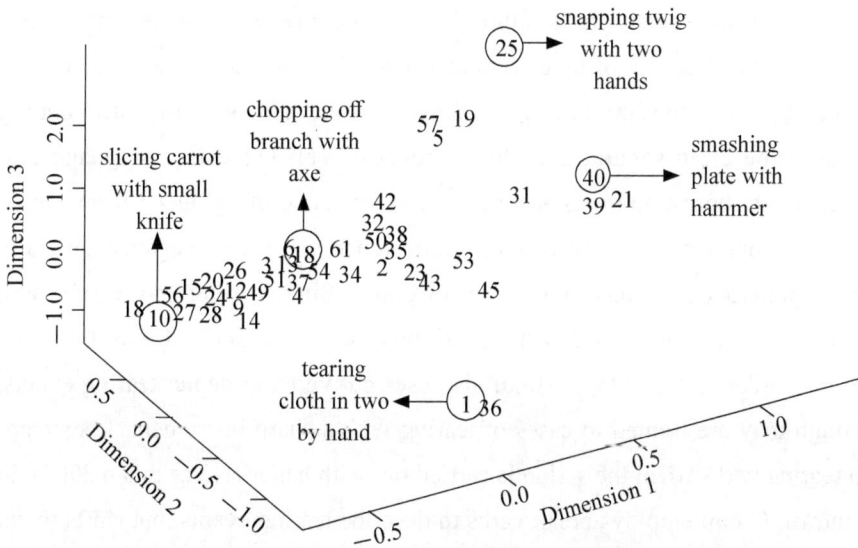

Figure 2.3 A three–dimensional plot of cutting and breaking events (Majid et al. 2007a)

As shown in Figure 2.3, chopping events (clip 48) constitute one example in the middle. Since English heavily weights the variable <instrument>, chopping is usually identified as a subtype of cutting in English. In contrast, other Germanic languages (Dutch, Swedish, and German) tend to group *chopping* together with *snapping* and *smashing*, because all of these actions are executed with a sharp blow (Majid et al. 2007b). Different from both English and Germanic languages,

Lao identifies chopping events as an independent category, because Lao is sensitive to the <degree of control> the agent has on the separation (Enfield 2007). Since chopping events are conducted with a flexible blade, the degree of control exerted in such events is lower than that of cutting events but higher than that of breaking events, thus they locate in the middle as an independent group. Another example in the middle is breaking a thread with hands (clip 38). With the same emphasis on <instrument>, English regards it as a different group from cutting a carrot with a knife (clip 10) and breaking a pot with a hammer (clip 39). But Sranan tells breaking a thread with a hand and cutting a carrot with a knife apart from breaking a pot with a hammer because the former two designate a clean separation while the latter denotes a messy one (Essegbey 2007). The third event group falling in the middle refers to the tearing events. Although the majority of languages consider this event type as an independent category, Levinson (2007) finds Yélî Dnye uses the same verb for carrot cutting to describe cloth separation. This is because Yélî Dnye is a language that categorizes separation verbs according to the variable of <grain> (fiber), which includes coherent severance with the grain, coherent severance against the grain, and incoherent severance (regardless of grain). Since cutting and tearing both denote coherent severance with grain, thus they are described with the same verb. Similar to Yélî Dnye, Hindi also uses cut verbs to depict tearing events, though they are limited to cases of tearing with a sharp instrument. It switches to tearing verbs when the action is carried out with hands (Narasimhan 2007). In contrast, Otomi employs break verbs to describe tearing events, but shifts to cut verbs when instruments are utilized (Palancar 2007).

Apart from the above variables and languages, some other variables and languages are also investigated. Ewe, a language similar to English, weights the variable of <instrument> heavily (Ameka and Essegbey 2007). But different from English, the other variables important in Ewe are <manner of separation>, <purpose of separation> as well as <direction of separation>. For instance, Ewe verb *tso* describes the process of cutting up vegetables for use in a sauce. In Jalonke, besides the abovementioned variables, <prototypicality of events>

also plays an important role (Lüpke 2007). For those non-canonical events, like cutting a carrot with hands, verbs used for corresponding canonical events are employed but the unusual instrument is indicated as well. Differently, Tzeltal and Lowland Chrontal regard <endstate> of the affected object as a critical variable (Brown 2007; O'Connor 2007). For instance, in Tzeltal, the verb *xet* depicts creating a simple break in a brittle object, while the verb *top'* describes shattering the brittle object completely. In Lowland Chrontal, when a cloth is torn or shredded but not necessarily torn apart, the verb *ts'ajl-* is used. Table 2.3 summarizes the specific studies that have investigated the categorization of break verbs.

Table 2.3 Cognitive linguistic studies on the categorization of break verbs (23 languages)

Languages	Semantic categorization	Syntactic categorization
General trend	Predictability of separation locus > affected object Cutting vs. breaking (Majid et al. 2007a)	Morpholexical transparency and complete linking −cut verbs vs. +break verbs (Bohnemeyer 2007)
Äiwoo	No study	Causative alternation single verb vs. +complex word forms vs. −serializations (Næss 2012)
Berber	No study	Causative alternation −cut verbs vs. +break verbs (Guerssel et al. 1985)
Biak	No study	Causative alternation bipolar verbs (Bohnemeyer 2007)
Dutch	Sharp blow > affected object Cutting vs. breaking (chopping) (Majid et al. 2007b)	No study
English	Instrument > affected object Cutting (chopping) vs. breaking (Majid et al. 2007b)	Causative alternation −cut verbs vs. +break verbs (Majid et al. 2007b)

Continued

Languages	Semantic categorization	Syntactic categorization
Ewe	Instrument, manner, purpose, direction of separation (lengthwise vs. crosswise) Cutting (highly agentive, agentive) vs. breaking (highly non-agentive, non-agentive) (Ameka and Essegbey 2007)	+highly agentive verbs vs. ± (agentive verbs and highly non-agentive verbs) vs. −non-agentive verbs vs.+lã (Ameka and Essegbey 2007)
German	Sharp blow > affected object Cutting vs. breaking (chopping) (Majid et al. 2007b)	Causative construction bipolar verbs (Majid et al. 2007b)
Hindi	Locus of separation > affected object Cutting (tearing) vs. breaking (Narasimhan 2007)	No study
Jalonke	Control over locus of separation, instrument, affected object, prototypicality Cutting vs. breaking (Lüpke 2007)	Causative alternation −cut verbs vs. −smash verbs vs. +break verbs (Lüpke 2007)
Kinyarwanda	No study	Causative alternation −cut verbs vs. +break verbs (Bohnemeyer 2007)
Kuuk Thaayorre	Instrument, affected object, manner, control, result Cutting vs. breaking (Gaby 2007)	Causative alternation −cut verbs vs. +break verbs (Gaby 2007)
Lao	Instrument blade position, affected object Cutting vs. chopping vs. breaking (Enfield 2007)	No study
Lowland Chrontal	Manner of action, manner, endstate Cutting vs. breaking (O'Connor 2007)	Causative alternation −cut verbs vs. +break verbs vs. +compound verbs (O'Connor 2007)
Mandarin	Instrument, manner, affected object Cutting (chopping, tearing with instrument) vs. breaking (tearing with hand) (Chen 2007)	Causative construction bipolar verbs (Bohnemeyer 2007; Chen 2007)

Continued

Languages	Semantic categorization	Syntactic categorization
Otomi	Instrument > affected object Cutting (tearing with instrument) vs. breaking (tearing with hand) (Palancar 2007)	No study
Spanish	No study	Causative alternation −cut verbs vs. +cortar vs. +break verbs (Spalek 2012, 2015)
Swedish	Sharp blow > affected object Cutting vs. breaking (chopping) (Majid et al. 2007b)	No study
Sranan	Mode of separation (clean vs. messy) No clear distinction (koti is generic) (Essegbey 2007)	Causative alternation +cut verbs vs. +break verbs (Essegbey 2007)
Tamil	Locus of separation > affected object Cutting vs. breaking vs. tearing (pirii for both tearing and opening) (Narasimhan 2007)	No study
Tidore	Instrument, manner, endstate Cutting (*tola* is generic) vs. breaking (*hoi* for both breaking and opening) (van Staden 2007)	Causative alternation −cut verbs vs. +*tola* vs.+break verbs (van Staden 2007)
Tzeltal	Affected object, direction of action, endstate 54 specific verbs (Brown 2007)	No clear syntactic division
Yélî Dnye	Mode of severance (along vs. against grain) Breaking events (Levinson 2007)	Causative alternation −*châp*wo vs. +break verbs (Levinson 2007)
Yukatek	No study	Causative alternation bipolar verbs (Bohnemeyer 2007)

(Note: This table only displays those languages of which research results are published. ">" stands for the priority status of variables, "−" for not allowing causative alternation, "+" for allowing causative alternation, "?" for unknown status about causative alternation.)

Besides the cognitive extensionalist studies on the extensional range of break verbs, Fujii (1999) compares the categorization of break verbs across languages with classifiers and languages without classifiers. Influenced by Thomason (1972) and Keil (1979), and drawing from Denny's (1986) claim that there might be a link between noun classifiers and verbs, Fujii argues that the categorization of break verbs is correlated to the categorization of affected objects. She proves that non-classifier languages like English, Hindi, Portuguese, Tibetan and Persian categorize break verbs and objects either in a two-way or three-way method. And the variables they are concerned with are <spatial configuration> and <strength of material>. In contrast, classifier languages like Japanese, Chinese, Korean and Indonesian adopt a four-way categorization of objects. The variables these languages take into consideration include not only <spatial configuration> and <strength of material> but also <functionality>. Comparing these two categorization systems, Fujii (1999) concludes that classifier languages have more differentiated varieties of verbs to describe the breaking of objects while non-classier languages have fewer.

2.4.1.2 *Cross-linguistic variations in the syntactic categorization of break verbs*

As summarized in Table 2.3, despite the general universal categorization trend revealed in Majid et al. (2007a), the conceptual boundary of breaking events is not a sharp line as it is supposed to be. Consistent with this trend, cognitive linguistic studies on the syntactic behavior of break verbs arrive at similar conclusions. Moreover, these studies also demonstrate that the diagnostic of causative alternation is not universally applicable.

Bohnemeyer (2007) reanalyzes the syntactic structure of break verbs and cut verbs against a corpus of 17 languages and comes out with four important findings.

Firstly, some languages, like Biak, German, Yukatek, and Mandarin, have neither break verbs nor cut verbs, but make prominent use of bipolar verbs to describe cutting or breaking events, for instance, Mandarin *bāi-duàn* 'bend-broken', Yukatek *xíik-ch'àak* 'burst-cut' and German *zer-schmetterte* 'apart-smash'. These bipolar or compound verbs denote both cause and change and do not form inchoative constructions, thus constituting a third class (beyond cut verbs and break verbs).

Secondly, languages such as Yélî Dnye lack cut verbs, while Sranan, Ewe, Spanish, and Tidore have cut verbs that form causative alternations. Yélî Dnye, as stated in Levinson (2007), makes no specific distinction between breaking and cutting events. Correspondingly, all Yélî Dnye separation verbs allow causative alternation, only with verb *châpwo* as an exception. In Sranan, cut verbs all form inchoative constructions as break verbs do (Essegbey 2007). Ewe *lã*, Spanish *cortar*, and Tidore *tola* are also special cases which denote cutting but appear in causative alternations.

Thirdly, Yukatek, Tzeltal, Hindi, and Mandarin are constrained by some polysemous structures. Since these structures denote both passive reading and inchoative reading, the discrimination of cut verbs from break verbs solely based on causative alternation becomes an equivocal issue. For instance, Hindi's suppletive intransitive form allows both passive and inchoative readings, and so far, there's no evidence to tell them apart (example 2.16).

Finally, Bohnemeyer (2007) arrives at the conclusion that there is no universal syntactic categorization of cut verbs and break verbs. If anything is universal, that is the abstract principle of Morpholexical Transparency and Complete Linking (refer to Bohnemeyer 2007: 158). By Morpholexical Transparency, he means that "productive Argument-structure alternations that relate two lexemes in a semantically transparent fashion can add or delete generic, but not specific, subevent representations from the event structure of the verb" (Bohnemeyer 2007: 158). In other words, only generic subevent can be added or deleted in the argument structure of words. Since the causing subevents of break verbs are generic, they can be freely added or deleted. Consequently, break verbs appear both in inchoative constructions and causative constructions. Complete Linking refers to "a well-formed syntactic projection from a verb lexeme requires all thematic relations spelled out in the verb's semantics to be linked to arguments or obliques specified in the verb's Argument-structure, unless they are blocked from linking by voice operations" (Bohnemeyer 2007: 158). That is, only in cases like passive constructions, thematic relations can be blocked. Otherwise, all thematic relations should be spelled out.

(2.16)

Ye   rasii kaT gaii kyOkii Floyd=ne
dem   rope   cut went because Floyd=ERG
'This rope got cut because Floyd tried to hit it with a knife.'

In addition to the insightful findings noted above, some other languages are also examined, among which some support the distinction between break verbs and cut verbs while others do not. For example, in Jalonke, cut and break verbs are distinctively categorized as English does, but smash verbs in this case do not behave the same as break verbs but as cut verbs (Lüpke 2007). More complicated than Jalonke, Ewe categorizes four subtypes of break or cut verbs, namely highly agentive verbs, agentive verbs, highly non-agentive verbs and non-agentive verbs (Ameka and Essegbey 2007). Among them, highly agentive verbs and agentive verbs are similar to English cut verbs, but some agentive verbs also occur in inchoative constructions in restricted contexts. Highly non-agentive verbs and non-agentive verbs are analogous to English break verbs, but a few non-agentive verbs do not participate in causative alternation. Similarly, Tzeltal also makes no clear syntactic categorization of break and cut verbs (Brown 2007). In this language, most of the verbs employed to describe either breaking events or cutting events allow both causative and inchoative reading. But this does not indicate all Tzeltal separation verbs are break verbs, because some of these verbs are transparently cut-like. Lowland chrontal is a language that distinguishes cut verbs from break verbs but also uses compound verbs as Biak, German, Yukatek, and Manrain do (O'Connor 2007). Äiwoo is an Oceanic language. It utilizes three forms to describe breaking events— single verbs, complex word forms, and serializations—among which complex word forms allow inchoative alternations (Næss 2012). Since complex word forms are composed of specific cut verbs and break verbs, their participation in inchoative alternation not only challenges Guerssel et al's (1985) dichotomy but also "violates" Bohnemeyer's (2007) abstract principles. Besides these divergent syntactic behaviors and language varieties, some languages behave more or less similar to English in the syntactic categorization of cut verbs and break verbs. These languages are Kuuk Thaayorre (Gaby 2007), Berber and Kinyarwanda (Bohnemeyer 2007).

In the case of Mandarin, to be specific, Chen (2007) finds that Mandarin does not completely support the binary categorization of break verbs and cut verbs. First of all, in Mandarin, besides monomorphemic break verbs and cut verbs, resultative verb compounds (combination of cut and break verbs like *bāi-duàn*, *dǎ-pò*) constitute a third category. This category is attested to be fairly productive and prominent in the expression of breaking and cutting events. Furthermore, concerning the argument structure of these three verb categories, cut verbs and resultative verb compounds only participate in causative constructions while break verbs only appear in inchoative constructions. For instance, break verbs like *duàn* does not participate in inchoative constructions (2.18). The seemingly causative alternations exhibited in cut verbs (2.17) and resultative compounds (2.19) are pseudo, because the pseudo-inchoative patterns in (2.17b) and (2.19b) do not allow inchoative interpretations. This indicates that neither Mandarin cut verbs nor break verbs allow causative alternation. So, the syntactic criterion of causative alternation does not work in Mandarin. Thirdly, the semantic categorization of Mandarin cut and break verbs, however, is to a large extent in line with that of English. To be specific, Mandarin cut verbs and break verbs are categorized in terms of variables including <instrument>, <manner of action> and <features of the affected objects>. Cutting actions are usually distinguished from each other based on the <instrument> and <manner of action>. The breaking states of objects are distinguished on the basis of the <features of the affected objects>. In this sense, the semantic categorization of cut and break verbs in Mandarin is consonant with the MPI findings.

(2.17)

a. 我**切**了苹果。

Wǒ **qiē** le píngguǒ.

I cut-LE apple.

"I **cut** the apple."

b. 苹果**切**了。

Píngguǒ **qiē** le.

apple cut-LE.

"The apple **cut**."

(2.18)

a. 棍子**断**了。

Gùnzī **duàn** le.

stick break-LE.

"The stick **broke**."

b. *我**断**了棍子。

Wǒ **duàn** le gùnzī.

I break-LE stick.

"I **broke** the stick."

(2.19)

a. 我掰**断**了棍子。

Wǒ bāi**duàn** le gùnzī.

I bend-break-LE stick.

"I bent-**broke** the stick."

b. 棍子掰**断**了。

Gùnzī bāi**duàn** le.

stick bend-break-LE.

"The stick bent-**broke**."

Different from Chen's conclusion, Bohnemeyer (2007) argues that

Mandarin has neither cut verbs nor break verbs for two reasons. For one thing, Mandarin, like Biak, German, and Yukateck, makes prominent use of bipolar verbs (Ackerman and Webelhuth 1998). Bipolar cut and break verbs are predominant in the description of breaking and cutting events in these languages. In addition, these bipolar verbs are inert in argument structure. Since they contain both cut verbs and break verbs, they undergo neither conative nor causative-inchoative alternations. Given these divergences, Bohnemeyer (2007) indicates that lexical classes with predictable morphosyntactic properties are not universal.

Overall, a wide range of crosslinguistic studies has been conducted to test whether the semantic and syntactic categorizations of break verbs are universal. As shown in Table 2.3, it's rather farfetched to either conclude that all languages distinguish break verbs following the same rule or simply summarize that languages are diversified in their categorization of break verbs. Obviously, on the one hand, languages like Sranan, Tzeltal, and Yélî Dnye do not support the symmetrical division between break and cut verbs, neither from the semantic nor the syntactic perspective. But on the other hand, most languages commonly emphasize variables like <instrument>, <affected object> and <manner of action>, etc. in the semantic categorization of break verbs and meanwhile resort to causative alternation as a diagnostic of the syntactic categorization of break verbs. In this sense, it might be safe to conclude that although there are linguistic variations in the categorization of break verbs, such variations are constrained within a semantic and syntactic space.

In general, cognitive extensionalist studies make a significant contribution to the categorization of breaking events and break verbs from a typological point of view. But be that as it may, some limitations should be noted. For one thing, despite the fact that the correspondence analysis reveals the three highly weighted variables employed in the categorization of break and cut verbs, it fails to show the specific variable combinations that give rise to these three variables. Furthermore, as noted above, MPI studies are constrained in the diversity of scenarios that they can afford to take into consideration. Consequently, they not only fail to consider metaphorical usages of cut and break verbs but also neglect some agentive or purposeful cutting or breaking events.

In addition, cognitive extensionalist studies are confined to the literal domain but neglect the metaphorical uses of break verbs (Taylor 2007). In view of this, some recent studies (Garib 2012; Spalek 2012, 2015; Kwon 2016) explore the linguistic uses of break and cut verbs across literal and metaphorical domains. Garib (2012) compares the LCS of Sorani Kurdish break and cut verbs in literal and metaphorical domains. She states that the conceptual structure of break and cut verbs is to some extent dependent on the object they describe and the contexts, literal or metaphorical, they occur in. Likewise, Spalek (2012, 2015) also finds that the syntactic behaviors of Spanish cut and break verbs depend on the semantics of the theme arguments. The other obvious characteristic (might not be a limitation) of the above studies is that most of them are conducted under the framework of cognitive semantics in a general sense but without any specific theoretical framework. The following parts review some studies framed under specific cognitive theories.

2.4.2 NSM studies on break verbs

NSM is a semantic explanatory framework developed by Wierzbicka and Goddard (Wierzbicka 1996, 2006; Goddard and Wierzbicka 1994, 2002; Goddard 1998, 2005). Characterized by its 60 or so semantic primes and attested semantic molecules, NSM explicates words' conceptual structure by means of extended explanatory paraphrases, known as explications. With regard to break verbs, Wierzbicka (1985: 1) points out that words for events and actions like *break* are not easy to define. Goddard and Wierzbicka (2009) conduct a specific study on break verbs with a six-part explanatory paraphrase, including [a] lexical-syntactic frame, [b] prototypical motivational scenario, [c] instrument, [d] how the person uses the instrument, [e] what is happening to the object, and [f] potential outcome. In what follows, we first review how NSM differentiates cut verbs from break verbs, then move on to how NSM accounts for the conceptual structure of cut verbs across different languages. Besides, as an alternative semantic typological approach, the advantages and downsides of NSM in contrast to the MPI typological investigation are compared and discussed.

First, in terms of the distinction between cut verbs and break verbs, NSM neither agrees with Guerssel et al.'s (1985) holding that *break* is monadic while *cut* is dyadic nor concurs with Rappaport Hovav and Levin's (1995) view that both *break* and *cut* are dyadic. The major reason is that NSM argues against taking the non-durative (eventive) structure as the basic, and insists that analyses doing so usually end up with circularity. Taking (2.20) as an example, NSM proposes that the imperfective structure (2.20c) represents the basic structure. This is because the imperfective progress only denotes the action in progress and does not indicate any final result. In contrast, the perfective structure (2.20a) presupposes the action in progress and adds to this the notion of the accomplished result. And given this point of view, cut verbs and break verbs are respectively distinguished as physical activity verbs and physical act verbs. Physical activity verbs denote activities that are extended in time and lead to a goal, while physical act verbs only denote an immediate result. In this sense, imperfective tense functions as diagnostic of physical activity and act verbs. Cut verbs do not allow causative alternation, but are compatible with imperfective tense, thus being diagnosed as physical activity verbs. Differently, although break verbs allow causative alternation, they are incompatible with the imperfective tense and thus are identified as physical act verbs (2.20a–2.20f). One more point, which might be controversial, and hence should be noted is that the NSM approach maintains that human languages are keener on physical activity verbs rather than physical act verbs (Goddard and Wierzbicka 2009). The underlying reason is that humans are always engaged in durative activities while physical acts are only confined to immediate speech acts or interpersonal acts, like hitting, kissing, and killing.

(2.20)

a. She **cut** the bread. b. *The bread **cut**. c. She is **cutting** the bread.

d. She **broke** the glass. e. The glass **broke**. f. * She is **breaking** the glass.

As noted above, NSM explicates the conceptual structure of cut verbs in terms of paraphrases composed of six parts. Although NSM is only adopted in a limited number of studies on cut verbs, its advantages in explicating word meanings are fully manifested. For instance, Otomo and Torii (2005) compare the meaning of *tear* and its three Japanese equivalents (*saku, chigiru, yaburu*) in terms of <instrument>, <object>, <manner> and <endstate>, framed under NSM. It is revealed that English *tear* and its Japanese equivalents share the same instrument. The tearing events in both English and Japanese are executed with hands. As for the manner of tearing, English *tear* does not specify any particular manner. In distinction, Japanese tear verbs do specify manners, such as "along the fiber" for *saku*, "with the finger" for *chigiru*, "making a sound" for *yaburu*. Concerning the affected object, as shown in Figure 2.4, English *tear* applies to any object that can be separated by hands. Japanese *saku* is restricted to 'flat', 'thin' objects made of 'fibers', like paper and cloth. *Chigiru* applies to things that are 'fragile' like paper, bread, cotton, sponge, and even lettuce. *Yaburu* is restricted to things that are 'flat' and 'thin' such as plastic bags.

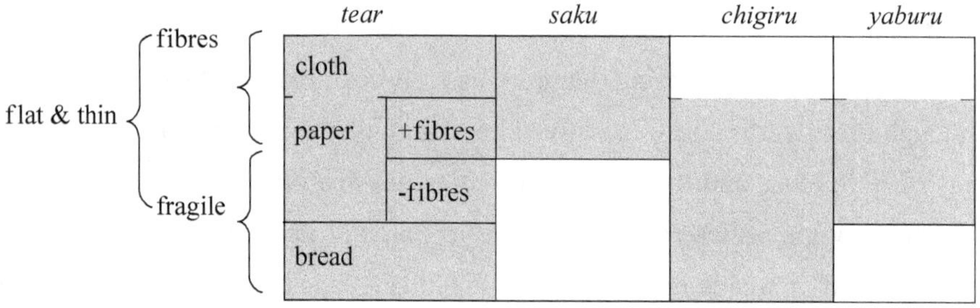

Figure 2.4 The affected objects of *tear* in English and Japanese (Otomo and Torii 2005)

Goddard and Wierzbicka (2009) explore cut and chop verbs across English, Polish and Japanese. They not only attend to the <instrument>, <manner>, <object> and <endstate> denoted by these verbs but also focus on their lexical-syntactic frame and prototypical motivational scenarios. Taking English *cut* as an example, its NSM explication is in the following paragraph. As revealed in this detailed explication, all minute semantic nuances are expounded by means of paraphrase. With such an explication template, NSM uncovers the subtle semantic distinctions between English *cut*, *chop*, *slice*, Polish *ciąć* "cut", *krajać* "cut/slice", *obcinać* "cut around", *rąbać* "chop" and Japanese *kiru* "cut", *kizamu* "chop". For instance, the explication template reveals that the agent's intention and instrument are two important variables in distinguishing cut verbs across the three languages. For instance, both Polish and English cut verbs are sensitive to the agent's intention. Polish *ciąć* and English *cut* are chosen when the agent wants to be precise about the objects' shape. Polish *krajać* and English *slice* are used when the agent is not concerned with the objects' shape. In contrast, Japanese cut verbs are indifferent to the agent's intention but sensitive to the employment of fingers. Japanese *kiru* is specifically used for cutting actions carried out either with fingers or with instruments like scissors.

[A] *someone (X) was cutting thing Y (e.g. some paper, a cake) with thing Z.*
LEXICO-SYNTACTIC FRAME

[a] someone X was doing something to thing Y with thing Z for some time
because of this, something was happening at the same time to thing Y
as this someone wanted
PROTOTYPICAL MOTIVATIONAL SCENARIO

[b] people do something like this when they do something to something
because a short time before, they thought about this something like
this:
"I want this something not to be one thing anymore
I want this something to be two things
I want these two things to have straight [M] edges [M]"
INSTRUMENT

[c] when someone does something like this, they do it with something
this something is not a part of this someone's body
this something has a sharp [M] edge [M]
HOW THE PERSON USES THE INSTRUMENT

[d] when someone does something like this with something,

53

one of this someone's hands [M] touches this thing in some places all the time

because of this, when this hand [M] moves as this someone wants, this thing moves at the same time as this someone wants

WHAT IS HAPPENING TO THE OBJECT

[e] when someone does something like this with something to something else,

The sharp [M] edge [M] of this thing touches this other thing in some places for some time

because of this, when this someone's hand [M] moves as this someone wants,

something happens to this other thing in these places.

POTENTIAL OUTCOME

[f] if it happens like this for some time,

after this, this other thing can be two things

In summary, NSM is an applicable approach for crosslinguistic semantic comparisons. Its advantages in comparison with MPI typological studies mainly lie in its demonstration of prototypical motivational scenarios and its adoption of semantic primes. For one thing, the prototypical motivational scenario shows the typical circumstances as well as the agent's intentions when a particular word is used. In contrast, the MPI description of the "objective" video clips fails to explicitly show the agents' intention when he or she is performing the action. Furthermore, NSM's employment of simple and translatable semantic primitives not only avoids explication circularity but also makes crosslinguistic research easy and transparent. But in this respect, MPI comparisons are constrained because they adopt English cut and break verbs as the starting point. Since some languages do not have the English cut type and break type verbs, this starting point renders the crosslinguistic comparison ineffective.

On the other way around, NSM also has its limitations. One particular point worth mentioning is its simplified identification of break verbs as physical acts.

On the one hand, although break verbs are non-durative, they are not limited to physical acts or speech acts. Break verbs as shown in cognitive extensionalist studies constitute an important subtype of separation verbs, and languages like English and Chinese have a great number of break verbs, for instance, English *snap, smash, shatter, crack, split, tear* and Chinese *duàn, suì, liè, shé*, etc. On the other hand, the relationship between cut verbs and break verbs is not as simple as being durative and non-durative. Both of the two verb classes depict the separation of material integrity. The only obvious semantic distinction is that break verbs specify results while cut verbs specify actions. Another limitation of NSM lies in its excessive emphasis on the variable combinations of specific break verbs, but fails to figure out the general categorization of different break verbs.

2.4.3 Frame semantic studies on break verbs

Frame semantics is another approach employed in the categorial analysis of break verbs. This approach, featured by its treatment of lexical items or constructions in terms of the frames they evoke (Fillmore 1982, 1985; Fillmore and Atkins 1992), attends to the categorization of break verbs by converting the multi-variables into varying frames. In doing so, this approach categorizes break verbs based on the frames they evoke and in the mean time brings to light more in-depth categorial frame variables. Moreover, this approach also provides an accessible means to the metaphorical frames of break verbs.

Firstly, frame semantics affords a multi-frame account for the complex semantic structure of break verbs, thus categorizing semantically similar break verbs in terms of the frames they evoke. As exemplified in Bouveret and Sweetser (2009), French separation verbs *casser, briser,* and *rompre,* though semantically similar, evoke different specific frames. To be specific, *rompre* evokes a break frame, where the affected object is a long thin object. When breakage happens, the object is no longer a whole. Correlated to this break frame is a function frame, simply because if the long thin object is a wire, breaking the wire will not only result in the separation of the wire but also disconnect a power source for an appliance. Similar to *rompre*, *casser* also evokes both break frame and function frame. But different from *rompre*, the break frame that *casser* evokes involves broken threads and yarns, and consistently the function frame it evokes is concerned with the dysfunction of complex objects. For instance, *ordinateur casser* (broken computer) describes the function loss of the computer rather than the power failure of the computer. In contrast to *rompre* and *casser*, *briser* evokes a shatter frame, which profiles the disintegration of objects into pieces, but does not indicate anything about the affected objects' function. For instance, *computer briser* (broken computer) only denotes that the physical computer separates into pieces but profiles nothing about its function. Besides, *rompre* and *casser* also evoke particular food frames in their idiomatic forms, like *rompre* a piece of bread, and *casser* an egg.

Secondly, as frame semantics treats lexical items in terms of the gestalt principle, it attends to the conceptual structures of break verbs more comprehensively. In this fashion, more variables, apart from those brought up in MPI studies, are put forward. These new variables include <loss of functionality>, <forceful bending>, <loss of integrity>, <focus on detachment of pieces> vs. <focus on degree of affectedness of the whole>, <functional division>, as well as <agentive intentionality> vs. <unintentionality> (Fujii et al. 2013b). Taking <loss of functionality> as an example, although English *break* and French *casser* both denote function loss in their extended frame, Japanese has a particular break verb—*kowasu*—which describes the loss of functionality. For instance, *kukkii o kowasite* (*cake breaks*) indicates that the cake can no longer function as a nice gift.

Thirdly, frame semantic studies reveal that some break verbs are semantically divergent in their metaphorical frames the same way as they are divergent in their literal frames. For instance, to the extent that *casser*, *briser*, and *rompre* are associated with different literal break frames, they are also attested to involve metaphorical frames in correspondingly different ways (Bouveret 2009; Bouveret and Sweetser 2009; Fujii et al. 2013b). To be specific, corresponding to their association in the break frame mentioned above, these three break verbs also describe breaking marriage from different perspectives. *Rompre un mariage* refers to legally ending a religious marriage, corresponding to its breaking a long thin object in the break frame. *Casser un mariage* is the standard use for ending a marriage by legal divorce in civil court, in correspondence to its reference to function loss in the functionality frame. In contrast, *briser un mariage,* however, refers to the breaking of a marriage due to the interference of an outside third party.

In general, frame semantic analysis on the categorization of break verbs manifests its advantages and weakness mainly from three aspects. In the first place, the frame semantic approach categorizes break verbs both in terms of the frames they evoke and in terms of the frame elements they profile. In other words, this approach attends to both the multiple variables involved in break verbs and the different weights assumed by these variables. The frame evoked by break verbs shows the variable combination, and the element profiled by the break verb demonstrates the proportion of weight assumed by different variables. But even so, it should be noted that frame semantics ceases at semantic interpretation, and neglects how the clustering of variables determines the categorization of different break verbs and how break verbs are differentially categorized on the basis of the weight assumed by different variables.

Secondly, frame semantics, similar to NSM, affords an easy way for crosslinguistic comparison. By comparing the frame that equivalent break verbs evoke and the elements they profile, crosslinguistic studies uncover a clear picture of crosslinguistic break verb categorization. What's more, in doing so, variables that have been neglected in previous studies are revealed and put forward. But in spite of this, these frame semantic studies only aim to complement cognitive extensionalist studies but fail to put forward a systematic set of principles that constrain the categorization of break verbs.

Thirdly, different from cognitive extensionalist studies and NSM studies, frame semantic investigations are not confined to prototypical breaking events. They afford a feasible way to delve into the metaphorical frames of break verbs by means of frame extension and frame mapping. The corresponding relations between the literal frames and the metaphorical frames of particular break verbs are also captured in detail. But despite this seeming advantage, more work needs to be done to specify the factors that drive and constrain the metaphorical frame extensions.

2.4.4 Causal chain studies on break verbs

The causal chain approach (Croft 2009, 2012, 2015) attends to the categorization of break verbs in terms of a three-dimensional event structure, which is composed of the qualitative dimension, the aspectual dimension, and the causal dimension. Such a three-dimensional model clearly displays the distinct contributions that aspectual structure and causal structure make to the linguistic representation of different verb classes. Besides these three dimensions, variables including <reversal>, <direction> and <increment> are also prominently considered.

To begin with, the three-dimensional event structure employed in the causal chain approach is exemplified in Figure 2.5 (Croft 2009, 2015): q stands for the qualitative dimension, t for the aspectual dimension, and the arrow line for the causal dimension. In this model, a complex verbal semantic structure is decomposed into two subevents. Each subevent involves only one participant with its own aspectual contour and is related to each other causally (Croft 2012: 212). To be specific, drawing from Talmy's (2000a) force dynamic theory, the causal dimension in this three-dimensional model represents a causal chain and denotes the transmission of force from one participant to another. The temporal dimension, represented as the x axis, describes how the event unfolds over time. As shown in the figure, the combination of solid lines and dash lines constitutes the temporal contour along which the event occurs. The solid line represents the profiled phase while the dashed lines represent the nonprofiled phases. For instance, the subevent "The vase broke" unfolds through three phases, among which the transition phase is profiled. The qualitative dimension, diagramed as the y axis, simply denotes the distinctively identified subevents. In this example, the two subevents are respectively "Jack impact the vase" and "The vase broke".

```
        Jack broke the vase.

              q
                      ┌----►  be broken
   OBJ    vase    � - - - - ┐
                            ▲
 y                          │          break
              q             │
                     ┌------┘
   SBJ    Jack    ┌--┴------ impact

                      t
         x
```

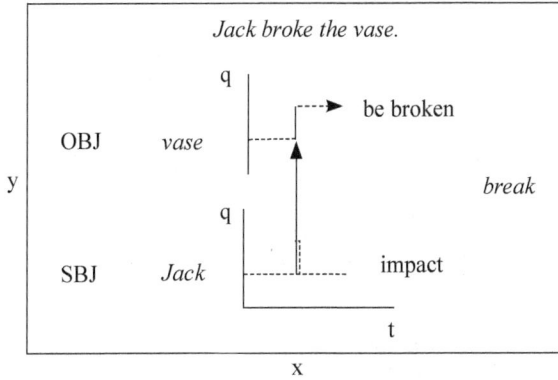

Figure 2.5　The event structure of *break* (Croft 2015: 13)

As noted above, the aspectual dimension describes the unfolding of events over the timeline. With regard to the categorization of break verbs, this aspectual dimension together with the variable <reversibility>[①] distinguishes open verbs from break verbs. As shown by the two different temporal contours in Figure 2.6, *open* (without the arrow) describes a reversible directed achievement result, which is transitory. In contrast, *shatter* (with an arrow) describes an irreversible directed result, which is permanent. To be specific, taking "The door opened" and "The window shattered" as examples, *open* depicts the directed change of the door from being closed to being open, and *shatter* denotes the directed change of the window from being intact to being fragmentary. In this sense, both *open* and *shatter* describe directed changes. But on the other hand, the reversibility correlated to these two directed changes is different. The change from closed to open is reversible because when the door is open, we can close it again. The change from intact to fragmentary is irreversible, since once the window is shattered, it cannot be integrated again. And for this reason, the result of the opening event is transitory while the result of the shattering event is permanent. Moreover, these two verbs are also similar in terms of being punctual. As shown in their aspectual contour, the door's opening and window's

---

① The variable of reversibility is described by Talmy as "resetability" (Talmy 2000b: 68) and by Clark et al. (1995) as "reversal".

shattering are both non-incremental.

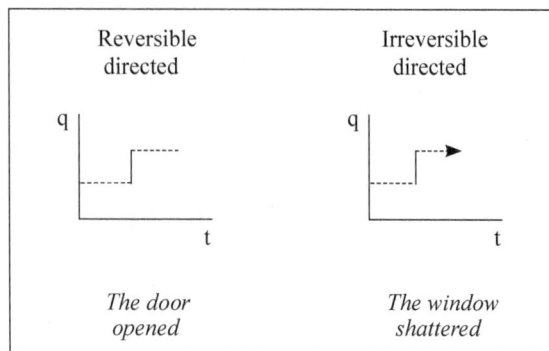

Figure 2.6 The event structures of *open* and *shatter* (Croft 2015: 8)

As for the categorization of cut verbs from break verbs, despite Levin and Rappaport Hovav's complementarity hypothesis (2008), the causal chain approach agrees with the proposal that verbs like *cut*, *schuss*, and *climb* encode both manner and result (Goldberg 2010: 46-50; Beavers and Koontz-Garboden 2012). Specifically speaking, Levin and Rappaport Hovav propose that *cut* is basically a result verb but in particular contexts also has its manner use. Taking the examples in (2.15) as instances, repeated here in (2.21), the manner use of *cut* (2.21b) and the result use of *cut* (2.21a) are represented in different temporal contours in Figure 2.7. In its manner use, *cut* denotes an undirected irreversible action, represented with broken lines. In contrast, in its result use, *cut* akin to *break* and *shatter* depicts a directed irreversible action. +*cut* indicates the specific manner of cutting. This is because if +*cut* is not indicated, it is impossible to tell the cutting action apart from other breaking actions.

(2.21)

a. … the rope ***cut*** on the rock releasing Rod on down the mountain.

b. Finally, she got the blade pulled out and started ***cutting*** at the tape on Alex…

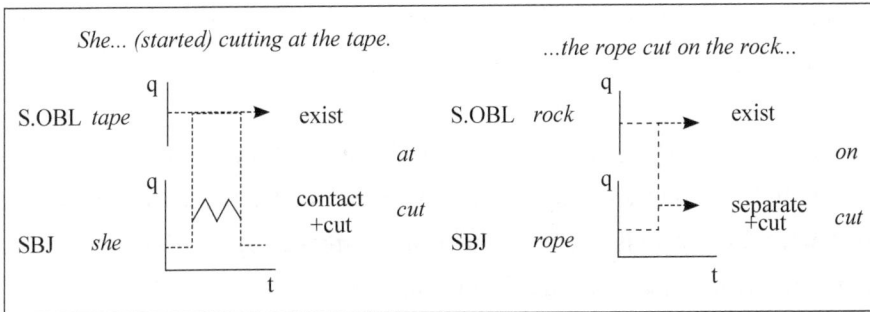

Figure 2.7 The event structures of *cut* (Croft 2015: 22–23)

Generally speaking, the causal chain approach contributes to verbal semantics by providing a geometrical representation for the event structures of verbs. In this fashion, the aspectual and causal structures of verbs are explicitly mapped out. As exemplified in the above figures, the two alternative aspectual contours of cut verbs (manner use vs. result use) clearly demonstrate the difference between its imperfective tense and its simple past tense. This to some extent supports Goddard and Wierzbicka's (2009) discrimination of *cut* from *break* by means of imperfective tense. And besides that, the causal chain approach further points out that *cut* also co-occurs with the simple past tense. And it is this co-occurrence that renders the categorization of cut verbs and break verbs a tricky issue.

One more point worth mentioning is that since the causal chain approach is developed to account for the argument realization of verbs, the event structure of verbs is represented in highly abstract structures. Consequently, the categorization of verbs is examined in a much coarser fashion. The specific affected objects and the specific endstate denoted by the verbs are neglected. As Croft (2015) suggests, it is necessary to further examine the qualitative dimension in the three-dimensional model. In addition, the causal chain approach also needs to take further steps to uncover the conditions that constrain verbs' alternation constructions. Although the three-dimension model implicitly shows that causative constructions describe complex causal event structures, it needs to be further examined as to why certain verbs allow causative constructions while others do not. For instance, why break verbs rather than cut verbs more often than not allow causative alternation.

2.4.5 Talmy's cognitive semantic study on breaking events

Talmy's cognitive semantic study addresses event categorization based on his finding that "there is a fundamental and recurrent category of complex event that is prone to conceptual integration and representation by a single clause" (Talmy 2000b: 216). For such a complex event category, the term macro-event is coined. This approach proposes five macro-event types, including motion events, events of state change, events of temporal contouring, events of action correlation, and realization events. Among these macro-event categories, it is the type of events of state change that is the most relevant to our proposed study.

As defined by Talmy (1991, 2000b: 237), an event of state change refers to "the case where it is conceived that a certain property is associated with a particular object or situation. Such a framing event consists of a change in, or the unchanging continuation of, that property". First, in terms of the internal structure of events of state change, the framing event of state change involves [Figure], [Ground], [Change/Stasis], and [Transition Type]. [Figure] is the entity associated with a property while [Ground] is the property *per se*. [Change/ Stasis] refers to the change or maintenance of the property associated with the entity. [Transition Type] refers to the direction of the relationship that the object or situation has with respect to the property. Co-events of state change are usually manner events or cause events that denote the manner pattern in which state change occurs or the causal reason that gives rise to the state change. Concerning the event types subsumed under events of state change, as shown in Table 2.4, two major categories of events of state change are state entry and state stasis. State entry includes a change in state of existence (2.22) and a change in condition (2.23). As the term suggests, change in the state of existence refers to the presence or absence of a certain state. Such changes are either punctual or gradual (discrete transition vs. bounded gradient transition) (2.22). Change in condition encompasses both physical integrity change and cognitive state change (2.23). For instance, objects' changing from intact to nonintact denotes the physical integrity change. In distinction, human's state changing from not knowing to knowing, or from unaware to aware denotes the cognitive change. In addition, different from other approaches, Talmy's cognitive semantics also categorizes the stasis or maintenance of the property as events of state change. As exemplified in (2.24), events being in a certain state or maintaining a certain state are also identified as events of state change.

Table 2.4 Classification of events of state change (Talmy 2000b: 237–253)

State entry	change in state of existence	from presence to absence	discrete transition (2.22a) The candle blew out.
			bounded gradient transition (2.22b) The meat rotted away.
		from absence to presence	discrete transition (2.22c) I boiled up some fresh coffee.
			bounded gradient transition (2.22d) The log burned up in 1 hour.
	change in condition	from intact to nonintact	(2.23a) The dog chewed the shoe up in 30 minutes.
		to readiness	(2.23b) *die Maschine einfahren* to warm up the machine for operating it
		to familiarity	(2.23c) *Ich habe mich in das Buch eingelesen.* I have read myself into the book.
		to awareness	(2.23d) *Sie hat ihr Kind herausgehört.* She has heard out her child.
State stasis	situatedness in a state		(2.24a) She is at home.
	maintenance of a state		(2.24b) I nailed the door shut.

Turning to the categorization of breaking events, although this event type is not explicitly mentioned in Talmy's macro-event, it is not uneasy to correspond it to the change from intact to nonintact. But generally speaking, Talmy's categorization is coarse and unsystematic. For one thing, Talmy's cognitive semantics puts forward a fine-grained analysis for change in the state of existence, but only talks about other types of events of state change in a piecemeal fashion. Taking change in condition as an instance, for physical change, Talmy only mentions the change from intact to nonintact with a marginal example (2.23a) while left changes like breaking, opening, cutting unattended. Similarly, for cognitive change, this approach only cites examples for change in readiness (2.23b), familiarity (2.23c), and awareness (2.23d) but fails to point out other cognitive changes. In addition, although Talmy innovatively identifies stasis as events of state change, he does not explain why that is the case.

Apart from these limitations, Talmy's fine-grained analysis of changes in state of existence brings to light some important variables that should be noted. First of all, it discriminates discrete transition from bounded gradient transition based on their co-occurrence with different types of temporal expressions. Discrete transition is consonant with punctual expressions while gradient transition is consonant with gradual expressions. Furthermore, it states that all particular state changes have a specific aspectual contour (Talmy 2000b: 244). This to a great extent corresponds to Croft's (2012) consideration of the temporal dimension and qualitative dimension. What's more, this approach advocates that although the event of state change in the majority of cases results from a certain causing event named by the verb, in some cases the action named by the verb is not one of the chained events but rather a manner event that accompanies the process of state change. In other words, manner is not part of the causal chain but an independent event co-occurring with the state change. This statement to a certain extent counters Croft's argument for the causal relationship between the manner event and state change (refer to Figure 2.5). Meanwhile, this statement is also inspiring for the binary division of manner and result, and further for the categorization of cutting events and breaking events. On the one hand, Talmy's cognitive semantics supports Levin and Rappaport Hovav's manner/result complementarity (2008), because it argues for the binary division of manner verbs and path verbs. But on the other hand, this approach rarely shows concern for some controversial cases like *cut*, *climb*, and *wipe*, etc. For cases like "He cut the bread into pieces", it insists that *cut* encodes the manner of cutting and *into pieces* encodes the transition type and ground. But if *cut*, as stated in the above-reviewed studies, is categorized as a break verb denoting separation, Talmy's analysis calls for further discussion.

2.4.6 Interim summary

The studies reviewed in this part are carried out under the framework of cognitive linguistics. Different from generative studies, these cognitive studies are more concerned with human construal in the categorization and conceptualization of breaking events. Consequently, more intricate perceptual and interactive variables are taken into consideration. For instance, the MPI project proves that <separation point predictability>, <rigidity>, and <dimensionality> are significant variables in predicting how different languages distinguish break verbs from cut verbs. The NSM approach accounts for break verbs by setting them in a detailed scenario and thus takes into consideration both the specific social context and human involvement. Frame semantics argues for the categorization of break verbs by means of the frames these break verbs evoke. That is, the specific breaking events and human perspectives that are encoded by those break verbs. The causal chain approach plots break verbs' event structure in terms of a three-dimensional model. In Talmy's cognitive semantics, breaking events constitute a subtype of events of state change. In events of state change, the four principle semantic components are [Figural entity], [Transition type], [State/change] and [Ground entity].

In a word, cognitive linguistic studies bring up more semantic or conceptual variables in the categorization of break verbs. But these studies still have their limitations. In the first place, although MPI studies reveal the underlying variables that distinguish break verbs from cut verbs, they do not mention the agent's intentionality in carrying out the breaking events. The NSM approach maps out the semantic structure of break verbs in an explanatory format, but the distinction between the break verbs relies on the researchers' format to format comparison. Similarly, Frame semantics describes break verbs in terms of the semantic frames they evoke, but the specific distinctions are contingent on the frame to frame comparison. The causal chain approach further shows the causal and temporal structures of break verbs, but as Croft (2015) himself admits, the qualitative dimension calls for more detailed characterization. Talmy's events of state change emphasize more on the general event structure, but overlook the conceptual boundary between different event types.

2.5 Diachronic Chinese linguistic studies on break verbs

2.5.1 Diachronic syntactic studies on break verbs

In Chinese linguistics, Chinese break verb *pò* has been the central concern. Two of the most controversial issues concerning Chinese break verb *pò* are: first, whether *pò* has grammaticalized as a verbal suffix; second, whether *pò* is originally a transitive verb or an autonomous verb.

First, in terms of the grammaticalization of *pò*, Sun (1999) demonstrates that *pò* has not grammaticalized as a verbal suffix while Xu (2001) proves that the semantic meaning of *pò* has changed from denoting concrete separation to denoting completion. Sun (1999) compares the grammatical distribution of *què*, *qì*, and *pò* in two syntactic patterns: collocation with verbs and collocation with nouns. He finds that neither the first nor the second syntactic pattern demonstrates that *pò* has grammaticalized as a verbal suffix.

Different from Sun's exclusive focus on the syntactic patterns, Xu (2001) emphasizes more on the semantic senses denoted by *pò*. In her analysis on the emergence of resultative constructions, Xu (2001) finds that *pò* was initially a verb expressing the starting of an action before the Han dynasty. But since then, *pò* has developed into a verb denoting the ending of an action. For instance in (2.25a), *pò* is in a juxtaposed position with 伐 *fá*, denoting the starting of defeating the enemy country. In contrast, *pò* in (2.25b) complements 打 *dǎ*, denoting the result of this action. Moreover, before the Han dynasty, *pò* usually referred to the destruction of utensils or the defeating of a country. But in its later development, *pò* is pervasively used to describe the completion of a certain action. In terms of the underlying mechanisms that give rise to such semantic changes, Xu (2001) reveals that both analogy and reanalysis play important roles. In other words, in analogous to V_1+V_2 (complete) (2.25c), V_2 in the serial verb constructions (2.25a) changed into a complement. Then after reanalysis, V_1 and V_2 formed the resultative construction. And as a consequence, V_1+V_2 (complement) (2.25b) and V_1+V_2 (complete) (2.25c) became two coexistent constructions that denoted the starting and ending of an action. But later, V_2 (complete) grammaticalized into an aspectual marker and V_1+V_2 (complete) was gradually replaced by V_1+aspectual marker. Therefore, resultative constructions and V+aspectual markers (*le, zhe,* and *guò*) remain as parallel forms denoting the completion of actions. But none of the V_2 (complement) forms have grammaticalized into aspectual markers.

(2.25)

a. 及燕使乐毅伐**破**齐，齐湣王出奔。（《田单列传》）

Jí   Yān shǐ Lèyì   fá**pò** Qí, Qímǐnwáng chū bēn.

when Yan send Leyi defeat Qí, king of Qí run away

"When Yan sent Leyi to **defeat** Qí, the king of Qí ran away."

b. 汝若会打**破**汝头。（《佛语录·禅林僧宝传》）

Rǔ ruò huì dǎ**pò** rǔ tóu.

you if can hit-break your head

"If you can, I will **break** your head."

c. 我已**饮**竟，水莫复来。（《百喻经·竹木筒水喻》）

Wǒ yǐ yǐn **jìng**, shuǐ mò fù lái.

I already drink finish, water no more

"I already **finished** drinking, so I don't need any more water."

Apart from the above studies on the grammaticalization of *pò*, the syntactic function of Chinese break verb *pò* also has aroused a wide range of discussions. Li (1994) classifies *pò* as a pseudo autonomous verb. Jiang (1999) insists that *pò* was originally a transitive verb. Taking sentence (2.26) as an example, Jiang claims that in this case *pò* is a transitive verb and the theme is the subject 卵 (*luǎn*). Wu (1999: 330) believes that *pò* was initially an autonomous verb. He analyzes *pò* in (2.26) as a verb describing the autonomous breaking of the egg. Wei (2000: 821) holds that *pò* could be used either as a causative verb in NP_1+V+NP_2 or as a resultative verb in $NP_1+V_1V_2+NP_2$. Xu (2001) claims that *pò* is a transitive verb before the Han dynasty.

(2.26)

卵**破**子死。（《荀子·劝学》）

Luǎn **pò**　zǐ　sǐ.

egg break young-bird die

"The egg **broke** and the young birds died."

To clarify the syntactic function of *pò*, Xu (2005, 2006: 174) conducts a diachronic syntactic study by observing the syntactic change of *pò* in structures like *pò*+NP, NP+*pò*, *pò*+V_2, V_1+*pò*. Through tracing the syntactic function of *pò* across different historical stages, she concludes that *pò*'s syntactic function change in *pò*+NP and V_1+*pò* demonstrates that *pò* progressively changes from a transitive verb (denoting both process and result) to an adjective or complement (denoting only result).

In general, diachronic studies on Chinese break verbs are particularly concerned with these verbs' syntactic changes. In spite of the disagreements on whether *pò* is initially a transitive verb or an autonomous verb, *pò* is attested to have changed from functioning as an independent predicate verb encoding both action and result to a verbal complement encoding only result. Such changes are involved in the formation process of resultative constructions. What's more, the attested coexistence of resultative constructions and V+aspectual markers proves that V_2 in resultative constructions, though not having grammaticalized as an aspectual marker, performs a quite similar function. This phenomenon demands further investigation to reveal the correlation between the temporal domain and the qualitative domain (Talmy 2000b: 244; Croft 2012). But despite such findings, the specific semantic readings of *pò* are greatly overlooked. Although Xu (2001) mentions that *pò* mainly denotes the destruction of utensils and the defeat of enemies before the Han dynasty, she fails to map out the diachronic variation of *pò* along the chronological timeline of Chinese.

2.5.2　Diachronic constructional studies on break verbs

The syntactic and semantic changes of *pò* recapped in the previous part indicate that Chinese break verbs are closely related to the formation of resultative constructions. This part reviews studies particularly on the relation between Chinese break verbs and the resultative constructions.

Hu (2005) proves that break verbs, like *pò*, *zhé*, *duàn*, *suì*, play a decisive role in the formation of resultative constructions. Based on the criteria of transitivity and semantic features, Hu classifies verbs in old Chinese into three groups, namely *shā* (杀) verbs, *pò* verbs, and *shú* (熟) verbs. Syntactically, *shā* verbs are prototypical transitive verbs (2.27a), *shú* verbs are prototypical intransitive verbs (2.27b), while *pò* verbs can be both transitive and intransitive (2.27c and 2.27d). Semantically, *shā* verbs denote action, *shú* verbs denote property, while *pò* verbs denote both action and property. More importantly, based on the current forms of resultative constructions, Hu deduces that the early forms of resultative constructions are mainly Vt *shā* O, Vt *pò* O, Vt O *shú*, and Vt O *pò*. In view of these linguistic facts, Hu (2005) proposes that the decreasing of action and the increasing of property in *pò* verbs may serve as decisive criteria to judge the appearance of resultative constructions. With these criteria, Hu (2005) finds that *pò* verbs began to function as intransitive verbs in the Han dynasty, the same time as the emergence of resultative constructions. Two conditions contribute to the change of *pò* verbs: 1) Serial verb constructions become increasingly pervasive; 2) V_2 in these serial verb constructions are mainly *pò* verbs. Driven by the mechanism of reanalysis, both Vt *pò* O and Vt

O *pò* changed to Vt *pò*_{complement} O. Meanwhile, motivated by the mechanism of analogy, Vt shā O shifted to Vt shā_{complement} O in analogous to Vt *pò* O. In the same vein, Vt O shú changed to Vt shú_{complement} O in the same way as Vt O *pò* did. In sum, *pò* verbs' turning into intransitive and complement verbs signifies the emergence of resultative constructions. Their initial transitivity (being both transitive and intransitive) affords an analogical impetus for the occurrence of *shā* and *shú* verbs in resultative constructions.

(2.27)

a. 秦人**杀**子金、子公。（《国语·周语上》）

　　Qínrén　**shā** Zǐjīn, Zǐgōng.

　　Qin-people kill Zijin, Zigong

　　"People from Qin **killed** Zijin and Zigong."

b. （熊蹯）未**熟**。（《左传·宣公二年》）

　　(Xióng fán) wèi **shú**.

　　bear foot not cooked

　　"The bear's foot is not **cooked**."

c. 伯牙**破**琴。（《吕览·本味》）

　　Bóyá **pò** qín.

　　Boya break qin.

　　"Boya **broke** the qin."

d. 军破身**死**。（《吕览·慎小》）

　　Jūn　　pò shēn sǐ.

　　army break self die

　　"The army would be defeated and the general himself would **die**."

Generally speaking, diachronic constructional studies shed insightful light on the co-occurrence of *pò* verbs and resultative constructions. Hu (2005) reveals the irreplaceable role of *pò* verbs in the emergence of resultative constructions. But in spite of this, these studies are only concerned with the syntactic structure of *pò* verbs but show little interest in their semantic change. Although they talk about the meaning of action and result encoded by *pò* verbs, they fail to go into the details. In other words, they do not mention the specific kind of actions and results denoted by *pò* verbs. Consequently, the categorization of break verbs is rarely talked about in Chinese linguistics. In addition, another point worth mentioning is that although Hu (2005) proves that simplex *pò* verbs encoding both action and result are replaced by complex V+*pò* constructions, he doesn't provide any explanation for such replacement. To this, Xu (2001) mentions that such a change results from the general trend that Chinese is turning from a synthetic language to an analytic language. Besides, based on Sapir's (1921) traditional typological scheme, Huang (2015) also notes that old Chinese is similar to English, packaging action and result within a single verb. But modern Chinese spells the action out and represents it explicitly by means of an extra action verb.

It goes without saying that diachronic studies on break verbs are rather limited. But this does not mean diachronic studies on other lexical items exhibit the same status quo. On the contrary, diachronic studies on lexical semantic change are fairly animate in Chinese linguistics. In the following section, diachronic Chinese linguistic studies on lexical semantic change are reviewed.

2.6 Diachronic Chinese linguistic studies on lexical semantic change

Early studies on Chinese lexical semantic change date back to the historical linguistic studies in 1950s. Wang (2013/1957–1958: 520) claims that language is dynamic and word meaning is variable. Inspired by historical-philosophical linguistics, he agrees that semantic change can be classified into semantic narrowing, semantic expanding, and semantic transfer (Wang 2013/1957–1958: 529). Jiang (1985) reexamines the threefold classification of semantic change and holds that it's too assertive to simply state a word's meaning is narrowed or expanded. Since some words are polysemous, he proposes to identify semantic change based on words' specific sememes. Moreover, based on the semantic component encoded in a word, Jiang finds that some semantic narrowing cases are actually semantic switch. For instance, the semantic meaning of *tì* (涕) has switched from denoting the fluid from the eyes to the fluid from the nose. What's more, Jiang (1985) further notes that semantic narrowing, semantic expanding, semantic transfer, and semantic switch are results of semantic change. These four types of semantic change result from the mechanism of semantic extension. Other mechanisms of semantic change proposed and further examined in Chinese linguistics include semantic contamination (Wu 1984), synchronous extension (Xu 1987), abbreviation as well as Traugott's Invited Inferencing (Jiang 2016).

In terms of research methodology, conceptual component analysis, conceptual field analysis, and cognitive typological analysis also have been widely adopted in studies on semantic change. For instance, Cui (2001) and Du (2002) investigate the semantic change of eat and drink verbs by examining the conceptual fields these verbs denote in their historical evolution. Likewise, Jiang (2005) examines how the Chinese motion verb *zǒu* (走) develops from expressing 'running' to 'walking' through conceptual component analysis. Jiang (2006) explores how the ten sememes of Chinese verb *tóu* (投) develops historically across eight conceptual fields. Dong (2009) reveals how the Chinese motion verb *tí* (提) gets the meaning of speaking in terms of its semantic variation across the conceptual fields of motion and speaking. Wang (2012) reexamines the semantic change of motion verb *tí* by observing its conceptual relation with the speaking verb *tí* (题). Jiang (2011, 2016) attends to the semantic change of eat and drink verbs through comparing their conceptual components and conceptual fields. Jia and Wu (2017) revisit the historical evolution of eat and drink verbs from a cognitive typological perspective. They address the semantic extensions of eat and drink verbs along with the semantic variables of <agent> and <patient> and conclude that the diachronic lexicalization and categorization of Chinese eat and cut verbs are highly consistent with that of other languages.

Apart from the above studies on diachronic semantic variation, some studies also concentrate on lexical grammaticalization. For instance, Li (2004) traces the grammaticalization of specific speech into abstract speech act verbs. For instance, he uncovers that speech act verbs like *zài-jiàn* (再见 goodbye) and *zhēn-zhòng* (珍重 take care) are developed from specific uttering of goodbye and take care. Wu (2007) probes the semantic change of the Chinese location word *hòu* (后), and formulates its evolution pathway as motion > space > time > time/ discourse > discourse/pragmatics. In his account for such changes, Wu indicates that the gramaticalization of *hòu* is a process of subjectification. The semantic change of *hòu* is greatly motivated by the mechanism of pragmatic inference. For instance, as a motion word, *hòu* indicates that Figure A moves behind Figure B. Based on this, it's not uneasy to infer that Figure B locates behind Figure A in the spatial dimension. In the same fashion, it's easy to further infer that Figure B will arrive at the terminal later than Figure B in the temporal dimension.

In general, lexical semantic change has been a central research topic in Chinese linguistics. The conceptual domains that have been focused on range from motion verbs (*tóu, tí*), eat and drink verbs, to location words (*hòu*), and speech act verbs. The research methodologies that have been employed vary from lexical substitution, conceptual component analysis, conceptual field analysis, and cognitive typological analysis. But be that as it may, as Jiang (2006) mentions, Chinese lexical semantic change is understudied and it's necessary to call for more attention to semantic change. As far as this literature review goes, such necessity can be outlined from two aspects. First of all, in terms of research methods, the majority of diachronic semantic studies rely on example enumeration. Admittedly, methods like conceptual component analysis, conceptual field analysis, and semantic typological analysis are adopted in prior studies. These methods have their own downsides. For instance, both conceptual component analysis and conceptual field analysis overlook the prototypical relationship between words' multiple sememes. Cognitive linguistic analysis compares words' semantic meanings in terms of variables like <agent> and <patient>, but disregards the interacting relationship between these variables.

Furthermore, concerning the range of words covered in prior studies, only a few words from the domain of motion, eating and drinking, as well as speech are examined. However, words of other conceptual domains like state change, weather, and cooking are rarely addressed. In view of this, our proposed study on the diachronic variation of break verbs is necessary and significant.

2.7 Summary

2.7.1 What has been done

Generally speaking, as shown in Table 2.5, a wide range of approaches have been employed in exploring the categorization of break verbs in terms of either syntactic means or conceptual variables. The syntactic means include not only the syntactic patterns and grammatically relevant meaning components, but also the temporal structure and causal structure that break verbs are involved with. Conceptual variables are simply the specific variables that the extensional reference of break verbs is related to, including <affected object>, <instrument>, <force>, <manner of action>, <reversal>, <endstate>, <functionality> and <intentionality>.

2.7.2 What needs to be done

Although break verbs have already been meticulously examined under a wide range of theoretical frameworks, there are some problems remain unresolved.

Firstly, previous studies attend to the argument realization and semantic structure of break verbs primarily from a synchronic perspective (Figure 2.8). They are more concerned with the crosslinguistic variations involved in the syntactic and semantic structures of break verbs. As a result, the diachronic variations of break verbs fall into oblivion. Even though generative semantic studies propose a dichotomy of break verbs and cut verbs (Guerssel et al. 1985; Hale and Keyser 1987), developmental psycholinguistic studies and cognitive

Table 2.5 Summary of research approaches on the categorization of break verbs

Research approaches		Categorization evidence and variables	Categorization results	General conclusion
Generative semantic approach	Generative derivational	Causative alternation	Cut *vs.* break	Universal
	Generative decompositional	Causative construction; Change of state; Manner/result complementarity	Externally caused change of state/result verbs (cut *vs.* break); Cut$_{manner}$ *vs.* break	Universal
Developmental psycholinguistic approach		Children's overextensions <affected object>, <reversal>, <instrument>, <action>, <endstate>	Overextension in different ways	Language specific but constrained by variables
Cognitive linguistic approach	Cognitive extensionalist approach	Event descriptions <locus of separation>, <affected object>, <instrument>, <endstate>, <manner of action>	Open *vs.* (cut *vs.* break)	Language specific but constrained within a semantic space
	NSM approach	imperfective tense	Cut *vs.* break	Universal
	Frame semantics	evoked frames <functionality>, <force>, <endstate>, <focus>, <intentionality>	Separation (cut *vs.* break (smash *vs.* shred *vs.* chip *vs.* slice))	Language specific, but constrained by frame variables
	Causal chain approach	aspectual structure and causal structure; <aspectual contour>, <reversibility>, <direction>, <increment>	Open *vs.* break; Cut$_{manner+result}$ *vs.* break	Universal
	Talmy's event categorization	[Figural entity], [State], [Transition type], [Ground entity]	break, cut and open are all state change events	Universal
Diachronic syntactic approach		transitivity of break verbs is dynamic		
Diachronic constructional approach		constructional patterns of break verbs are dynamic		

typological studies reveal that there's no sharp line between breaking events and cutting events (Bowerman 2005; Majid et al. 2007a, etc.). Our concern on this point is whether the conceptual boundary of break verbs was different when culture and tools were less developed, whether events like cutting and opening were subcategories of breaking events in ancient times. To answer these questions, we believe it is necessary to trace the diachronic pathway of break verbs.

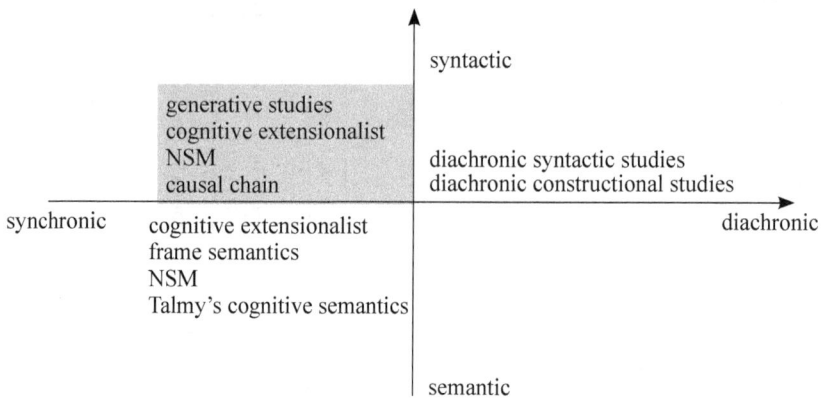

Figure 2.8 Research gap

Secondly, in terms of Chinese break verbs, previous studies are more concerned with the syntactic structure of break verbs, but pay little attention to the conceptual structure of break verbs, let alone the diachronic conceptual variation of break verbs. Previous syntactic studies on Chinese break verbs already make outstanding achievements but semantic or conceptual studies lag far behind. In view of this, this book decides to concentrate on the conceptual range of Chinese break verbs and aims to reveal how the conceptual range of Chinese break verbs change by bringing together those conceptual variables sporadically investigated in previous studies.

Thirdly, there is no denying that a limited number of studies (Garib 2012; Spalek 2012, 2015; Kwon 2016, etc.) have compared the extensional-intensional uses of break verbs, but few studies have systematically attended to the corresponding relation between extensional usages and intensional readings.

Given this, this study lends itself also to revealing how intensional readings are extended from their corresponding extensional usages.

Finally, in terms of research methods, as mentioned above, classical linguistics, generative semantics as well as Chinese linguistics are constrained to example enumeration (Table 2.6). Although developmental psycholinguistic studies take notice of the multiple variables that more or less determine the conceptual boundary of break verbs, they fail to account for the weight assumed by these variables in a comprehensive fashion. Cognitive typological studies, especially the MPI studies, employ the method of correspondence analysis, but the three dimensions they uncover do not correspond to any of the specific variables (Moore *et al.* 2015). In view of this, our proposed study only takes into consideration specific perceptual and interactive variables. To reveal the matrix variable combination as well as the specific weight assumed by different variables, we make use of corpus data and resort to statistic methods like correspondence analysis, Ctree, and random forest for data analysis.

Table 2.6 Research methods employed in previous studies

Research methods	Data source	Data analysis
Generative studies	example enumeration	manual comparison
Developmental psycholinguistics	examples, elicitation	manual comparison, CA
Cognitive typological studies	elicitation	CA
Diachronic syntactic studies	examples	manual comparison
Diachronic constructional studies	examples	manual comparison
Diachronic conceptual variation	corpus data	MCA, Ctree, random forest

CHAPTER 3

Research methodology and design

This chapter presents the research methodology adopted in this study and the research design of three specific studies. The research methodology includes both theoretical framework and research methods. Section 3.1 introduces the theoretical framework under which this study is conducted. Section 3.2 expounds the research target and the research design of the three studies. Section 3.3 gives an account of the specific research methods. Section 3.4 specifies the detailed data retrieval, data annotation, and data analysis procedures. Section 3.5 is the summary of the chapter.

3.1 Theoretical framework

As demonstrated in the literature review, there are numerous applicable theoretical approaches for surveying conceptual variation, such as Frame Semantics, NSM, Causal Chain. DPS is adopted primarily for two reasons. Firstly, DPS brings together prototype theory and diachronic semantics, and thus happens to afford a feasible framework for investigating how the conceptual structure of break verbs varied diachronically. Moreover, DPS integrates extensional usages and intensional readings and thus makes it possible to trace break verbs both in terms of their extensional and intensional evolution. But DPS is not accepted completely as it is. We propose a revised version of DPS and put forward a tentative model of diachronic conceptual variation.

In what follows, section 3.1.1 reviews briefly how prototype theory evolves from classical theory. Section 3.1.2 traces the extension from prototype theory to DPS. Section 3.1.3 proposes a revised version of DPS.

3.1.1   From classical theory to prototype theory

Throughout the twentieth century, much work in philosophy, psychology, linguistics, and anthropology advocate that categories are internally unstructured, category members are equivalent, and category boundary is well defined in terms of criterial features (Taylor 2003: Cha 2). Such proposals on categorization are subsumed under the node "classical theory" and usually trace back to Aristotle. With his most frequently cited example "man", Aristotle insists that category should be delineated in terms of necessary and sufficient features. For instance, the category "man" is defined in terms of two features, "two-footed" and "animal" (Aristotle 1933).

Against such a research background, Rosch and her colleagues (Rosch 1973, 1975, 1977; Rosch and Mervis 1975; Mervis and Rosch 1981) prove with psychological experiments that natural categories are highly structured internally, with a prototype surrounded by nonprototype members. The prototype is the best exemplar of the category and bears a family resemblance to its nonprototype members. More importantly, they find that the boundary of a category is not clear-cut. A category cannot be defined in terms of necessary and sufficient features. In view of this, they conclude that the majority of categories are prototypical in nature and are thus should be referred to as "prototypical categories".

To corroborate their proposal, Rosch and her colleagues probe into the internal structure of both perceptual categories (color, form) and semantic categories (furniture, bird) (Berlin and Kay 1969; Rosch 1973, 1975; Kay and McDaniel 1978; Mervis and Rosch 1981). And their claims on the internal structure of categories can be summarized in terms of four prototypicality effects, including the degree of typicality, family resemblance, blur edge, and indiscrete definition. By degree of typicality, they emphasize that prototypical categories exhibit degrees of typicality, and not every member is equally representative for a category. By family resemblance, they mean that prototypical categories exhibit a family resemblance structure and their semantic structure takes the form of a radial set of clustered and overlapping readings (Rosch and Mervis 1975; Wittgenstein 1953/2001). By blur edge, they indicate that prototypical categories are blurred at their edges. Finally, by indiscrete definition, they highlight that prototypical categories cannot be defined by means of a single set of criterial (necessary and sufficient) attributes.

3.1.2 From prototype theory to DPS

Despite the fact that prototype theory has been tested against both natural and semantic categories, it is primarily employed to work on categories existent in a certain culture at a given time (Rosch 1977). In view of this, Geeraerts (1983, 1997, 1998) extends prototype theory into historical semantics and put forward DPS.

Further summarizing those four prototypicality effects, Geeraerts (1997: 11) reduces them into a distinction between non-equality and non-discreteness. And by crosscutting this distinction with the distinction between extensional and intensional levels, he puts forward a contingency table (Table 3.1) which shows extensional non-equality, extensional non-discreteness, intensional non-equality, and intensional non-discreteness. And then these four effects are further turned into four statements on semantic change, as shown in Table 3.2 (Geeraerts 1997: 23).

Table 3.1 Prototypicality effects at extensional and intensional levels (Geeraerts 1997: 11)

Prototypicality effects	Extensional (on the referential level)	Intensional (on the level of senses)
Non-equality (salience effects, internal structure of core and periphery)	(a) Differences of salience among members of a category	(c) Clustering of readings into family resemblances and radial sets
Non-discreteness (demarcation problems, flexible applicability)	(b) Fluctuations at the edges of a category	(d) Absence of definitions in terms of necessary and sufficient attributes

Table 3.2 Four statements on diachronic categorical variation (Geeraerts 1997: 23)

(1) By stressing the extensional non-equality of lexical-semantic structure, prototype theory highlights the fact that changes in the referential range of one specific word meaning may take the form of modulations on the core cases within that referential range.

(2) By stressing the extensional non-discreteness of lexical semantic structure, prototype theory highlights the phenomenon of incidental, transient changes of word meaning.

(3) By stressing the intensional non-equality of lexical-semantic structure, prototype theory highlights the clustered set structure of changes of word meaning.

(4) By stressing the intensional non-discreteness of lexical semantic structure, prototype theory highlights the encyclopedic nature of changes in word meaning.

Extensional non-equality indicates that central members of prototypical categories are usually stable, whereas noncentral members change based on the modulation of central members. For instance, in the diachronic development of Dutch *legging*, its prototype member remains stable and takes on features like "from below the calves to the ankles, tight-fitting, no crease, smooth material, upper wear, worn by woman", whereas its peripheral members are less stable and change in the form of gradually losing these prototypical features (Geeraerts 1997: 35-44). Non-discreteness instantiates that the conceptual boundary of lexical categories may fluctuate diachronically. That is, some lexical meanings may come into being and then disappear all through the diachronic development of lexical categories. For instance, the transient meaning of Dutch verb *vergraven*, "to hide something by burying it", first cropped up in the sixteenth century, disappeared after the sixteenth century, and showed up again in the nineteenth century (Geeraerts 1997: 65-66).

Intensional non-equality highlights that the various meanings of a lexical item constitute a clustered set structure. Its central meanings are structurally more weighted based on which its peripheral meanings are usually extended from. Diachronically, central meanings are relatively stable while peripheral meanings do not subsist. Taking Dutch verb *vergrijpen* as an instance, "to use physical violence against (someone)" is one of its central meanings, based on which extended peripheral meanings like "to oppose someone to whom one owes respect and obedience", "to do something forbidden" and "to commit suicide" arise in later stages. Among them, "to commit suicide" did not subsist after the 18th century (Geeraerts 1997: 59). Intensional non-discreteness claim stresses that there is no fault line between encyclopedic knowledge and semantic senses. It is precisely this encyclopedic nature that gives rise to the indefinite intensional boundary of lexical items. Diachronically, the semantic change of a lexical item may start from the extensional level just as well as from the intensional level, or from the encyclopedic information just as well as from the semantic information. For instance, Dutch verb *kruipen* originally meant "move on hands and knees" with "to move slowly on hands and knees" as its salient subset. But in a later phase, the peripheral encyclopedic information "to move slowly" has successfully developed as a new meaning.

3.1.3 From DPS to revised DPS

Admittedly, DPS brings prototype and semantic change together into an overall model of the diachronic structure of semantic categories. But in spite of this, DPS is not thoroughly adopted as it is. The present study maintains that the non-equality and non-discreteness claims need further revisions (Table 3.3). In the first place, DPS supports that prototypical members are always stable in the diachronic variation of lexical categories. Our present study insists that this hypothesis should be a bit weaker in the sense that prototypical members are relatively but not always stable in the course of diachronic variation. This is because categories are dependent upon social and cultural context, the change of which will give rise to fluctuations in the categorical structure (Rosch 1975; Györi 1996; Taylor 2003: 59). When enough changes have happened in the categorical structure, the core meaning will also change and so does the prototypicality (Winters 1987). For instance, Chinese "tì" (涕) refers to fluid from the nose or eyes in ancient Chinese but now only denotes nasal discharge in Mandarin (Jiang 2016). In addition, concerning extensional non-discreteness of category boundary, DPS holds that some transient meanings could spring into existence at any moment in the history of the word. But this study considers that transient meaning is a bit farfetched to verify extensional non-discreteness. Extensional non-discreteness can be better elaborated in terms of the diachronic boundary variation between semantically similar categories. That is, this study believes that it is the diachronic variation in the categorical belonging of certain category members that gives rise to the diachronic boundary fluctuation.

As for intensional non-equality and non-discreteness, apart from the above-mentioned claims, this study aims to emphasize that there exists a cross-domain correspondence between extensional references and intensional readings. In terms of intensional non-equality, among the varying intensional readings of a lexical item, it is its literal reading that makes up the prototypical core while those intensional readings extended from this literal reading are peripheral. As noted above, the literal reading *per se* is structured prototypically. It subsumes all the extensional references of the lexical item. By non-discreteness, we want to point out that intensional readings of a lexical item always arise from its extensional usages. We can always find the extensional origins of the intensional senses. Moreover, even if the extensional origin of an intensional reading has died out, this later emerged intensional reading might still subsist and be further extended to give rise to new intensional readings.

Table 3.3   Revisions of the statements on diachronic categorical variation

---

（1）Extensional non-equality does not necessarily indicate that prototypical members are always stable, because when enough of the categorical structure of a lexical item has changed, the core meaning will change and so will the prototype;

（2）Extensional non-discreteness can be better elaborated in terms of the conceptual boundary variation among near-synonymous semantic categories;

（3）Intensional non-equality and non-discreteness emphasize the cross-domain correspondence between extensional references and intensional readings. It is always possible to figure out the extensional origins of the intensional readings of a lexical item. Even when their extensional usages have faded away, the intensional readings will still subsist and can be further extended to give rise to novel intensional readings.

3.2 Research design

Framed under revised DPS, this study extends previous studies on object categorization to event categorization and attends to the categorization of breaking, cutting, and opening events. This section first defines our research target in 3.2.1. Then the research design of three specific studies is sketched in 3.2.2.

3.2.1 Research target

This study defines break verbs as any verbs which denote the transition of an object from a complete state to an incomplete state. In this sense, break verbs are rather broad in their range, including *pò, làn, liè, duàn, qiē, shé*, and *kāi*, etc. This study does not aim to encompass all these verbs but home in on *pò, qiē*, and *kāi*. These three keywords are targeted based on both qualitative and quantitative criteria.

In the first place, we choose to focus on *pò, qiē* and *kāi* because the classification of their English counterparts constitutes a controversial issue in previous synchronic studies. For instance, generative syntactic studies (Guerssel et al. 1987) insist that English *break* and *open* belong to the same class while *cut* behaves differently from them. In contrast, generative semantic studies (Levin and Rappaport Hovav 1995, 2008) hold that these three lexical items should be subsumed under the node of result verbs because they all encode the semantic element [state change]. Cognitive extensionalist studies (Majid et al. 2007a, 2007b) point out that crosslinguistic classification of these three and their semantically similar verbs displays typological universals. In view of these disagreements in synchronic studies, this study turns to a diachronic investigation of these three lexical items and aims to reveal their dynamic conceptual relationship. Since historical Chinese corpora avail us to trace the conceptual development of break verbs, we opt for Chinese *pò*, *qiē*, and *kāi*.

More importantly, these three keywords have been used for a long time from ancient Chinese to modern Chinese, and thus lay the groundwork for our diachronic investigation. Specifically, among them, *pò* and *kāi* are the most frequently used and their token frequencies are above 3000. Although *qiē* is comparatively lower in its token frequency, its type frequency is relatively high all through ancient and modern Chinese. In stark contrast, the other verbs like *làn* and *liè* only show up in modern Chinese but are rarely used in ancient Chinese. As a result, we cannot trace their diachronic development simply based on corpora and they are thus beyond our research scope.

Another important point we need to bring forward is that *pò*, *qiē*, and *kāi* have undergone syntactic changes in the development of Chinese. In ancient Chinese, *pò* and *kāi* were more prototypically used as monomorphemic verbs and encoded both action and result. But in modern Chinese, they have relegated to verb complements and more frequently show up in forms like V∣*pò* and V+*kāi*. Like *pò* and *kāi*, *qiē* was also used in its monomorphemic form and denoted the action and result of object separation. But different from *pò* and *kāi*, *qiē* does not develop into a verb complement but grow into an action verb which is complemented by preposition phrases or adjectives (in the form of *qiē*+PP or *qiē*+AP). This study sets such syntactic changes as the background for our study on diachronic conceptual variation. These keywords are regarded as anchor verbs in their collocation patterns. On the one hand, this study attends to the diachronic variation of these three lexical items in their conceptual range. A detailed elaboration on their syntactic variation will repeat previous studies and leave this study far afield from its central goal. On the other hand, even though *pò* and *kāi* have relegated to verb complements and *qiē* has developed into an action verb, their application ranges are in the same line as their monomorphemic forms. In this sense, it is still feasible to trace the conceptual ranges of *pò*, *qiē*, and *kāi* even when they have changed in their existing forms.

3.2.2 Research design

With *pò*, *qiē*, and *kāi* as the research target, three studies are conducted to answer our proposed research questions.

Chapter 4 presents the first study which attends to the diachronic conceptual variation of extensional *pò*. The extensional *pò*'s diachronic trajectory is characterized in terms of the distribution of its extensional usages. The underlying cognitive mechanism is explored by revealing the weight assumed by different conceptual variables. This study reveals how the working principle of "conceptual adjustment" operates in the process of conceptual variation.

Chapter 5 captures the second study which is on the conceptual boundary variation of *pò*, *qiē*, and *kāi*. This study shows how the three lexical items reorganize their conceptual ranges along the timeline and demonstrates the operation of the principle "conceptual reorganization".

Chapter 6 addresses the intensional readings of *pò*. The corresponding relationship between extensional usages and the intensional readings are matched in terms of the specific type of events of separation state change they denote. The working principles of "conceptual alignment" and "conceptual independence" are characterized.

In what follows, detailed procedures of data retrieval, annotation, and analysis are described.

3.3 Research methods

Situated in the framework of revised DPS, the conceptualization and categorization of break verbs are explored by means of multiple multivariate methods. Section 3.2.1 first accounts for the reason why multivariate methods are resorted to. Section 3.2.2 presents the specific multivariate methods employed in this study, including MCA, Ctree, and random forest.

3.3.1 Multivariate methods

Self-evidently, multivariate methods emphasize the multivariate nature of the semantic structure and advocate for the statistical analysis of linguistic phenomena with the help of multivariate techniques (Geeraerts 2006: vi).

In the first place, the semantic structure is multivariate in nature. Semantic structures of any degree of complexity (lexeme, construction, or syntactic rule) vary from speaker to speaker, from context to context, and from time period to time period (Glynn 2010: 9). Consequently, either manual abstraction from these multiple variates (or variables) or any focus on one single variate is overly ideal and unnatural. Multivariate methods, however, confront the inevitability of this linguistic complexity directly and prove to be powerful in dealing with the multivariate dataset. For one thing, multivariate methods help to identify the associations and disassociations between different variate types. This is especially tricky when the dataset is large and the number of variates is numerous. In other words, multivariate methods substitute intuitive analysis of co-occurrence information with objective and exploratory statistics (Jansegers and Gries 2020). In addition, multivariate methods render the measurement of the internal structure of variates possible. Language usages of a certain linguistic pattern show the simultaneous interaction of different variables which assume a differential weight in determining these usages. With multivariate methods, the conditional importance of those different variables can be revealed.

More importantly, multivariate methods offer a multitude of applicable techniques for data processing. Such techniques release manual identification, and thus reduce subjectivity and afford more objectivity in the data processing. Moreover, these techniques transform data matrix into dot plots and allow visualization. Such techniques are great in number and different in algorithm.

The most frequently used multivariate techniques can be classified into three types, namely exploratory analysis, confirmatory analysis, and machine learning model (Zhang and Liu 2016). Exploratory analytical methods include correspondence analysis, multidimensional scaling, cluster analysis, and mosaic plots etc. Confirmatory analytical methods include different kinds of regression analysis like linear regression analysis, logistic regression analysis as well as poison regression analysis. Machine learning model refers to methods like conditional inference tree, random forest and naïve discriminative learning, etc. It should be noted that these techniques are usually not individually employed but most often go hand in hand in analyzing a certain linguistic phenomenon. For more information on these methods, please refer to Glynn (2010), Levshina (2015) as well as Zhang and Liu (2016). Section 3.2.2 introduces those methods that are employed in this study of break verbs.

Despite the advocation for multivariate analysis in recent linguistics, it is necessary to mention that multivariate analysis is not brand new in linguistics. Some linguists already noticed the importance of multiple variates decades ago. The difference is that their multivariate studies are manually conducted but recent linguistics propose statistic-technique-based multivariate analysis. For instance, Labov (1973) in his study on the lexeme *cup* finds that the categorical boundary of *cup* is demarcated by variables like <function>, <material>, <width> and <length> etc. Likewise, Chinese historical linguist Jiang (1985, 2016) states that the diachronic variations of lexical items are co-determined by different semantic variables. For instance, the usages of knocking verbs like *qiāo* and *jī* are driven by variables like <action>, <force>, <object>, and the <result sound> (Jiang 2016: 122).

3.3.2 MCA, Ctree, and Random forest

In view of the above mentioned advantages that multivariate methods display, this study addresses the diachronic conceptual variation of break verbs in terms of a set of multivariate methods, including MCA, Ctree as well as random forest.

MCA (Multiple Correspondence Analysis)

MCA constitutes a further extension of simple CA. It is an explanatory technique for complex categorical data and identifies the association or disassociation between different usages of a linguistic form and its various categorical variables (Glynn 2014: 443). The rationale behind this is that MCA (like CA) converts the frequency of co-occurring features into a distance matrix, which is then plotted, revealing how far or close the variables are in a two-dimensional or three-dimensional space (Greenacre 1984). MCA takes into consideration not bivariate but multivariate categorical data. MCA plot shows the association both between multiple variable levels and between varying individual usages of the lexical categories. The association between variable levels indicates how strongly they are related and whether they can be interpreted by means of common dimensions of variation as shown in Figure 3.1 (Greenacre 1984). The association between individual usages reveals the category structure of the lexical item, including both its center and periphery as shown in Figure 3.2 and Figure 3.3 (Levshina 2015: 375).

Figures 3.1, 3.2 and 3.3 are three MCA plots showing the conceptual ranges of two German lexical categories *Stuhl* (chair) and *Sessel* (armchair) (Levshina 2015: Cha 19). They are presented to give an impression of how MCA plots visualize the lexical conceptual structure. To be specific, Figure 3.1 displays the association between variable levels. The short distance indicates close association while the long distance suggests independent relation. For instance, conceptual variable levels like *Back_Adjust* and *SeatDepth_Adjust* are close and are associated while *Back_Adjust* and *Rock_Rock* are far in distance and thus are less associated with each other. The first dimension differentiates variable levels associated with *work* from those associated with *outdoor*. The second dimension tells variable levels associated with *AddFucntions_Table* from *AddFunctions_Bed*. As *Stuhl* locates at the upright and *Sessel* at the low left, we can see that these two lexical categories are fairly different in their associated variables. Figure 3.2 and Figure 3.3 demonstrate specific usages of the two lexical categories which constitute their conceptual range.

MCA also allows us to draw confidence ellipse around the centroids and conceptual boundary of the keywords by setting the logistic value of addEllipses as "addEllipses=TRUE". With the value of ellipse.level set as "ellipse.level=0.05", an ellipse will be drawn around the prototypical center of the keywords (enclosing 5% of the exemplars). By setting the ellipse level at 0.95, an ellipse will be drawn around the conceptual boundary of the keyword (enclosing 95% of the exemplars). With confidence ellipses, Figure 3.2 shows the category centers of the two lexical categories are distant from each other, whereas Figure 3.3 exhibits that their peripheral boundaries are overlapped. Such distribution indicates that these two lexical categories are different in their central members but their peripheral members sometimes overlap.

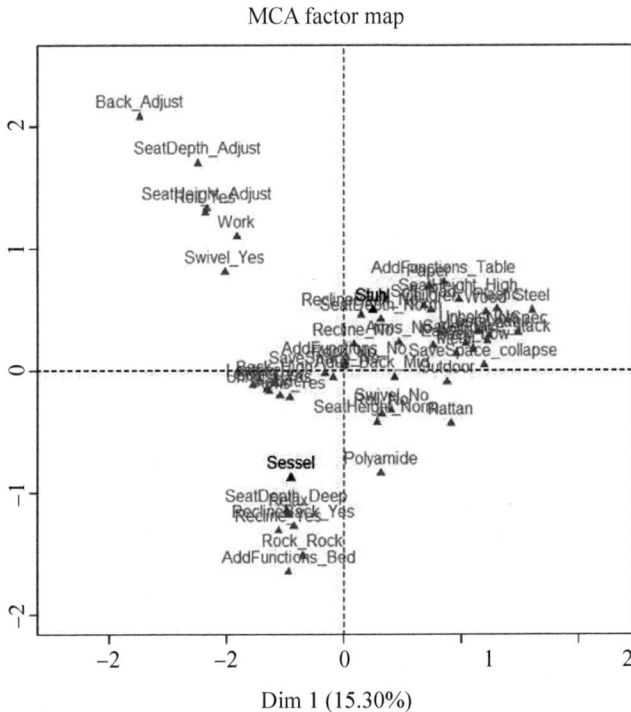

Figure 3.1   Association between variable levels (Levshina 2015: 276)

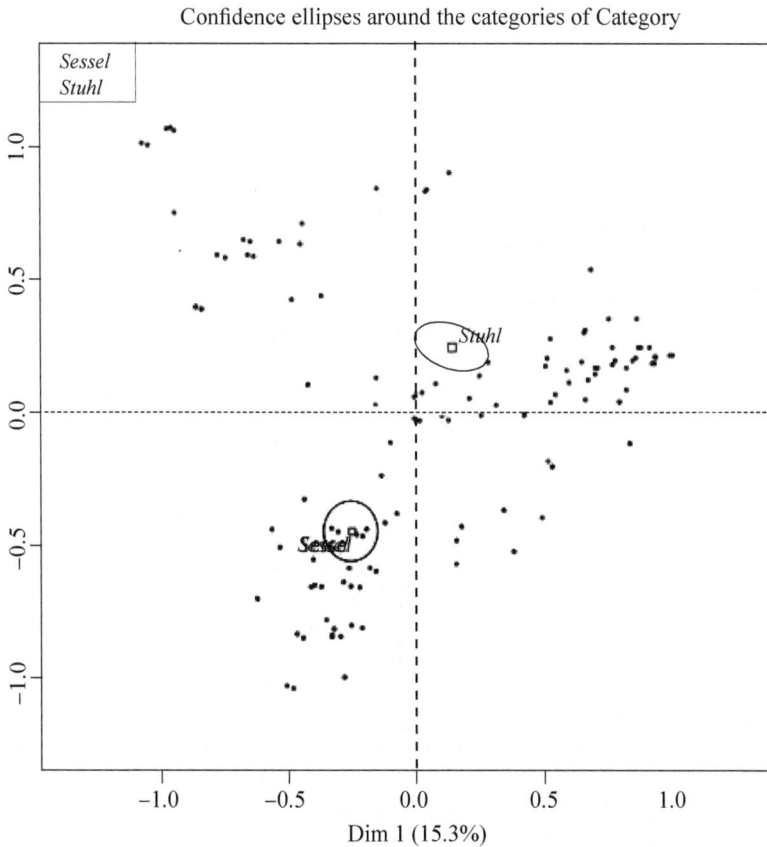

Figure 3.2 **Association between individual usages and category center (Levshina 2015: 380)**

Further speaking, MCA draws upon both variable levels and lexical usages and henceforth brings together prototype and usage (Divjak and Arppe 2013). It should be noted that MCA is a "fishing" technique. By "fishing", it means that one should bear in mind a target correlation he or she intends to locate in advance. This is because MCA is a tool for identifying correlations, but whether the correlation is significant or meaningless depends on the researcher's pre-determined target. R packages should be installed and loaded for MCA include {FactoMineR}, {factoextra} and {mjca}.

Ctree (conditional inference tree)

Ctree is a machine learning method for regression and classification based

Confidence ellipses around the categories of Category

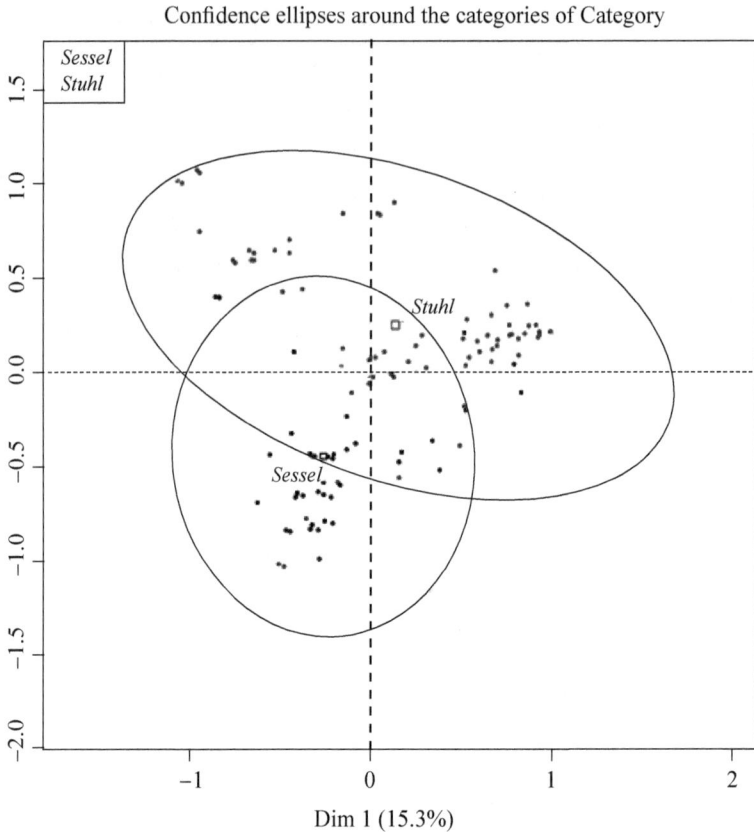

Dim 1 (15.3%)

Figure 3.3 Association between individual usages and the category periphery

(Levshina 2015: 381)

on binary recursive partitioning. It is especially useful in cases where the sample size is small but the predictor size is large (Levshina 2015: Cha 14). Specifically speaking, Ctree involves three steps. In the first step, the algorithm tests and chooses the variables that are most strongly associated with the response variables. Then in the second step, those variables are binarily split with a certain *p*-value. These two steps are recursively executed until the *p*-value is under the pre-defined threshold. Finally, the result of Ctree forms a tree model with nodes and branches and shows the interaction between those differential variables. Ctree demonstrates two advantages in the data processing. For one thing, its algorithm can effectively avoid bias and overfitting. Moreover, the algorithm returns the *p*-value which shows how confident one can be about the split.

Random forest

From many conditional inference trees, we can grow random forest. The random forest algorithm seeks to predict which of the alternatives is most probable. Random forest works through the data and establishes whether a variable is a useful predictor. The basic algorithm used by the random forest constructs conditional inference trees. Random forest constructs a large number of conditional inference trees (Tagliamonte and Baayen 2012). Each tree in the forest is grown for a subset of the data generated by random sampling without replacement from observations and predictors. It yields a variable importance measure reflecting the impact of each variable in both main effects and interactions (Strobl et al. 2009). In other words, random forest displays the importance of predictors while Ctree visualizes how multiple predictors operate in tandem. To realize Ctree and random forest, R packages like {mclm} {lmerTest} {car} {effects} {party} and {Rling} should be loaded.

3.4 Data retrieval, annotation and analysis

3.4.1 Data retrieval

To trace break verbs' diachronic conceptual variation, this study resorts to CCL corpus (Center for Chinese Linguistics PKU)[①]. CCL corpus is composed of two sub-corpora, namely the ancient Chinese sub-corpus and the modern Chinese sub-corpus. The ancient Chinese sub-corpus comprises 20 billion characters of classical texts in Chinese, covering a period from the 11th century BC to the 20th century. The modern Chinese sub-corpus comprises 50 billion characters of modern Chinese texts. The varied genres of both sub-corpora range from novels, fiction, poems, and prose to scriptures etc. Only the ancient Chinese sub-corpus is employed for data collection in this study.

---

① The website of CCL corpus is http://ccl.pku.edu.cn:8080/ccl_corpus/index.jsp?dir=gudai.

Chronological stages of Chinese

As a diachronic study, it is the varied usages of break verbs across different chronological stages that form the research baseline. To set up this baseline, we first explore how the usages of break verbs change across four chronological stages. In terms of Chinese historical stages, we refer to Wang (2013/1957–1958: 35) and Traugott and Dasher (2002: xiii). They divide the history of Chinese into the following seven developmental stages:

Pre-Archaic Chinese (PAC) (1400 BC—1100 BC)

Early Archaic Chinese (EAC) (1100 BC—500 BC)

Late Archaic Chinese (LAC) (500 BC—200 BC)

Early Middle Chinese (EMC) (200 BC—AD 600)

Late Middle Chinese (LMC) (600—1250)

Early Mandarin (EMand) (1250—1800)

Modern Mandarin (MdMand) (1800—present)

It should be noted that this periodization is not determined arbitrarily but based on specific considerations. The factors that have been taken into consideration for the division of these stages include phonological evolution, language development, social-cultural advancement as well as dynastic changes. Meanwhile, previous studies conducted upon these seven chronological stages have already captured some historical regularities of language development.

Among these seven stages, this study chooses to focus on the final four stages to facilitate our discussion on diachronic change. The first three stages are disregarded because data on break verbs in these three stages are very limited. As Table 3.4 shows, the EMC stage embraces the Han dynasty, the Three Kingdoms, the Jin dynasty, and Northern and Southern dynasties and the Sui dynasty, and runs roughly from 200 BC to AD 600. The LMC stage starts from 600 and ends in 1250. The Tang dynasty, the Five dynasties, and the Song dynasty fall into this stage. The EMand stage incorporates the Yuan, Ming and Qing dynasties and lasts from 1250 to 1911. The MdMand stage refers to the time of the Republic of China and runs from 1912 to 1949.

Table 3.4 Four developmental stages[①]

Chinese	Chronological stages	historical dynasties	Time periods
Ancient Chinese	Early Middle Chinese (EMC)	the Han dynasty the Three Kingdoms, the Jin dynasty, and Northern and Southern dynasties the Sui dynasty	200 BC—AD600
	Late Middle Chinese (LMC)	the Tang dynasty the Five dynasties the Song dynasty	600—1250
Mandarin Chinese	Early Mandarin (EMand)	the Yuan dynasty the Ming dynasty the Qing dynasty	1250—1911
	Modern Mandarin (MdMand)	the Republic of China	1912—1949

Data collection

To make sure the dataset is controlled within a manageable range, for each keyword, we set 10,000 as a threshold. If its frequency is above the threshold, 10,000 concordance lines are randomly extracted from the corpus. If not, all the data are retrieved in that stage. For instance, the frequency of *pò* in EMC is below 10,000, thus we adopt all of them. Whereas its frequency in MdMand is above 10,000, thus we randomly extract 10,000 of the concordance lines and then retrieve the extensional usages. Additionally, speaking of intensional usages, almost two-thirds of the 10,000 concordances of *pò* in LMC, EMand, and MdMand are intensional usages. To strike a balance between the extensional and intensional usages of *pò*, we randomly take into consideration 30% of the intensional usages in LMC (6,188) and EMand (6,829) respectively and 20% of the intensional usages in MdMand (3,426). In doing so, altogether 12,830 extensional usages of *pò*, *qiē*, and *kāi* and 5,668 intensional usages of *pò* are collected (Table 3.5 and Table 3.6). The disproportionate distribution of the

---

① Different from the developmental stages mentioned in Wang (2013/1957—1958:35) and Traugott and Dasher (2002:xiii), EMand ends in 1911 and MdMand starts from 1912. This is because we take dynasty division into consideration, following CCL corpus.

extensional usages of *pò*, *qiē*, and *kāi* indicate that *pò* and *kāi* are more widely used than *qiē*.

Table 3.5 Frequency of extensional *pò*, *qiē* and *kāi* across the four stages

Key words	EMC	LMC	EMand	MdMand	Total
extensional *pò*	193	693	1,507	1,233	3,626
extensional *qiē*[①]	106	44	228	79	457
extensional *kāi*	59	1,664	3,252	3,772	8,747

Table 3.6 Frequency of extensional and intensional *pò* across the four stages

Key words	EMC	LMC	EMand	MdMand	Total
extensional *pò*	193	693	1,507	1,233	3,626
intensional *pò*	439	1,730	1,908	1,591	5,668

Specific procedures for data collection are as follows:

Step 1: Extract concordance lines of *pò, qiē* and *kāi* from CCL and single out the extensional usages of *pò, qiē*, and *kāi* according to the above-mentioned four chronological stages, namely EMC, LMC, EMand, and MdMand. By extensional usages, here we indicate cases where these keywords are used to denote concrete object separation, no matter the separation of melon or the separation of water.

Step 2: Delete the adjective and noun uses of *pò, qiē*, and *kāi*. This study only takes into consideration their verb uses, while adjective and noun forms are beyond our research scope.

Step 3: Delete repetitive concordances, because some concordance lines are quoted or repeated in later historical works.

Step 4: Keep a separate record of the intensional usages of *pò*. Chapter 4

---

① Through comparing the frequency of *qiē* across different corpora, we find this key word is relatively constrained in its token frequency but this does not indicate it is only used in one circumstance. It is applicable to describe different types of events of separation state change.

and Chapter 5 focus on the extensional usages[①] of *pò*. Chapter 6 is concerned with the intensional readings.

Step 5: Number each concordance line in terms of the combinations of the four historical stages, the keywords it contains, and its numerical order, like EMandqie24, MdMandkai23. Meanwhile, to distinguish extensional *pò* from intensional *pò*, the former is marked as *poe* and the latter as *poi*.

3.4.2 Data annotation

Situated in a usage-based background, specific usages of the above mentioned keywords are coded in accordance with the distributional hypothesis, namely differences in function/meaning are reflected in the difference in distribution (Harris 1954; Firth 1957; Bolinger 1968). In this study, the distribution of break verbs is closely related to the events of state change proposed by Talmy (2000b: 237) because break verbs represent a subtype of events of state change, namely events of separation state change. Talmy proposes that events of state change are composed of five semantic elements, including [Agent], [Figure], [Change], [Transition type] and [Ground]. The [Agent] initiates a causal chain that culminates with a state change. The [Figure] is the object associated with a particular property while the [Ground] is the property. The [Change] is the transition of the object with respect to the property. The [Transition type] is the direction of relationship that the object has with respect to the property. It is based on these five semantic components that the conceptual variables of break verbs will be annotated.

Data annotation for extensional *pò*

To answer our first research question, the extensional usages of *pò* are manually coded in terms of four conceptual variables, including <Spatial Configuration> (SC), <Material Composition> (MC), <Functional Change> (FC) as well as <Endstate> (ES). The reason why these four variables are chosen is

---

① Extensional usages of *pò* refer to the cases where *pò* is used to describe the breaking of concrete and visible objects. In contrast, the breaking of abstract and invisible objects is regarded as its intensional usages.

that they correspond to the basic semantic components of events of state change (Talmy 2000b: 237-238), namely [Agent], [Figure], [Change], [Transition type] and [Ground].

To be specific, FC corresponds to [Agent] and suggests the agent's intentionality or purpose in carrying out the breaking events. This variable includes four levels, namely *function affected, no longer an impediment, new function*, and *function neutral. Function affected* means the agent breaks the object to affect its function, such as breaking the ship. *No longer an impediment* refers to situations where the agent breaks the object to get rid of impediments, like breaking the door. *New function* denotes cases when the agent breaks the object to make further uses, for instance breaking meat into parts for eating. *Function neutral* represents breaking events when objects are broken by natural forces with no particular purpose.

SC and MC stand for the spatial configuration and material composition of the Figure. SC represents the physical dimensionality of the objects that *pò* describes. This variable includes two levels, namely *two-dimensional* and *three-dimensional*. For instance, clothes, skin, paper, or window glass are two-dimensional while stones, human organs (head, gut, belly), bridges, or ships are three-dimensional. MC indicates the material that the objects are made of. This variable includes five levels, *fleshy, fragile, flexible, stiff*, and *tender*. Fleshy objects are normally human organs, fragile objects are glassware, flexible objects are cloth or paper, stiff objects are bamboo or bridges and tender objects include fruit or vegetables.

ES shows the objects' resulting state after the breaking action and corresponds to [Transition type] and [Ground]. This variable includes three levels, namely *surface breaking, breaking into parts*, and *breaking into pieces*. Skin breaking is an instance of surface breaking, bamboo, or door breaking shows partial breaking while glass breaking stands for breaking into pieces.

Table 3.7 demonstrates the corresponding relationship between the semantic components and the four conceptual variables. The variable levels are the specific values of each conceptual variable. They are represented by means of short forms (as listed in the annotation column) in the MCA plot. The example column cites specific usages of each variable level.

Table 3.7　Conceptual variables and variable levels of extensional *pò*

Semantic components	Conceptual variables	Variable levels	Examples	Annotations
Agent	Functional Change (FC)	function affected	他刺破了窗户纸 (he pierce break window paper)	aff
		no impediment	某公破门而入(someone break door and come in)	noimp
		new function	生姜拍破 (ginger slap break)	new
		function neutral	岩石破碎(rock break pieces)	neu
Figure	Spatial Configuration (SC)	two-dimensional	布(cloth), 纸(paper)	2
		three-dimensional	石头(stone), 箱子(box)	3
	Material Composition (MC)	fleshy	牛肉(beef), 手(hand)	fles
		fragile	杯子(cup), 碗(bowl)	fra
		flexible	布(cloth), 纸(paper)	flex
		stiff	桌子(table), 船(boat)	sti
		tender	橙子(orange), 茄子(eggplant)	ten
Transition type +Ground	Endstate (ES)	surface breaking	破其棺，棺中有人 (break that coffin, coffin inside have person)	sur
		partial breaking	卷子上纸已戳破 (paper puncture break)	par
		pieces breaking	衣服破碎 (clothes break pieces)	pie
Total	4	14	14	14

To code the extensional usages of *pò,* variable levels are concatenated together. It should be noted that since SC is proved to assume the lowest weight in later random forest and Ctree analyses, it is disregarded in the data coding process. The rest three variables MC, FC, and ES are concatenated to represent the specific usages of *pò*. After variable concatenation, we arrive at 34 extensional usages of *pò* (see Table 3.8). Explanations and examples are listed for better understanding.

For instance, *flex_affpar* stands for the affected partial separation of flexible objects like the foot wrapping cloth in (3.1a). Likewise, *ten_newpar* represents the partial separation of tender objects for new use, like peeling an orange to dispel the effect of alcohol (3.1b).

(3.1)

a. EMandpol126: 两条脚布**破**了。(*flex_affpar*)

        Liǎng-tiáo jiǎobù   pò le.

        two-CL   foot-cloth   break LE

        'Two pieces of cloth for wrapping foot were torn.'

b. MdMandpol4: 随命梅妃**破**橙醒酒。(*ten_newpar*)

        Suí   mìng Méifēi   pò   chéng xǐng jiǔ...

        then ask Mei-concubine   break orange decant alcohol

        'Then he asked his concubine Mei to break the oranges to dispel the effect of the alcohol.'

Table 3.8 34 usages of *pò* across the four chronological stages[①]

Usages	Explanations	Examples
fles_affsur	surface separation of fleshy objects to affect their functions	额头跌破。 "forehead fall break"
fles_affpar	partial separation of fleshy objects to affect their functions	马脊破烂。 "horse back break mushy"
sti_noipar	partial separation of stiff objects to remove impediments	撞破门。 "crash break door"
sti_affpar	partial separation of stiff objects to affect their functions	踢破木板。 "kick break wooden board"
flex_affpar	partial separation of flexible objects to affect their functions	撕破衣服。 "tear break clothes"
fles_noipar	partial separation of fleshy objects to remove impediments	破肚取肠。 "break belly get intestine"

① English translations of the Chinese examples are in Appendix 2.

Continued

Usages	Explanations	Examples
fra_affpie	fragmentary separation of fragile objects to affect their functions	打破碗盏。"hit break bowl"
flex_noipar	partial separation of flexible objects to remove its impediments	戳破窗户纸。"puncture break window paper"
fra_affpar	partial separation of fragile objects to affect their functions	摔破镜子。"throw break mirror"
ten_newpar	partial separation of tender objects to create new functions	葱破成段。"onion break into parts"
sti_noisur	surface separation of stiff objects to remove impediments	破柱取朔。"break pillar get Shuo"
fra_neupie	fragmentary separation of fragile objects with neutral functions	疾雷破石。"rapid thunder break stone"
fra_noipie	fragmentary separation of fragile objects to remove impediments	破石而出。"break stone and out"
fra_noipar	partial separation of fragile objects to remove impediments	破竹而下。"break bamboo and down"
fles_newpar	partial separation of fleshy objects to create new functions	将羊肉破成片。"make mutton break into pieces"
fra_noisur	surface separation of fragile objects to remove impediments	打破鸡子。"hit break egg"
sti_newpar	partial separation of stiff objects to create new functions	破棍为杖。"break stick into cane"
fles_affpie	fragmentary separation of fleshy objects to affect their functions	腹破肠流。"belly break intestine run"
flex_affpie	fragmentary separation of flexible objects to affect their functions	衣衫破碎。"clothes break pieces"
fra_neupar	partial separation of fragile objects with neutral functions	雨不破块。"rain not break soil block"
fra_newpie	fragmentary separation of fragile objects to create new functions	搦破块。"nik break soil block"
ten_noipar	partial separation of tender objects to remove impediments	擘破，取子。"thumb break, get seed"
sti_affpie	fragmentary separation of stiff objects to affect their functions	船头破碎。"boat head break pieces"
sti_neupar	partial separation of stiff objects with neutral functions	破金刚石。"break diamond"
ten_affpar	partial separation of tender objects to affect their function	踢破翠苔。"kick break moss"

Continued

Usages	Explanations	Examples
ten_neupar	partial separation of tender objects with neutral functions	破青萍。"break duckweed"
ten_newpie	fragmentary separation of tender objects to create new functions	擘破饭块。"thumb break rice block"
sti_newpie	fragmentary separation of stiff objects to create new functions	以巨竹破为四片。"with great bamboo break into four pieces"
fles_newpie	fragmentary separation of fleshy objects to create new functions	破果为六片。"break fruit into six pieces"
fra_newpar	partial separation of fragile objects to create new functions	破碎大块的油页岩。"break oil shale of big block"
sti_noipie	fragmentary separation of stiff objects to remove impediments	园篱破碎。"hedge break pieces"
ten_affpie	fragmentary separation of tender objects to affect their functions	花被狂蜂破残。"flower BEI wild bee break damage"
ten_neusur	surface separation of tender objects with neutral functions	石榴裂破。"pomegranate split break"
ten_noisur	surface separation of tender objects to remove impediments	破橙醒酒。"break orange and dispel the effect of alcohol"

Total 34

Data annotation for extensional *pò*, *qiē* and *kāi*

To further explore the conceptual boundary between Chinese *pò*, *qiē*, and *kāi*, these three keywords are further annotated in terms of a wider range of conceptual variables which are adapted from previous literature (Shaefer 1979, 1980; Bowerman and Majid 2003; Bowerman 2005; Majid et al 2007a; Chen 2007; Bouveret and Sweetser 2009; Fujii et al. 2013a). These conceptual variables include not only the abovementioned conceptual variables (MC, FC and ES) but also additional vital variables like <locus predictability>, <initiation of force>, <reversibility>, <separation mode> and <change pattern> (Table 3.9). These variables are added because they are considered criterial in differentiating break, cut, and open verbs in previous studies (Shaefer 1980; Majid et al. 2007a; Fujii et al. 2013b). SC is ignored because Ctree and random forest analyses show it assumes a very limited weight in accounting for the differential usages of extensional *pò*.

Table 3.9 Conceptual variables and variable levels of extensional pò, qiē and kāi

Semantic components	Conceptual variables	Variable levels	Examples	Annotations
Agent	Functional change	affected, noimped, new, neutral	Table 13	Table 13
	Initiation of force	onset	他踢开了箱子。(he kick open box)	onset
		extended	他把牛肉切片。(he BA beef slice pieces)	extended
Figure	Material composition	fleshy, fragile, flexible, stiff, tender	Table 3.7	Table 3.7
Change	Locus predictability	predictable	他打开门。(he hit open door)	predictable
		unpredictable	他打破玻璃。(he hit break glass)	unpredictable
	Change pattern	incremental	他切开西瓜。(he cut open melon)	incremental
		nonincremental	他跌破头。(he fall break head)	nonincremental
Transition type + Ground	Endstate	surface, partial, pieces	Table 3.7	Table 3.7
	Separation mode	clean	他把茄子切丁。(he BA eggplant cut dices)	clean
		messy	他打破了花瓶。(he hit break vase)	messy
	Reversibility	reversible	他打开壶盖。(he hit open teapot)	reversible
		irreversible	他把土豆切块。(he BA potato cut dice)	irreversible
Total	8	22		

103

<Initiation of force> refers to how the Agent exerts force on the Figure to cause state change, namely whether the causing force is initiated coextensively or only at the onset (Talmy 2000b: 418). For instance, breaking a plate only requires initial force while tearing a cloth needs extensive force. <Locus predictability> indicates if it is possible to predict where exactly the change or the separation will happen (Majid et al. 2007a). When cutting an apple with a knife, we are pretty sure where the apple will sever, whereas when smashing a bottle on the ground, it is hard to tell where the bottle will partition. <Change pattern> is related to the internal temporal process of the separation, distinguishing incremental from nonincremental changes (Croft 2015). Different from <ES>, <separation mode> here is associated with the effect of state change, namely whether the cross-section of the affected object is clean or messy after separation (Essegbey 2007). <Reversibility> is concerned with the direction of [Transition type], being reversible or irreversible (Talmy 2000b: 68; Croft 2015). The partition of the lid from the teapot is reversible because we can cover the teapot with the lid again. In contrast, the slicing of meat is irreversible. Once the meat is sliced, it cannot be together again.

Data annotation for intensional *pò*

Intensional *pò* is relatively simply encoded in terms of three variables. The first variable is the intensional readings of *pò* in a different context. Major specific intensional readings are tablelized and exemplified in Chapter 6. The second variable is the functional change of the figural entity after being "*pò*" and the variable levels are correspondent with the four levels based on which the extensional usages are annotated. The third variable is the figural entity that undergoes state change, no matter it is an emotional state, a cognitive state, or a temporal state.

3.4.3 Data analysis

As alluded to, this study adopts a multivariate research method. The dataset of all those three keynotes is analyzed with multivariate methods, such as MCA, Ctree, and random forest. As these methods have already been detailed in 3.2.2, this part only explains the specific procedures for data analysis.

Data analysis for extensional *pò*

Step 1: Represent specific usages of *pò* in the form of *mc_fces*, namely the concatenation of MC, FC, and ES.

Step 2: Calculate frequencies of *pò*'s specific usages across the four chronological stages and identify the prototypical extensional usages based on relative frequencies.

Step 3: Load the coded data matrix into R. Table 3.10 demonstrates a snapshot of the coded scheme or matrix.

Table 3.10 Snapshot of the coded scheme for extensional *pò*

Number	MC	FC	ES	CT
EMC1	stiff	noimped	surface	EMC
EMC2	tender	affected	partial	EMC
EMC3	tender	new	partial	EMC
EMC4	tender	new	partial	EMC
EMC5	stiff	new	partial	EMC
EMC6	stiff	new	pieces	EMC
EMC7	stiff	new	partial	EMC
EMC8	tender	noimped	partial	EMC
EMC9	tender	new	partial	EMC
EMC10	tender	new	pieces	EMC
EMC11	tender	new	partial	EMC
EMC12	tender	new	partial	EMC
EMC13	tender	new	partial	EMC
EMC14	tender	noimped	partial	EMC
EMC15	tender	new	pieces	EMC
EMC16	tender	new	pieces	EMC
EMC17	tender	new	pieces	EMC
EMC18	tender	new	pieces	EMC
EMC19	tender	new	pieces	EMC
EMC20	tender	new	pieces	EMC

Continued

Number	MC	FC	ES	CT
EMC21	tender	new	pieces	EMC

Step 4: Convert the coded dataset of extensional *pò* into a two-dimensional MCA plot with R packages including {FactoMineR},{factoextra} and {ca} and visualize its diachronic variation in terms of its prototypical structures across the four chronological stages.

Step 5: Draw confidence ellipses to encircle the centroid and boundary of the extensional usages of *pò* in the MCA plots by setting ellipse.level=0.05 and ellipse.level=0.95 respectively.

Step 6: Explore the weight assumed by the four variables in determining the diachronic variation of extensional *pò* with Ctree and random forest.

Spatial distribution of the prototypical center of extensional *pò* across the four stages reveals *pò*'s diachronic trajectory. Fluctuation of the conceptual boundary of extensional *pò* displays *pò*'s conceptual range variation. Ctree and random forest analyses demonstrate the weight assumed by different variables in accounting for the diachronic variation of extensional *pò* and further indicate the operation of the underlying mechanism of conceptual reorganization.

Data analysis for extensional *pò, qiē* and *kāi*

Step 1: Transform the cross-tables of individual usages and multiple variables into MCA plots. Table 3.11 shows a snapshot of the coded scheme of extensional *pò, qiē*, and *kāi*.

Step 2: Add *pò, qiē* and *kāi* as supplementary variables in the MCA plots.

Step 3: Draw confidence ellipses around the centroids and boundaries of *pò, qiē* and *kāi*.

Step 4: Explain the diachronic boundary variation through observing and comparing the MCA plots across the four historical stages.

Table 3.11 Snapshot of the coded scheme for extensional *pò*, qi ē and *kāi*

Number	Locus	MC	Aspect	FC	ES	Reversabiligy	Incrementality	Separation	Keynote
po1	unpredictable	tender	onset	new	partial	irreversible	nonincremental	messy	po
po2	unpredictable	tender	onset	neutral	partial	irreversible	nonincremental	messy	po
po3	predictable	tender	onset	new	partial	irreversible	nonincremental	messy	po
po4	predictable	tender	onset	new	partial	irreversible	nonincremental	messy	po
po5	predictable	tender	onset	new	partial	irreversible	nonincremental	messy	po
po6	predictable	tender	onset	new	partial	irreversible	nonincremental	messy	po
po7	unpredictable	tender	onset	new	partial	irreversible	nonincremental	messy	po
po8	predictable	tender	onset	new	partial	irreversible	nonincremental	messy	po
po9	unpredictable	tender	onset	affected	partial	irreversible	nonincremental	messy	po
po10	unpredictable	tender	onset	affected	partial	irreversible	nonincremental	messy	po
po11	unpredictable	tender	onset	neutral	partial	irreversible	nonincremental	messy	po
po12	unpredictable	tender	onset	neutral	partial	irreversible	nonincremental	messy	po
po13	unpredictable	tender	onset	neutral	partial	irreversible	nonincremental	messy	po
po14	unpredictable	tender	onset	neutral	partial	irreversible	nonincremental	messy	po
po15	unpredictable	tender	onset	neutral	partial	irreversible	nonincremental	messy	po
po16	predictable	tender	onset	new	partial	irreversible	nonincremental	messy	po
po17	predictable	tender	onset	affected	partial	irreversible	nonincremental	messy	po
po18	unpredictable	tender	onset	neutral	partial	irreversible	nonincremental	messy	po
po19	predictable	tender	onset	new	partial	irreversible	nonincremental	messy	po
po20	unpredictable	tender	onset	affected	partial	irreversible	nonincremental	messy	po
po21	unpredictable	tender	onset	affected	partial	irreversible	nonincremental	messy	po

By comparing overlapping areas among these three lexical items, we can summarize conceptual boundary variations among these three lexical items. By observing their prototypical centers and peripheral boundaries, we can reveal their labor division in categorizing events of separation state change. Moreover, the distribution of those variable levels indicates how the underlying mechanism of conceptual reorganization motivates the diachronic conceptual variation of these three lexical items.

Data analysis for intensional *pò*

Step 1: Classify intensional readings of *pò* into different semantic categories.

Step 2: Analyze the conceptual parallel between intensional readings and extensional usages of *pò* and identify its diachronic lineages.

Step 3: Analyze the grammaticalization trend of *pò* to reveal it is at the incipient stage of grammaticalization.

Step 4: Demonstrate the diachronic semantic change trajectory of *pò* and explain the interaction between its extensional usages and intensional readings.

A detailed comparison of the extensional usages and intensional readings shows their corresponding relationship and reveals the important diachronic lineages. The underlying mechanisms that motivate the rise of these multiple intensional readings will also be uncovered. Moreover, a simple observation of these numerous intensional readings will show that *pò* is undergoing grammaticalization.

3.5 Summary

In general, this study adopts revised DPS as the theoretical framework and multidimensional analysis as the research method. Revised DPS affords both extensional and intensional viewpoints on the internal conceptual structure of lexical categories. The extensional viewpoint is concerned with how extensional usages of break, cut, and open verbs varied across the four historical stages. The intensional viewpoint focuses on the diachronic variation of the intensional senses of break verbs in resonance with their corresponding extensional usages. The multidimensional analysis offers a multivariate approach to annotate and plot the internal conceptual structures of lexical items in terms of these multiple variables. Specifically, algorithms like MCA and Ctree are conducted to process the association between the individual usages and the multiple variables of break verbs. And in so doing, the prototypical conceptual structures of these break verbs are mapped out.

With such research methodology in stock, in what follows, we first explore how the extensional usages of *pò* change diachronically in Chapter 4. Then the conceptual boundary variation of *pò, qiē*, and *kāi* is addressed in Chapter 5. Finally, Chapter 6 attends to the diachronic variation involved in the intensional readings of *pò*.

CHAPTER 4

Diachronic conceptual variation of extensional *pò*

This chapter explores how the conceptual range of extensional *pò* with regard to events of separation state change varies diachronically across four chronological stages. Two specific variation types, category member variation and conceptualization pattern variation are addressed. Category member variation is elaborated in section 4.1, focusing on extensional members of *pò* and describes how prototypical and peripheral extensional members of *pò* gradually change and vary. Conceptualization pattern variation is expounded in 4.2, demonstrating an in-depth investigation of the conceptual variables along which *pò* undergoes conceptual change. Section 4.3 summarizes that when these two variation types are covered, we are able to answer our research questions (1a) and (2a): What conceptual variation pathway is exhibited in the extensional reference of *pò*? What cognitive mechanisms motivate such conceptual variation?

4.1 Category member variation

As a prototypical category, *pò* represents events of separation state change. Its category members are specific events of separation state change. To reveal what conceptual variation pathway extensional *pò* undergoes, MCA is utilized to map its category members across EMC, LMC, EMand, and MdMand. By observing how its category members vary across these four chronological stages, its diachronic conceptual variation pathway will be uncovered.

In what follows, we first report our research findings concerning the category member variation of extensional *pò* in section 4.1.1. Then section 4.1.2 and section 4.1.3 specify the diachronic variation of *pò* in terms of its prototypical and peripheral members. Section 4.1.4 is an interim summary. One point that should be repeated at this stage is that both prototypical and peripheral members of *pò* are its specific usages in referring to specific events of separation state change.

4.1.1 Research findings

To interpret our findings on the diachronic conceptual change of *pò*, both raw data (Table 3.9) and association measures shown in the MCA plots (Figure 4.1 to Figure 4.3) are referred to. Raw data demonstrates the relative frequency of multiple usages of *pò* across the four historical stages. These usages are concatenations of the three coded conceptual variables <material composition>, <functional change> and <endstate>. For instance, *fles_affsur* represents the employment of *pò* to describe surface damage of fleshy objects like body parts, such as injuring one's head or finger. The conceptual variable <spatial configuration> is neglected for reasons to be addressed below. MCA plots map out the association between specific usages and between different variable levels.

Both relative frequency and association are drawn upon because they complement each other in reflecting the diachronic variation of extensional *pò* across the four stages. Relative frequency presents the rank of different usages employed in the four stages, indicating which usages are continuously frequently used and which usages are gradually given away. Association measure shows relativities of these usages among the four stages. A usage may display a higher frequency in EMC than in LMC, but it may have a strong association with LMC because it is much more above the average than the other usages in LMC. Reflected in the MCA plot, the further these usages are from the origin, the more discriminating they are, while the closer they are to the origin, the less distinctive they probably are.

Research finding 1:

Our constructed dataset displays 34 varying usages of extensional *pò* (Appendix 1). To save space, this study takes into account the first 22 usages, the absolute total frequency of which is greater than or equals 15. The absolute frequency of these 22 usages accounts for 96% of the total frequency, thus they are thorough enough to reflect the extensive usage of *pò*. Table 4.1 shows the relative frequencies of these 22 usages across the four chronological stages (please refer to Appendix 2 for more concrete examples). At first glance, relative frequencies from this table demonstrate that extensional usages of *pò* vary notably across the four chronological stages. As shown in Table 4.2, in EMC, the top usages whose relative frequencies are above 5.0 include *fra_affpie*, *sti_affpar*, *fles_affsur*, *sti_noisur*, *fles_noipar*, *fles_newpar*, and *ten_newpar*. Differently, the most frequent usages in LMC are *sti_affpar*, *sti_noipar*, *fles_ affpar*, *flex_affpar*, and *fra_affpie*. *Fles_affsur*, *fles_affpar*, *sti_noipar*, *sti_affpar* and *flex_affpar* constitute the most frequent usages in EMand and MdMand. That is to say, some usages are stable across the four stages, while others are fluctuating. But even so, it is hard for us to generalize the rough diachronic trajectory of the category member variation simply based on frequency comparison. The association between specific instances of extensional *pò* and the four chronological stages should be further explored. To this end, for further data mining, MCA algorithms are made use of to measure the association strength between numerous individual usages and between different variable levels.

Table 4.1 The first 22 extensional usages of *pò*

Usages	EMC	LMC	EMand	MdMand	Examples
fles_affsur	9.3	6.2	21.8	12.7	头被打破了。(break head)
fles_affpar	2.6	15.9	16.9	22	挖眼睛，破肚子。(break belly)
sti_noipar	3.6	15.9	11.2	9.9	杨生破门而入。(break door)
sti_affpar	10.9	18.2	9.5	9.4	木鱼子敲破了。(break woodblock)

Continued

Usages	EMC	LMC	EMand	MdMand	Examples
flex_affpar	1.0	13.0	10.3	8.3	他撕破了衣服。(he tear break clothes)
fles_noipar	6.2	3.0	9.1	4.1	破腹出脏。(break belly)
fra_affpie	11.4	6.9	3.0	4.4	既讫，掷破瓯走去。(break vase)
flex_noipar	1.0	0.1	7.0	0.8	撕破窗纸一看。(break window paper)
fra_affpar	1.0	4.7	1.9	3.8	三尺杖子破瓦盆。(break vase)
ten_newpar	5.7	1.6	0.7	5.0	破石榴以献。(break pomegranate)
sti_noisur	7.3	1.2	0.9	2.4	破其外青皮，得白心。(break skin)
fra_neupie	4.1	1.2	0.3	3.6	温差风化隧使表层岩石破裂。(break rock)
fra_noipie	4.7	0.9	2.6	0.7	凿山破石，勿使阻碍。(break rock)
fra_noipar	0.5	2.3	0.9	2.5	此古器，当是破冢得之。(break tomb)
fles_newpar	6.2	0.6	0.3	1.9	破雁，炙而分食之。(break wild geese)
fra_noisur	3.6	0.7	0.3	2.2	卵破，有婴儿出焉。(break egg)
sti_newpar	3.6	1.9	0.3	0.5	逃者隧取竹一竿，破以为蔑。(break bamboo)
fles_affpie	2.6	0.1	0	1.3	扑的一声，把头颅轰破。(break head)
flex_affpie	0	0	0.4	1.0	衣服破碎。(break clothes)
fra_neupar	0.5	0.9	0.5	0.2	风鸣条，雨破块。(break soil)
fra_newpie	1.0	0.1	0	1.0	碾破青山作路。(break road)
ten_noipar	3.1	0	0.1	0.6	青椒破口去籽切粗丝。(break pepper)

Table 4.2 Frequent extensional usages of *pò* across the four stages (relative frequency >5.0)

Four stages	Top extensional usages
EMC	*fra_affpie* (玻璃破了 glass break-LE); *sti_affpar* (桌子敲破了 table knock break-LE); *fles_affsur* (手指割破了 finger cut break-LE); *sti_noisur* (木箱子打破了 wooden case hit break-LE); *fles_noipar* (破肚取肠 break belly get intestine); *fles_newpar* (破首以为饮器 break head into drinking vessels); ten_newpar (破瓠为瓢)

Continued

Four stages	Top extensional usages
LMC	*sti_affpar* (门敲破了 door knock break-LE); *sti_noipar* (撞破门 knock break door); *fles_affpar* (刺破心脏 pierce break gut); *flex_affpar* (衣服破了 clothes break-LE); *fra_affpie* (玻璃破了 glass break-LE)
EMand MdMand	*fles_affsur* (脚磨破了 foot abrade break-LE); *fles_affpar* (破肚子 break belly); *sti_noipar* (破门而入 break door and come in); *sti_affpar* (木鱼子敲破 woodblock knock break); *flex_affpar* (衬衫破了 shirt break-LE)

Research finding 2:

To further explore the association between individuals and between variables, MCA plots are generated to demonstrate the prototypical conceptual structure of extensional *pò*. The first two dimensions of the following three MCA plots account for 69.9% of the variations (as shown in Table 4.3), thus they are reliable for uncovering the diachronic variation of extensional *pò*. First, Figure 4.1 reveals the association between specific instances of extensional *pò* (grey dots) and between different variable levels of MC, FC, and ES (black triangles). Specifically, the grey dots are specific instances like EMC2, LMC5, EMand38 and MdMand100. The variable levels are *stiff*, *new*, *noimped*, and *tender* etc.

From a closer observation of this MCA plot, we can find that along the first dimension (from right to left), MC levels *tender* and *fragile* are distinguished from *stiff*, *flexible*, and *fleshy*, FC levels *new*, *neutral*, and *noimped* are set apart from *affected*, and ES level *pieces* is differentiated from *partial* and *surface*. In the same vein, along the second dimension (from top to bottom), *stiff* and *flexible* depart from *fleshy* and *fragile*, *new* and *noimped* depart from *affected* and *neutral*, and *partial* departs from *surface* and *pieces*. Further speaking, the four quadrants demonstrate different conceptual variable clusters. These variable levels are extracted from their corresponding individual usages.

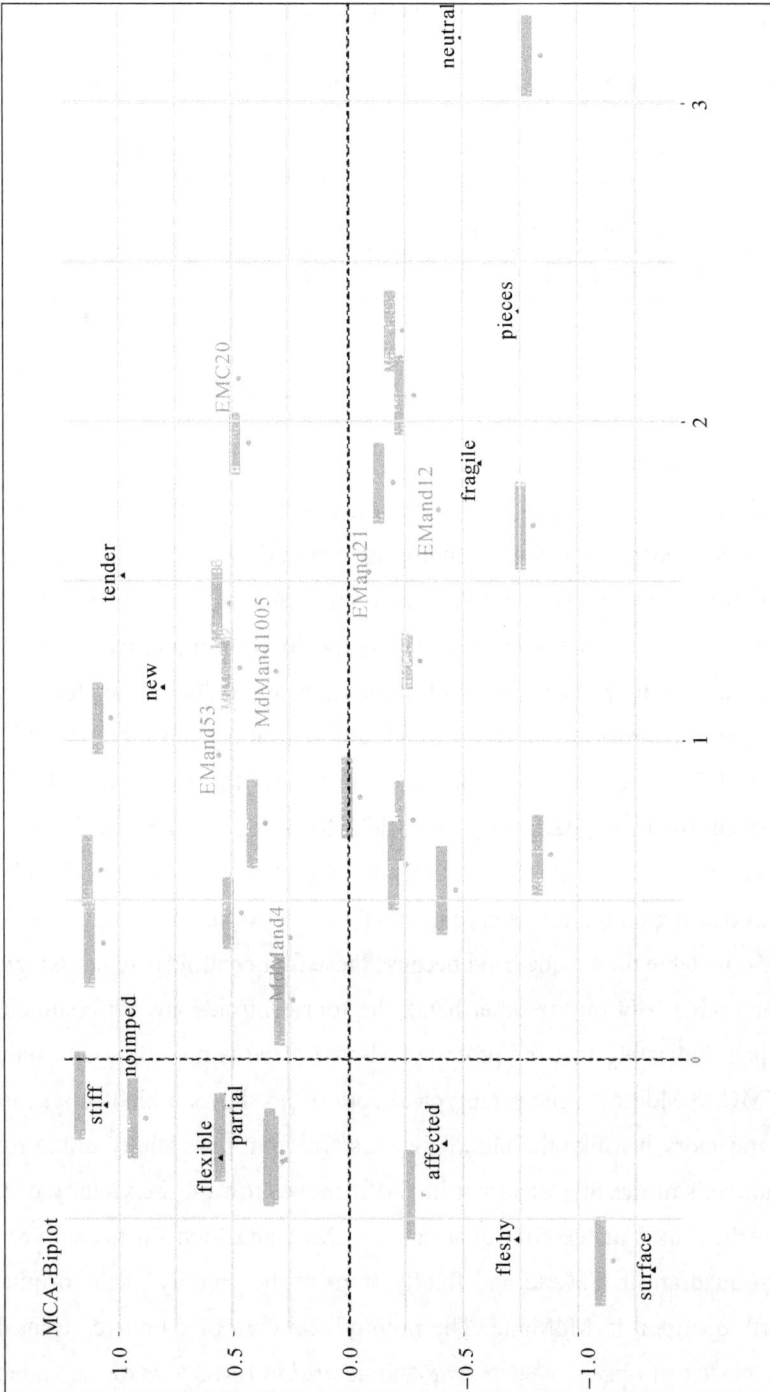

Figure 4.1 The MCA plot for individual usages and variable levels of extensional *pò*

Table 4.3 Scree plot of extensional *pò*

Dim	Value	%	Cum %	Scree plot
1	0.177581	45.2	45.2	*************
2	0.096852	24.7	69.9	*******
3	0.055809	14.2	84.1	****
4	0.003742	1.0	85.0	
		......		
Total:	0.392833			

Research finding 3:

The MCA plot in Figure 4.2 marks the prototypical core of extensional *pò* with a confidence ellipse surrounding its centroid. What is enclosed within this centroid are 5% of the prototypical extensional usages of *pò*. In this way, prototypical cores of extensional *pò* across the four chronological stages are mapped out. The four chronological time periods are added as supplementary variables. As demonstrated in the legend, colored ellipses in these two MCA plots stand for extensional members of *pò* across the four chronological stages, blank for EMC, dark grey for LMC, streak for EMand, and light grey for MdMand. Levels of the three conceptual variables are marked with black squares. Focusing on the four centroids, it is pretty obvious that the prototypical core of *pò* is stable on the one hand because these four centroids are not far away from each other. But on the other hand, the four centroids are not completely overlapped, indicating that the prototypical core of *pò* is not absolutely stable. From EMC to MdMand, the prototypical core of *pò* shows a kind of a spoon-shaped trajectory just like the big dipper. It starts from the vicinity of the right horizontal axis at the first quadrant in EMC, moves toward the vicinity of the upper vertical axis at the first quadrant in LMC, and then further moves to the third quadrant in EMand and finally stops at the vicinity of the origin at the fourth quadrant in MdMand. The prototypical core of *pò* moves from the variable cluster of *tender*, *new*, *fragile* and *neutral* in EMC toward the variable

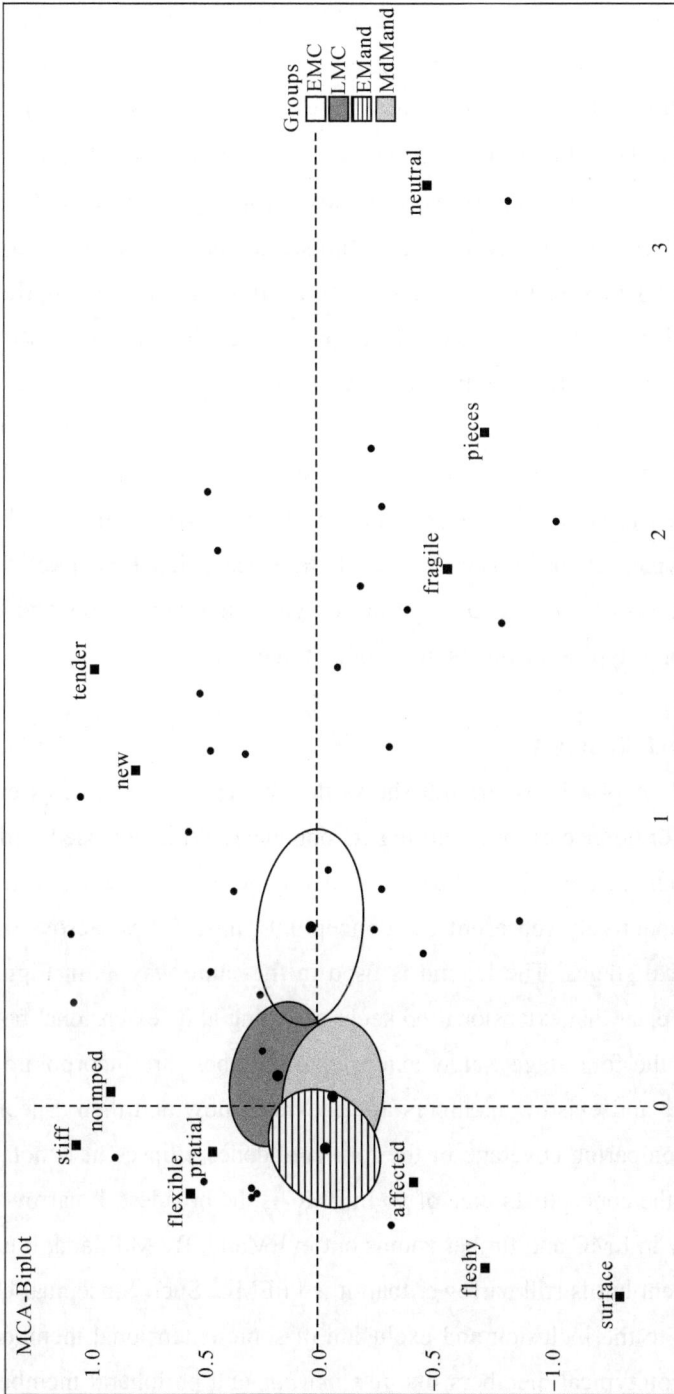

Figure 4.2 The MCA plot for prototypical core of extensional *pò*

cluster of *partial*, *flexible*, and *stiff* in LMC, then toward the variable cluster of *affected*, *fleshy*, and *surface* in EMand and finally toward the vicinity of the origin in MdMand. The close distance between the two prototypical cores in EMand and MdMand indicates little variance between these two stages.

In addition, specific usages near these prototypical cores indicate that prototypical core stability arises from the stable status of some prototypical members and prototypical core variation stems from certain fluctuant prototypical members. As Table 4.1 and Figure 4.2 demonstrate, extensional members displaying features like *affected*, *partial*, and *flexible* are not distinct from the four historical stages. They are prototypical members of extensional *pò* in all of the four time periods. In contrast, extensional members showing features like *fragile*, *tender*, *pieces*, and *new* are prototypical in EMC but lose their prototypical status in later stages. Likewise, extensional members showing features like *fleshy* and *surface* are prototypical members in EMand but are secondary prototypical members in the other three stages.

Research finding 4:

The MCA plot in Figure 4.3 shows the conceptual range of extensional *pò* with a confidence ellipse marking its boundary. What enclosed within the confidence ellipse are 95% of the extensional usages of *pò*. The four confidence ellipses respectively represent the conceptual ranges of *pò* across the four chronological stages. The legend is used in the same way as in Figure 4.2. Firstly, it is clear that extensional *pò* keeps changing at its extensional boundary all through the four stages. New extensional members are incorporated from time to time and existing members are got rid of now and then. Specifically speaking, comparing coverage of the four confidence ellipses, it is not uneasy to find that the conceptual range of *pò* in EMC is the broadest. It narrows down significantly in LMC and further zooms out in EMand. By MdMand, it expands to some extent but is still narrower than it is in EMC. Such conceptual changes are owning to the inclusion and exclusion of some extensional members. For instance, prototypical members like *ten_newpar* and peripheral members like *sti_newpar* and *ten_noipar* in EMC gradually fade away from the conceptual range of extensional *pò* by LMC and later stages. In the same vein, prototypical usages such as *sti_noisur* and peripheral usages like *fra_affpar* and *fra_noipar* also move out of the conceptual range of *pò* from LMC to EMand. But by MdMand, some of the disappeared members come into being again, such as *ten_ newpar* and *fra_affpie*. The difference is that they are becoming less prototypical members.

Secondly, when concentrating on specific instances encircled within the conceptual range of *pò*, it can also be found that *pò* has undergone a specialization trajectory. Its conceptual range narrows down over time (Geeraerts 2010: 26; Colleman and Clerk 2011). Specifically speaking, the specialization of *pò* is embodied in the decreasing variety of events of separation state change it can be used to denote. To illustrate, EMC locates at the first quadrant, where there are usages like *fra_newpar*, *ten_noisur*, *ten_affpar*, and *fles_newpar*, denoting breaking objects into pieces, revealing the objects' inside, or turning the objects into something new. Differently, LMC is located in the vicinity of the upper vertical axis, in proximity to usages like *fra_neupar*, *fra_affpie*, *sti_ affpar* and *fra_affpar*, referring to objects' function being damaged or breaking objects to get rid of impediments. EMand is situated in the third quadrant, near usages like *fles_affpar*, *fles_affsur*, and *flex_affpar*, denoting opening objects or destructing objects in the surface or into parts. MdMand is located close to the origin, near usages like *fles_affpar* and *fra_affpar*, expressing fleshy or fragile objects' functional disruption. Such varied usage distribution evinces that *pò*'s referential range is zooming out from all kinds of events of separation state change to only disruptive events of separation state change.

Thirdly, as for the contributing weight for diachronic change assumed by the four time periods, the two-dimensional distribution of these four periods reveals that they should not be equally ranked. The four column stages show that EMC accounts for the greatest proportion of variation, followed by EMand. LMC and MdMand are close to the origin and assume the least variation. This suggests that EMC and EMand are important turning points for the diachronic

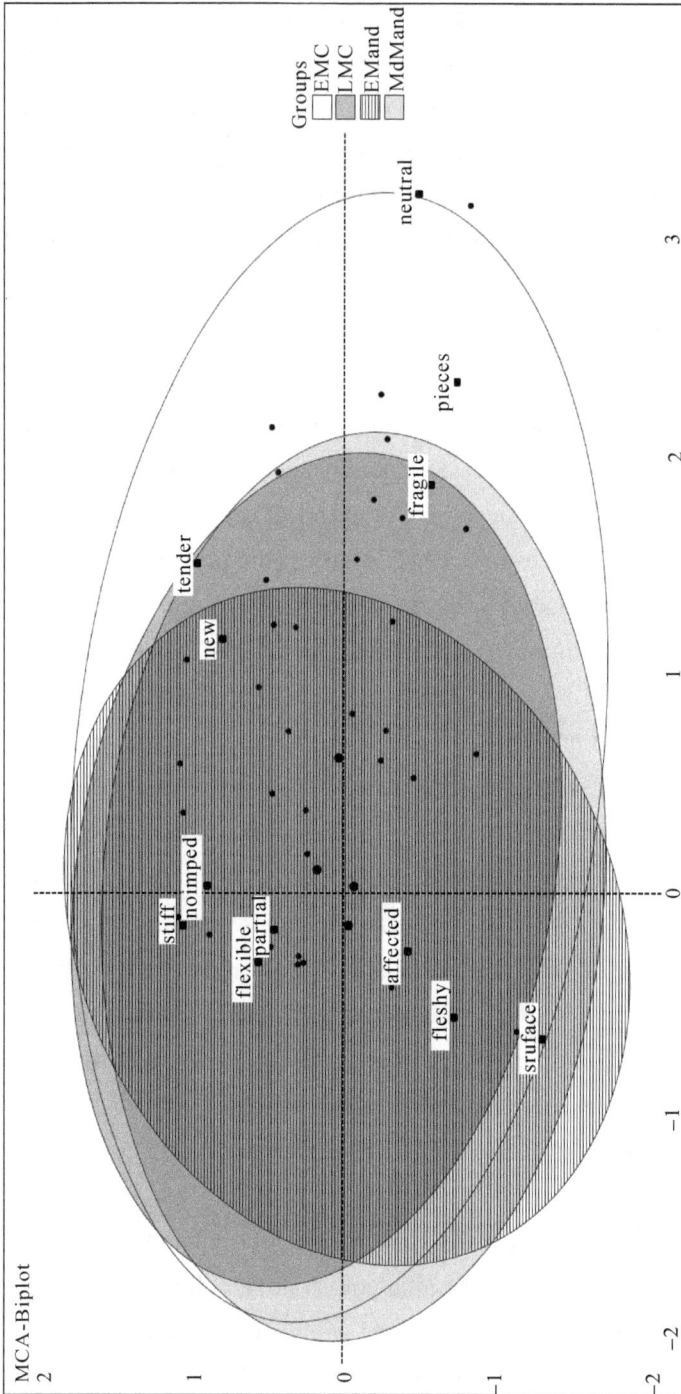

Figure 4.3 The MCA plot for the referential range of extensional *pò*

variation of extensional *pò*. However, LMC and MdMand are relatively stable stages.

Generally speaking, the above measurements of frequency and association contribute to our exploration of diachronic variation from different perspectives. Frequency affords a measurement of the relative frequency of each usage across different historical stages. A comparison of the relative frequency of those multiple usages allows us to better understand the regularity and principle of linguistic categorization (Hilpert 2013). Association, on the other hand, opens a way for further data mining. By observing the association between specific instances and variable levels, we are able to reveal and highlight those usages that vary most significantly and those usages that are most saliently used in one particular stage (Glynn 2014: 447). But in spite of this all-around information of frequency and association, to unravel the diachronic pathway of extensional *pò,* a more detailed analysis per stage is required.

4.1.2　Prototypical member variation

As stated in Chapter 3, our proposed revision for extensional non-equality is that prototypical members are relatively but not always stable in the course of diachronic variation. To specify how prototypical members of *pò* vary diachronically, we make use of the prototypical usages of *pò* in each of the four chronological stages and substantiate these usages with specific instances. Then through a cross-stage comparison, we highlight the pathway along which the prototypical members of *pò* vary diachronically.

4.1.2.1 Prototypical member identification

Prior to an elaboration on *pò*'s prototypical member variation across the four stages, the criteria applicable for identifying prototypical members should be first ascertained. In terms of prototype identification, a variety of criteria has been brought forth in previous studies, including the asymmetrical judgment of goodness or similarity, ease of elicitation, gradation within the category, earliest attested meaning, centrality/predominance in the semantic network, and use in composite forms (Gries 2006: 75). However, there are still controversies concerning which of these criteria should be adopted. What's more, these criteria are put forward with the assumption that the prototypical usage of a lexical item is always the same. That is, there is no diachronic change involved in the prototypical structure of the lexical category. To correctly identify prototypical usages of *pò*, the present study appeals to converging evidence (Langacker 1999) and at the same time adopts a dynamic perspective.

The very first two criteria we take into consideration for identifying prototypical members are relative frequency and family resemblance structure. Although Rosch argues against frequency as a determinant of prototypical member identification, linguists like Nosofsky (1988) and Bybee (2010) state that categorical center shifts towards the member with a higher frequency. Consent with this latter assertion, this study treats frequency as a vital identification criterion of prototypical members in the consideration that only the most frequently employed usages form psychologically valid prototype. Table 4.1 shows the relative frequency of our observed extensional members of *pò*. As for family resemblance structure, Rosch and Mervis (1975) assert that family resemblance is one of the major principles that govern the formation of semantic categories. Prototypical members are located near the centroid and nonprototypical members gradually deviate from the prototypical center and cluster to the boundary. The closer the extensional members are to the centroid, the more central they are as prototypical members. Figure 4.2 and Figure 4.3 demonstrate the family resemblance structure of *pò* both in terms of the association between individual usages and the association between conceptual variables.

Other evidence we also take into account includes etymology, first attestation as well as elicitation. Etymology refers to the origin of a word. According to the etymological dictionary[1], the Chinese character 破 (*pò*) is composed of two parts. The left part represents its semantic meaning and the

---

[1] Here is the website: https://www.yellowbridge.com/chinese/character-etymology.php?zi=%E7%A0%B4#.

right stands for its phonological form. With these two componental parts, *pò* refers to the breaking of stones, namely the breaking into pieces of stones. The first attestation indicates the earliest attested instance. The first attestation of *pò* is recorded to appear in the *Book of Odes* (6th century B.C.). This attestation is *Jì pò wǒ fǔ, yòu quē wǒ qiāng* (break my axe and deprive my spear). In this example, *pò* denotes the separation of an axe, namely the destruction of an instrument made of stone. Elicitation evidence shows native speakers' first impression. Although it is impossible to trace ancient people's first impression of *pò*, in ancient dictionaries'[1] enumeration of *stone shattering* as the first entry of *pò* tells us that the shattering of stone is psychologically the most salient reference of *pò* in ancient people's mind. In contrast, when Mandarin speakers are asked to describe a great variety of breaking events with different break verbs, they more often than not use *pò* to name scenarios like *Tā qiē-pò shǒu* (He cut-break his hand) and *Tā chě-pò bù* (He tear-break cloth) (Pye et al. 1995; Chen 2007).

4.1.2.2 Prototypical member variation

Starting with EMC, the prototypical core of extensional *pò* at this time period is located at the first quadrant, near the right horizontal axis. Prototypical members at this stage are numerous, including *fra_affpie*, *sti_affpar*, *fles_affsur*, *sti_noisur*, *fles_newpar*, *fles_noipar*, as well as *ten_newpar* (Table 4.2). Among these usages, *fra_affpie*, *fles_newpar*, and *ten_newpar* are most pronouncedly associated with EMC. As shown in Figure 4.2, these usages are associated with the most distinctive variable levels such as *pieces*, *fragile*, *tender* and *new* and drive the prototypical core of *pò* in EMC away from that in the latter three stages. Specifically speaking, in its etymon, *pò* is composed of "stone" and "surface", and etymologically encodes the disintegration of stones (Hu 2005). This etymological origin fleshes out in the prototypical usage of *fra_affpie,* which describes the functionally-affected piece breaking of three-

---

[1] Ancient Chinese Frequent-used Character Dictionary.

dimensional fragile objects, such as stones or porcelains (4.1a and 4.1b). But this etymological usage does not persist for a long time. Similarly, *fles_newpar* and *ten_newpar* are another two prototypical members that do not sustain in the evolution of *pò*. *Fles_newpar* represents the partial breaking of fleshy objects to make new things, for instance, breaking the head to make a drinking vessel or breaking fish in order to cook it (4.1c and 4.1d). *Ten_newpar* denotes the separation of tender objects like melon to create a container or the partition of vegetables for further use (4.1e and 4.1f). These usages gradually fade away from the conceptual range of extensional *pò* in the three succeeding stages.

(4.1)

a. EMCpoe182: 元康七年，霹雳**破**城南高禖石。

　　　　　　Yuánkāng qī nián, pīlì pò chéng nán Gāoméi shí.

　　　　　　Yuankang seven year, light smash city south Gaomei stone

　　　　　　"In the seventh year of Yuankang, a light smashed the stone in Gaomei temple which lay in the southern part of the city."

b. EMCpoe185: 时有一人，驴负瓦器至市欲卖，须臾之间，驴尽**破**之。

　　　　　　Shí yǒu yī rén, lú fù wǎqì zhì shì yù mài, xūyúzhījiān, lú jìn pò zhī.

　　　　　　once there one-person, donkey carry earthenware to market to sell, a while, donkey all smash earthenware

　　　　　　"Once there is someone who used his donkey to carry earthenware to the market, but after a while, the donkey smashed all the earthenware."

c. EMCpoe39: 大败知伯，**破**其首以为饮器。

　　　　　　Dà bài Zhìbó, pò qí shǒu yǐwéi yǐn qì.

　　　　　　utterly defeat Zhibo, break his head into drinking vessel

　　　　　　"They defeated Zhibo utterly and broke his head into a drinking vessel."

d. EMCpoe100: 四**破**，於大釜煮之。

　　　　　　Sì pò, yú dà fǔ zhǔ zhī.

four break, with big pot boil it

"Break it into four parts and boil it with the pot."

e. EMCpoe3: 瓠一行……黄色好，**破**以为瓢。

　　　Hù yī háng, …huáng-sè hǎo, pò yǐ wéi piáo.

　　　gourd a line, …yellow good, break into ladle

　　　"Some gourds, yellow, break them into gourd ladle."

f. EMCpoe28: 焦茄子法：用子未成者，……以竹刀骨刀四**破**之。

　　　Fǒu qiézǐ　fǎ: yòng zǐ wèi chéng zhě ... yǐ zhúdāo gǔdāo　sì pò zhī.

　　　cook eggplant method: use seed not tough … use bamboo-knife bone-knife four break it.

　　　"Method for cooking eggplants: use a tender eggplant and break it into four parts with bamboo knife or bone knife."

Apart from the above transitory prototypical usages, there are some relatively stabilized prototypical usages, such as *sti_affpar, sti_noisur, fles_affsur*, and *fles_noipar*. These usages are close to the origin and are tightly associated with less distinctive variable levels like *affected, fleshy, noimped*, and *partial* which are not far from the origin. For instance, *sti_affpar* refers to the functionally-affected partial breaking of three-dimensional stiff objects, like a boat, musical instruments, or wood (4.2a and 4.2b). *Sti_noisur* indicates breaking the surface of three-dimensional objects so as to get rid of the impediment, for instance, breaking the cover of a coffin, breaking the surface part of bamboo, or a wooden post (4.2c and 4.2d). *Fles_affsur* describes the surface breaking of fleshy objects, such as the slight wounding of a head, a finger, or an arm (4.2e and 4.2f). *Fles_noipar* represents the partial breaking of three-dimensional fleshy objects to reveal the inside, for instance, breaking the belly to get rid of the internal organs, or breaking the fish to get a knife out (4.2g, 4.2h).

(4.2)

a. EMCpol38: 水戾**破**舟。

Shuǐ   lì   pò zhōu.

water rapid break boat

"The rapid stream broke the boat."

b. EMCpoe41: 是故钟子期死而伯牙绝弦**破**琴。

Shì-gù Zhōng Zǐqī sǐ   ér Bóyá jué   xián pò   qín

so   Zhong Ziqi die and Boya damage string destroy qin

"So when Zhong Ziqi died, Boya destroyed his qin."

c. EMCpoe135: **破**其棺，棺中有人。

Pò   qí guān, guān zhōng yǒu rén

open that coffin, coffin inside have person

"Opened that coffin, and there was someone inside."

d. EMCpoe110: **破**竹，得男。

Pò   zhú,   dé nán

open bamboo, find boy

"Opened the bamboo and found a boy."

e. EMCpoe141: 以梨打我，头**破**乃尔。

Yǐ lí dǎ wǒ , tóu pò   nǎi ěr

use pear hit me, head wound and stop

"He hit me with a pear, and stopped until my head was wounded."

f. EMCpoe163: 粮尽，杀马步行，足**破**，卧岩石下。

Liáng jìn, shā mǎ bùxíng, zú pò,   wò yánshí xià.

food over, kill horse on foot, foot wounded, lie stone down

"no food, killed the horse and walked on foot, foot wounded and lay down near the stone."

g. EMCpoe126: 见尼裸身挥刀，**破**腹出脏。

Jiàn ní luǒ shēn huī dāo, pò fù chū zàng.

see nun naked body take knife, break belly get inwards

"saw the nun naked with a knife in hand, opened her own belly and got the internal organs."

h. EMCpoe125: **破**鱼腹，得瓜刀。

Pò   yúfù, dé guādāo.

open fish-belly, get melon-knife

"open the fish belly and get the knife."

By the time period of LMC, the prototypical core has shifted from the vicinity of the right horizontal axis toward the vicinity of the upper vertical axis. Prototypical members of extensional *pò* have reduced to *sti_affpar*, *sti_noipar*, *fles_affpar*, *flex_affpar*, and *fra_affpie*. Compared with EMC, major changes at this stage reside in three aspects. Firstly, the relative frequency of *sti_affpar* dramatically increases from 10.9 to 18.2 and it becomes the most prominent usage of *pò* in this stage. Secondly, the extensional usages of *pò* no longer include *fles_newpar* and *fles_noipar*. That is, the partial breaking of fleshy objects to make new things or to get rid of impediments are no longer within the extensional core of *pò*. Meanwhile, although *fra_affpie* is still within the prototypical core, its frequency has dropped dramatically from 11.4 to 6.9. Such diachronic variation is also manifest in Figure 4.2, because variable levels like *new*, *fragile*, and *pieces* are relatively far away from the upper vertical axis. The decreasing of these four usages indicates that although *pò* is still used to refer to object disintegration, it is becoming less predominant in denoting smashing, opening or cutting types of separations.

Along with this trend, usages like *fles_affpar*, *flex_affpar*, and *sti_noipar* remain stable and gradually take over the prototypical core of extensional *pò*. *Fles_affpar* refers to the breaking of human organs into parts, such as the breaking of back, liver or guts (4.3a–4.3b). *Flex_affpar* describes the partial breaking of two-dimensional flexible objects like cloth and paper (4.3c–4.3d). The occurrence and development of this usage are closely tied up with the invention and the wide use of flexible materials like cloth, glass, and paper. *Sti_noipar* shows the partial breaking of stiff objects in order to get rid of impediments, such as breaking a door, a wall, or a lock (4.3e–4.3f).

(4.3)

a. LMCpoe34: 至横灞，便属马脊**破**，烂溃特甚。

　　　　　　Zhì　Héngbà, biàn　　zhǔ　　mǎjǐ　　pò，　lànkuì　　tè
　　　　　　shèn

　　　　　　arrive Hengba, then　happen to　horseback injured, festered
　　　　　　pretty　severe

　　　　　　"When arrived at Hengba, the horse's back happened to be
　　　　　　injured and festered severely."

b. LMCpoe146: 刀剜骨肉斥斥**破**，剑害肝肠寸寸断。

　　　　　　Dāo　wān　gǔròu　　chì　chì　pò，　jiàn　hài　gāncháng cùn
　　　　　　cùn duàn.

　　　　　　knife scoop bone-meat piece piece break, sword cut　liver-
　　　　　　gut　inch inch break

　　　　　　"the knife broke the bones and flesh, and the sword cut the
　　　　　　liver and gut."

c. LMCpoe115: 幞头巾子露，衫**破**肚皮开。

　　　　　　Fú　tóujīnzǐ lù，　shān pò　dùpí kāi.

　　　　　　cover head-scarf worn, shirt tear belly reveal

　　　　　　"The headscarf was worn, the shirt was torn and revealed
　　　　　　the belly."

d. LMCpoe212: 骑兵三千余人袭**破**其牙帐。

　　　　　　Qíbīng　sānqiān　　yú rén xípò　　qí yázhàng.

　　　　　　cavalrymen three-thousand more people attack-break their
　　　　　　tent

　　　　　　"More than three thousand cavalrymen attacked and broke
　　　　　　the tent."

e. LMCpoe463: 复**破**之，中有一蚕。

　　　　　　Fù　pò zhī, zhōng yǒu yī cán.

　　　　　　again open it, inside have a silkworm

　　　　　　"Opened it again and found a silkworm inside."

f. LMCpoe441: 儿就岸**破**之，有婴儿长尺余，遂迅走。

Ér jiù 　àn　 pò zhī, yǒu yīngér cháng chǐ　yú, suì　xùn
zǒu.

kid near riverside open it, have baby　long　feet more, then
quick run

"The kids opened it at the riverside and found a baby. The
baby ran away immediately."

Moving into EMand, the prototypical core of *pò* has further moved to
the third quadrant which incorporates variable levels like *affected*, *fleshy*, and
surface. Three striking points should be noted in terms of prototypical member
variation. Firstly, the etymological force of *pò* has disappeared and *fra_affpie*
has completely lost its prototypical status. The piece breaking of fragile objects
is no longer prototypically categorized as *pò*. As noted above, such a diachronic
prototypical change is also reflected in Figure 4.2. When the prototypical core
moves to the third quadrant, it becomes farther away from variable levels like
fragile and *pieces*. Secondly, as revealed in the frequency matrix and MCA
plots, it is the functionally-affected breaking of objects that is taking up the
prototypical core of extensional *pò*. For instance, usages like *fles_affsur, fles_
affpar, flex_affpar* as well as *sti_affpar* constitute the prototypical members
in both EMand and MdMand (4.4a–4.4h). That is, as time goes by, *pò* has
developed from a polarity-neutral disintegration verb to a disruptive (negative)
disintegration verb. Besides these usages, although *sti_noipar* is still frequent,
it is no longer productive in EMand and MdMand. It only reserves breaking
event scenarios particularly in the form of idioms and allusions, like *pò-zhù-qǔ-
shuò* (破柱取朔）, *pò-zhú-zhī-shì* (破竹之势）, *chéng-fēng-pò-làng* (乘风破浪）.
Moreover, it is obvious that the description of the breaking of body parts turns
out to be the most prototypical usage of *pò*. In both EMand and MdMand, *fles_
affsur* and *fles_affpar* are the two most frequent extensional usages of *pò*. Such
diachronic variation suggests that "our embodiment is directly responsible for
structuring concepts" (Evans and Green 2006: 176).

(4.4)

a. EMandpoe38: 吃了一跌，把鼻子跌**破**了。

        Chī lē yīdiē, bǎ bízī diēpò le.

        eat-LE one-fall, BA nose fall-hurt-LE

        "fell down and hurt nose."

b. EMandpoe84: 后军急忙救起，头已跌**破**。

        Hòu jūn jímáng jiù qǐ, tóu yǐ diēpò.

        behind army hurry save up, head already fall-hurt

        "The soldier following him saved him but his head was broken."

c. EMandpoe240: 他把我一口吞下肚去，我就捻**破**他的心肝。

        Tā bǎ wǒ yīkǒu tūn xià   dù qù, wǒ jiù niǎnpò tā-de xīngān.

        he BA me one-mouth swallow down belly-DEIXIS, I then twist-break his heart-liver

        "He swallowed me into his belly, and I broke his heart and liver with my hands."

d. EMandpoe978: 出来把八个人的左肩头都扎**破**了。

        Chū lái bǎ bā gè rén de zuǒ jiāntóu dōu zhāpò le.

        out-DEIXIS BA eight-CL person-DE left shoulder all puncture-break-LE

        "When he got out, he punctured each of the eight people's left shoulder."

e. EMandpoe126: 买糖儿吃，两条脚布**破**了。

        Mǎi tángér chī, liǎng tiáo jiǎobù pò le.

        buy candy eat, two-CL foot-cloth tear-LE

        "bought candy, his foot wraps were worn."

f. EMandpoe145: 令左右将伞扯**破**，每人分一半去。

        Lìng zuǒyòu jiāng sǎn chěpò, měirén fēn yī bàn qù.

        ask left-right JIANG umbrella tear-break, each take a half-DEIXIS "ask attendants to tear the umbrella and order each take a half."

g. EMandpoe157: 取出细斧，将牌劈**破**。

Qǔ chū xì fǔ, jiāng pái pīpò.

take out fine saw, JIANG board chop-break

"took out a fine saw and chopped open the board."

h. EMandpoe177: 命左右将大鼓砍**破**了。

Mìng zuǒyòu jiāng dà gǔ kǎnpò le.

ask left-right JIANG big drum chop-break-LE

"ask attendants to chop break the drum."

Coming to MdMand, the prototypical core has moved from the third quadrant to the vicinity of the origin and falls in the fourth quadrant. This is mainly because the referential range of *pò* broadens to some extent in comparison with EMand. The inclusion of nonprototypical usages like *fra_affpie* and *ten_newpar* drives the prototypical core to the origin. On the one hand, according to the relative frequency table, prototypical members of extensional *pò* remain relatively stable in comparison with EMand. Usages like *fles_affpar*, *fles_affsur*, *sti_affpar*, and *flex_affpar* maintain their prototypical status. In consequence, MdMand is fairly close to EMand, indicating constrained variance. But on the other hand, compared with EMand, the relative frequencies of usages like *ten_newpar* and *fra_affpie* have increased from 0.7 to 5.0 and from 3.0 to 4.4 respectively. As a result, the prototypical core of *pò* has moved from the third quadrant to the vicinity of the origin. Example (4.5) shows specific instances of *ten_newpar* and *fra_affpie* in MdMand. *Ten_newpar* is popular in the cooking context, denoting the separation of plants for further use (4.5a). *Fra_affpie* is consistent with the etymological origin of *pò,* designating the partition of dishes (4.5b).

(4.5)

a. MdMandpoe25: 把姜葱洗净拍**破**，与花椒一起下锅同猪舌同煮。

bǎ jiāng cōng xǐjing   pāipò, yǔ huājiāo   yīqǐ   xià

guō tóng zhūshé   tóng zhǔ

BA ginger onion wash-clean pat-break, with wild-pepper

together into pot together pork-tongue together boil

"Wash the ginger and pat it into parts, then boil it with wild

pepper and pork tongue."

b. MdMandpoe561: 打**破**了碗盏，想必是要赔的

dǎpò le wǎnzhǎn, xiǎng bì shì yào péi−de

hit-break-LE dishes, think must need compensate

"If you break the dishes, you must compensate for it."

Another point that should be mentioned is that the usage of two-dimensional *fles_affpar* also evolves into the prototypical core of extensional *pò*. This usage refers to the breaking of the skin of body parts, such as facial skin, scalp, and belly (4.6a and 4.6b). In this way, the prototypical core of extensional *pò* has been overwhelmingly taken up by the disruptive separation of body parts.

(4.6)

a. MdMandpoe918: 他用利器刺**破**皮肤。

Tā yòng lì qì cìpò   pífū.

he use sharp weapon pierce-break skin

"He pierced through the skin with a sharp weapon."

b. MdMandpoe1176: 你是否把头皮抓**破**了？

Nǐ shì fǒu bǎ tóupí zhuāpò le?

you are not BA scalp scratch-break-LE

"Have you scratched your scalp?"

Along with the conceptual variation of extensional *pò,* the syntactic pattern of *pò* also has undergone diachronic variation. When extensional *pò* has gradually developed to only denoting disruptive separation in Mandarin, its syntactic pattern also has changed from monomorphemic verb to verb complement (in the form of V+ *pò*). In other words, monomorphemic *pò* is used to denote more varied events of separation state change, while verb-complement *pò* is constrained to only denoting the result of actions. This suggests a correlation between conceptual variation and syntactic change. We leave this correlation to future studies.

To conclude, relative frequency and association measures demonstrate that prototypical usages of extensional *pò* have undergone significant diachronic variation. Although some stabilized prototypical members occupy the prototypical core all the time, those discriminating prototypical usages indicate that the prototypical core is moving along a spoon-shaped diachronic trajectory of specialization. As summarized in Figure 4.4, this specializing trajectory manifests itself in two prominent aspects. First of all, the extensional range of *pò* gradually departs from its etymological origin. Over time, the usage of *fra_affpie* has lost its prototypical status. Only the separation of fleshy objects and the separation of stiff objects remain as prototypical usages of extensional *pò*. Such a diachronic variation on the one hand shows that although lexical items are relatively stable in terms of their prototypical members (Geeraerts 1997: 23), their etymological origin may gradually become less explicit in accounting for its extensional usage. Furthermore, words are not used according to their historical value but always have a current value limited to the moment when they are employed (Vendryes 1925: 176).

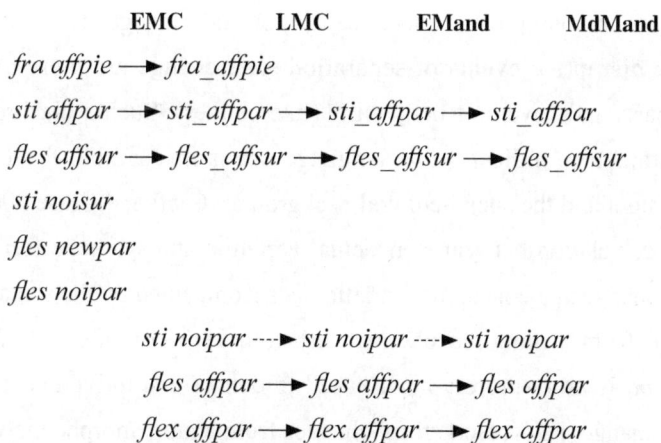

	EMC	LMC	EMand	MdMand

fra affpie ⟶ *fra_affpie*

sti affpar ⟶ *sti_affpar* ⟶ *sti_affpar* ⟶ *sti_affpar*

fles affsur ⟶ *fles_affsur* ⟶ *fles_affsur* ⟶ *fles_affsur*

sti noisur

fles newpar

fles noipar

　　　　sti noipar ----▶ *sti noipar* ----▶ *sti noipar*

　　　　fles affpar ⟶ *fles affpar* ⟶ *fles affpar*

　　　　flex affpar ⟶ *flex affpar* ⟶ *flex affpar*

Figure 4.4　Prototypical member variation

Moreover, despite the fact that *pò* is used to denote both positive and disruptive separation in EMC, it is more likely to be used to describe disruptive separation exclusively in later stages. Positive separation usages gradually recede from the prototypical core and degrade to the peripheral fringe. This diachronic variation indicates that the categorization of events of separation state change varies across stages (Shi 2003). As for reasons, both embodied experience and onomasiological saliency account for this categorization change. For one thing, *pò* is generally used to describe any kind of separation in EMC, but as more advanced instruments are invented, coarse separation like breaking and tearing are gradually distinguished from fine separations like cutting and opening. More exactly, there exists an onomasiological saliency effect when alternative conceptual categories are available to name the same events (Geeraerts 2018: 47). The dwindling away of usages like *fles_newpar*, *sti_newpar* as well as *ten_noipar* are attributed to near-synonym competition. When fleshy objects like fish are separated finely with a knife instead of messily with hand, and when stiff objects like doors are separated in a neat way, the linguistic way of categorizing and naming such events as *pò* is substituted by verbs like *kāi* and *qiē*.

In a nutshell, prototypical members of extensional *pò* have undergone a specialization trajectory and display a "disruptive separation" bias and a "body-related" orientation. That is, what *pò* most saliently evokes in the mind of Mandarin speakers are disruptive events of separation state change. The affected objects in these disruptive events of separation state change are more often than not body parts and covers of body parts (like clothes). Such a diachronic specialization trajectory indicates that language use is inseparable from our situated embodiment and the social-cultural background (Croft and Cruse 2004). Concerning the correlation between conceptual variation and syntactic form, it should be noted that such a conceptual variation is accompanied by the syntactic relegation of *pò* from a monomorphemic verb to a verb complement. That is to say, when *pò* is more prototypically used to denote disruptive events of separation state change, its syntactic form changes from a monomorphemic verb to a verb complement in the form of V+ *pò*.

4.1.3 Peripheral member variation

Diachronic variation at the peripheral aspect of extensional *pò* is characterized by its flexible adaptability. Such flexible adaptability renders the extensional boundary of *pò* not rigid and allows it to flexibly adapt to changing circumstances. In spite of such flexible adaptations, in response to the prototypical member specialization, the conceptual range of *pò* also undergoes a specialization trajectory. As noted above, the conceptual range of *pò* is rather broad in EMC, but it gradually narrows down in LMC and EMand. And by MdMand, the conceptual range expands to some extent but is still narrower than it is in EMC. In what follows, we will explain how the conceptual range of *pò* narrows and expands by means of reducing or incorporating extensional members.

First of all, the referential range of *pò* is fairly broad in EMC because prototypical members are widespread in this stage and peripheral members that arise from these prototypical members are also numerous and extensive. As noted above, prototypical members include *fra_affpie*, *sti_affpar*, *fles_ affsur*, *sti_noisur*, *fles_newpar*, *fles_noipar* as well as *ten_newpar*. Peripheral members that arise from deviations of these prototypical members are even more widespread. The deviations take the form of modulation or adjustment on the basis of those prototypical members (Rosch and Mervis 1975; Geeraerts 1997: 24). For instance, *fra_affpie* constitutes a prototypical usage. *Fra_neupie* is one of its peripheral members at this stage. Apparently, *fra_neupie* deviates from *fra_affpie* along with the variable of FC, changing from functionally affected to functionally neutral (4.7a). Similarly, *fles_affsur* also gives rise to a great number of peripheral members. *Fles_affpie* deviates from it along with the variable of ES, changing from surface breaking to fragmentary breaking (4.7b). *Fles_newpie* deviates from it along the variable of FC, varying from the function being affected to a new function (4.7c). But despite such transparent deviations, it needs to be pointed out that it is not always easy to figure out exactly from which prototypical member these peripheral members come into being. It seems that all the peripheral and prototypical members are to varying degrees clustered together. Such an equivocal relevance highlights the family resemblance relationship among these category members (Rosch and Mervis 1975; Geeraerts 2007).

(4.7)

a. EMCpoe40: 疾雷**破**石。

        Jí   léi   pò shí.

        swift thunder break stone

        "The swift thunder broke the stone."

b. EMCpoe72: 五内屠裂，肝心**破碎**。

        Wǔnèi túliè,   gānxīn pòsuì.

        Belly disintegrate, liver-heart break-smash

        "The belly disintegrated and the liver and heart broke."

c. EMCpoe93: 用牛、羊、獐、鹿肉之精者……**破**作片。

        Yòng niú, yáng, zhāng,   lùròu zhī jīngzhě ... pò zuò piàn.

        With cow, sheep, roebuck, venison ZHI best ... break into pieces

        "Cut the best beef, mutton, roebuck and venison into pieces."

Secondly, the conceptual range of *pò* significantly narrows down in LMC and EMand mainly because some prototypical members gradually lose their central status. Their corresponding peripheral members gradually fade away from the extensional range of *pò*. As noted above, prototypical usages like *fles_noipar*, *sti_noisur*, *fles_newpar* lose their central status from LMC onward. Further tracing their peripheral usages, it is found that such usages like *ten_newpie* and *fles_newpie* by and by disappear from the referential range of *pò*. The degrading of prototypical members and the disappearance of peripheral members demonstrate that the linguistic categorization of events of separation state change is evolving along with the development of our corporeal, cognitive and social experiences (Li 2008: 77). But the disappearance of these peripheral members does not mean their corresponding events of separation state change no longer exist, but tells that these events are linguistically categorized otherwise.

The conceptual range of *pò* in MdMand is also narrower than in EMC. But compared with LMC and EMand, the conceptual range of *pò* in MdMand is relatively broader. This is because some disappeared peripheral members show up again in MdMand. For instance, *ten_noipar* and *fra_newpie* disappear in EMand but show up again in MdMand. *Ten_noipar* refers to the separation of tender objects in order to get into its inside, like breaking plants to get rid of their seeds (4.8a). *Fra_newpie* indicates segmenting fragile objects into pieces for new uses, like breaking stones for metallurgy (4.8b). In addition, those peripheral members which deviate from prototypical members also contribute to the broad extensional range of *pò* in MdMand. For instance, *fles_newpar* constitutes a prototypical member that describes those breaking events when fleshy objects like fish are separated into parts for new uses in EMC. Although this prototypical member gradually moves away from the central core in LMC, EMand, and MdMand, we can still find its peripheral usages in MdMand. They are constrained to peripheral cooking context or marginal cases like breaking fingers to write words (4.8c and 4.8d). Similarly, *sti_noisur* is frequently used in EMC to denote breaking stiff objects in the surface to reveal the inside but degrade to the peripheral edge in MdMand (4.8e and 4.8f).

(4.8)

a. MdMandpoe75: 青椒**破**口去籽切粗**丝**。

        Qīngjiāo   pò kǒu qù zǐ qiē cū sī.

        green-pepper break open rid seed cut thick slice

        "Broke the green pepper, get rid of its seed and cut it into slices."

b. MdMandpoe660:矿石经过**破**碎、粉磨等逐级加工后可以应用在金属矿山、冶金工业。

        Kuàngshí jīngguò pòsuì, fěnmó děng zhújí jiāgōng hòu kěyǐ yīngyòng zài jīnshǔ kuàngshān, yějīn gōngyè.

ore through break-smash, grind etc. each step process later can apply in metal mining, metallurgical industry

"After being smashed and ground step by step, the ore can be used in metal mining and metallurgical industry."

c. MdMandpoe367: 截**破**右手两指，沥血成书。

Jiépò   yòu shǒu liǎng zhǐ,   lì xuè chéng shū.

truncate-break right hand two fingers, run blood into book

"Broke two of his right-hand fingers and wrote the words with the blood."

d. MdMandpoe492: 胡氏义不受辱，咬**破**手指在墙上题了一首血诗。

Húshì   yì   bú shòu rǔ,   yǎopò   shǒuzhǐ zài qiángshàng tí le yī shǒu xuè shī.

Hu righteous not stand insult, bite-break finger on wall-LOC write-LE a-CL blood poem

"Hu rejected the insult, bit her finger and wrote a poem with blood on the wall."

e. MdMandpoe745: **破**棺裸尸。

Pò   guān luǒ   shī.

open coffin expose corpse

"Open the coffin and expose the corpse."

f. MdMandpoe761: **破**茧而出。

Pò   jiǎn   ér chū.

break cocoon and out

"Breakaway from the cocoon."

In sum, diachronic variation at the aspect of peripheral members demonstrates a flexible evolving pathway and thus contributes to the flexible boundary of extensional *pò*. Firstly, peripheral members arise from variable deviations from the prototypical members. Such peripheral members differ from the prototypical members along with variables of MC, FC as well as ES. Secondly, peripheral members are simply degraded prototypical members which lose their central status. Thirdly, peripheral members may gradually disappear from the referential range. In consideration of these three major ways of peripheral member variation, it is not uneasy to understand that the referential range of *pò* narrows down in LMC and EMand because some prototypical members lose their central status and some peripheral members fade away from the referential range. The referential range broadens in MdMand because some prototypical members retreat themselves into the peripheral fringe and some new peripheral members come into being. In this way, the categorical boundary of extensional *pò* fluctuates diachronically across the four stages and also undergoes a specialization trajectory.

Further exploring such boundary fluctuation and referential specialization, the first reason goes to the accommodation to social-cultural changes, or more cognitively, embodied experience changes (Györi 2002). For one thing, in ancient times, when human needed to slice an object or check the inside of an object, what they could do was to break those objects in a rough way. But nowadays, along with the development of technology, instruments like knives, saws, locks are invented and popularized. As a consequence, it is not necessary to break open or slice objects by hand. Human can use particular instruments to open or cut objects. In this way, prototypical breaking events like *fles_noipar*, *sti_noisur*, *fles_newpar* in EMC are becoming marginal and gradually fade away from the referential range of extensional *pò* in later stages. Moreover, the invention of new materials like paper and cloth enlarges the extensional boundary of *pò*. Given the expressive need to describe new experiences of breaking paper and breaking cloth, speakers evoke their old experience of breaking stiff or fleshy objects and categorize these new experiences in the same way as *pò* (Geeraerts 1988).

Extending further from the first reason, another important reason for the varying boundary is the differential linguistic ways of categorizing events of separation state change. As mentioned above, with social progress, some breaking events have receded from the extensional range of *pò* and are no longer identified or categorized as *pò*. The decreasing of these usages on the one hand is attributed to social development, and on the other hand, results from categorization variation. That is, these usages move away from the extensional range of *pò* and step into the referential range of other lexical items like *kāi* and *qiē*. In EMand and MdMand, events of state change like objects designed to be separable are separated and categorized in terms of *kāi*. State change events like separating objects in a clean way for further use are more often than not linguistically categorized as *qiē*. To prove this conclusion, Chapter 5 further explores conceptual boundary variation of *pò, qiē,* and *kāi*.

4.1.4 Interim summary

To conclude, along with cognitive, social, and cultural development, the conceptual range of *pò* evolves through a specialization trajectory. The prototypical core of *pò* narrows down its scope through giving up the coverage of opening stiff objects and cutting fleshy and tender objects, and instead centers on the characterization of body part partition. Meanwhile, the conceptual range of *pò* broadens and narrows simultaneously as new experiences arise and old experiences die out, but generally displays a specialization trajectory. In general, the prototypical-structured categorical system of *pò* shows the mutual check between flexible adaptability and structural stability (Geeraerts 1988). On the one hand, in its adaptation to social-cultural changes, the extensional range of *pò* flexibly evolves. It not only admits the degrading of prototypical members but also incorporates new peripheral members. On the other hand, the categorical system of *pò* maintains its overall organization. It does not change fundamentally anytime. Old information needs to be restructured, new information needs to be incorporated or extant information needs to be eliminated. Further speaking, the organization of human cognition follows the principle of maximizing the richness of each category and at the same time conforms to the rule of structural stability.

Extending beyond the surface prototype-based category member variation, the underlying concept formation patterns abiding by which specific events of separation state change are categorized also need exploration. In what follows, the conceptual variables that motivate the above-mentioned category member variation are further explored.

4.2 Conceptualization pattern variation

Conceptualization pattern refers to the formation of concepts or relations in the human mind. It shows how concepts are formed and categorized in terms of variable attributes that human is concerned with and thus reflects the segmentation and organization of the conceptual system (Evans and Green 2006: 170). Conceptual pattern variation, self-evidently, means the variation or shift of different conceptualization patterns. As for the conceptualization pattern of events of state change, previous studies prioritize the conceptualization pattern variation of events of state change at the superordinate level. For instance, Talmy (2000b: 237-238) proposes three potential conceptualization patterns of events of state change and states that it is the third pattern that is the most basic and preponderant. This third pattern is "the object or situation could be conceptualized as a figural entity with respect to the property as a ground entity, as if coming to or occurring in the property". In contrast, this study focuses on the conceptualization pattern variation at the basic level and intends to prove that the conceptualization pattern variation of events of separation state change takes the form of conceptual range re-segmentation or reorganization.

Simply speaking, this section argues that members of a prototypically-organized category can be defined as the combination of values on the underlying variables (Geeraerts 2007). The referential range of extensional *pò* undergoes a specialization trajectory because human conceptualization of events of separation state change is readjusted and fine-tuned on the basis of the multiple variables. In other words, diachronic conceptual variation can be further interpreted in terms of how speakers make use of these specific variables as well as the values located on these continuous variables in their categorization of events of separation state change. To this end, section 4.2.1 runs the dataset in Table 3.7 with Ctree and random forest to uncover the importance measure assumed by those multiple variables in accounting for the diachronic variation of extensional *pò*. Section 4.2.2 describes how the structural weights of the conceptual variables vary in the conceptualization of extensional *pò*. Section 4.2.3 explains how the underlying conceptualization patterns drive category member variation. Section 4.2.4 is an interim summary.

4.2.1 Research findings

To explore the differential weight assumed by each variable in determining category member variation, the dataset in Table 3.7 is further processed through Ctree and random forest. As algorithms of Ctree and random forest have been elaborated in 3.2.2, this section concentrates on reporting the research findings. Figure 4.5 demonstrates the importance rank of different conceptual variables with a conditional inference tree. The layout of those tree branches displays how much weight each conceptual variable assumes for the conceptualization pattern of extensional *pò*. Figure 4.6 shows the conditional importance of each conceptual variable after running numerous conditional inference trees with the algorithm of random forest.

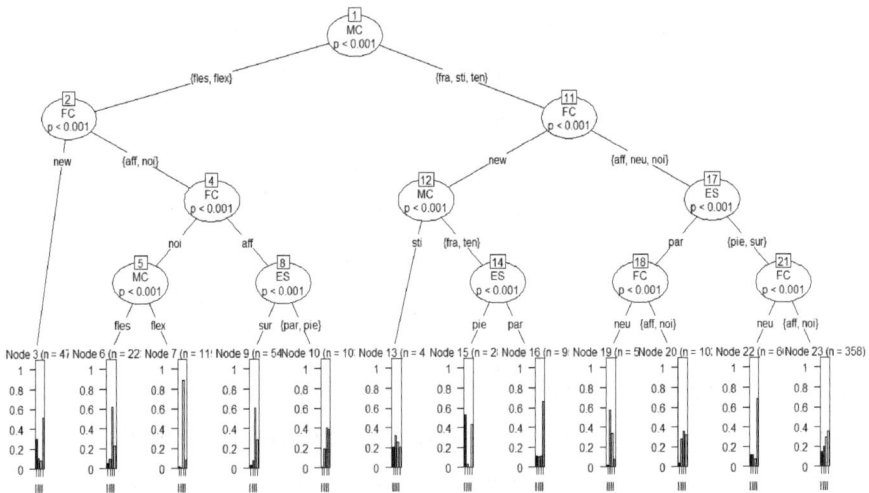

Figure 4.5 Ctree analysis of conceptualization pattern variation

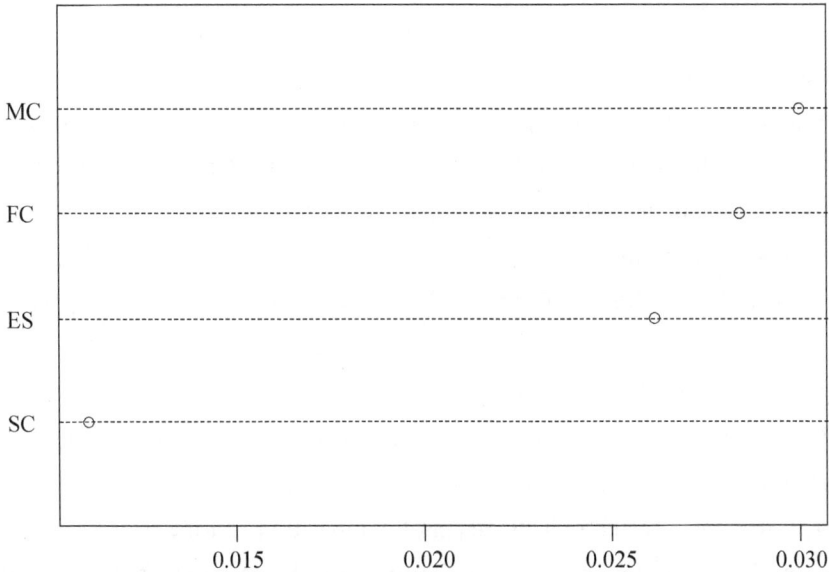

Figure 4.6 Conditional importance of variables from random forest

Research finding 1:

Both Ctree and random forest demonstrate that the four underlying variables are unequally distributed in accounting for category member variation. Comparing Figure 4.5 and Figure 4.6, it can be found that both Ctree and random forest show that the conditional importance of these four variables is ranked as MC>FC>ES>SC. Such weighted distribution indicates that the referential range of *pò* is comprised of multiple variables on the one hand and evinces that there is weight difference among the underlying variables in motivating *pò*'s diachronic variation on the other hand.

Research finding 2:

Figure 4.5 demonstrates the first four tree levels at which different variables account for the diachronic variation of extensional *pò*. The very first tree level shows that MC foremost sets fleshy and flexible objects apart from objects of other materials. This indicates that the separations of fleshy and flexible objects are diachronically categorized rather differently from other objects. At the second tree level, FC first distinguishes the new function from the rest. Such distinction suggests that events of separation state change which describe the breaking of objects to create new functions vary most significantly. At the third tree level, ES tells partial separation from surface separation and fragmentary separation. This suggests that it is surface and fragmentary separation that are gradually categorized differently from partial separation.

Research finding 3:

According to Figure 4.6, among the four variables, the importance measure of MC, FC and ES are above 0.025 and assume higher weight for the diachronic variation of extensional *pò*. In contrast, the variable of SC is less salient. This indicates that the first three variables equate with less "psychological distance" from the lexical category of *pò* than others (Pullman 1983: 112). In other words, it is the affected objects' material composition and the Agent's purpose that motivate the conceptual variation of *pò* to a great extent. Besides, the resulting state of the affected object after the breaking action also to some extent contributes to the diachronic variation of *pò*. In contrast, <spatial configuration> is a less criterial variable in *pò*'s referential variation. *Pò,* as a lexical category, is indifferent to the spatial configuration of the affected objects. This is the reason why we neglect spatial configuration in our MCA analysis in Section 4.1.

Overall, it is borne out through Ctree and random forest analyses that category members are in fact combinations of multiple variable levels. Since different variables assume different weights for the diachronic variation of extensional *pò*, the category members that arise out of these variables also exhibit diachronic variation, as described in the foregoing section.

4.2.2 Conceptual variable variation

As revealed through Ctree and random forest analyses, three of the four underlying variables are pinpointed to assume a significant structural weight in the conceptualization pattern of *pò,* namely MC, FC, and ES. This section elaborates how these three conceptual variables vary in contributing to the categorization of extensional *pò*.

To begin with, MC contributes the highest weight in the conceptual variation of extensional *pò*. As mentioned above, <material composition> refers to the material that the affected objects are made of. In this case of events of separation state change, the material is also attested to be a predominant variable in motivating the diachronic variation of extensional *pò*.

As shown in Figure 4.7, the underlying variable of <material composition> is measured in terms of five specific values, namely *fleshy, flexible, fragile, stiff*, and *tender*. Firstly, with regard to relative frequency, from EMC onward to MdMand, these five variable levels vary significantly in motivating the categorization of extensional *pò*. Specifically, it is found that fleshy (26.94 to 41.98) and flexible objects (2.07 to 10.07) exhibit a general increasing trend in driving the emergence of the categorical system of extensional *pò*. In contrast, *stiff, fragile* and *tender* objects all display a decreasing trend and are becoming less important in contributing to the lexical categorization of *pò*. More exactly, in EMC, variable levels of *fleshy, stiff* and *fragile* are equally important in stimulating the formation of lexical concept *pò*. But in LMC, only *fleshy* and *stiff* make such a contribution. In EMand, *flexible* turns up as a third vital variable level while in MdMand *flexible* is replaced by *fragile* in driving the categorization process of *pò*.

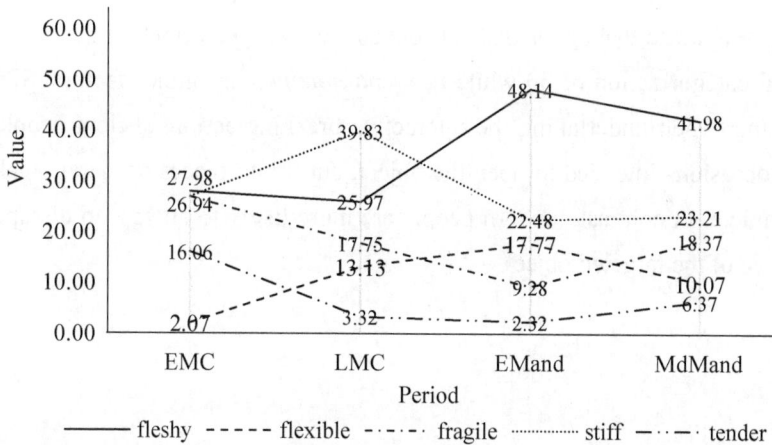

Figure 4.7 Diachronic variation along <material composition>

As for the prototypical core of *pò,* the range of material type is rather extensive in EMC but gradually narrows down in LMC, EMand, and MdMand. In EMC, no matter the disintegration of fragile objects like stones, the rupture of fleshy objects like body parts, the partition of stiff objects like boats, or the division of tender objects like fruit, all to some extent motivate the concept formation of *pò.* But as time goes by, the disintegration of fragile and the separation of tender objects are less frequently related to *pò.* Only the separation of stiff, fleshy as well as flexible objects, maintain their contributing importance to the concept formation of *pò.* In other words, the lexical categorization of *pò* is becoming increasingly sensitive to the material composition of the affected objects.

The second important structuring variable is functional change. Functional change stands for the interaction between the affected object and the Agent, namely the Agent's purpose in carrying out breaking events (Pullman 1983: 103; Lakoff 1987: 392). As the following Figure 4.8 demonstrates, in EMC, *new*, *noimped*, and *affected* are three salient contributing values on the variable of <functional change>. But after this stage, the *affected* increases dramatically from 39.90 to 64.22 and becomes most salient in the categorization of extensional *pò.* On the contrary, *new* undergoes a sharp decrease from 25.39 to 8.70. The *noimped* also decreases to a small extent from 30.05 to 23.13. Such measurable changes along the underlying variable of <functional change> indicate that *affected* stands out as the major contributing factor for the lexical categorization of *pò* while *new* and *noimped* are minor factors. Simply speaking, when undertaking the interactive breaking action, ancient people on most occasions intended to open the object, cut it into pieces or merely make it incomplete. In contrast, modern people are more likely to attempt to disrupt the function of the targeted object.

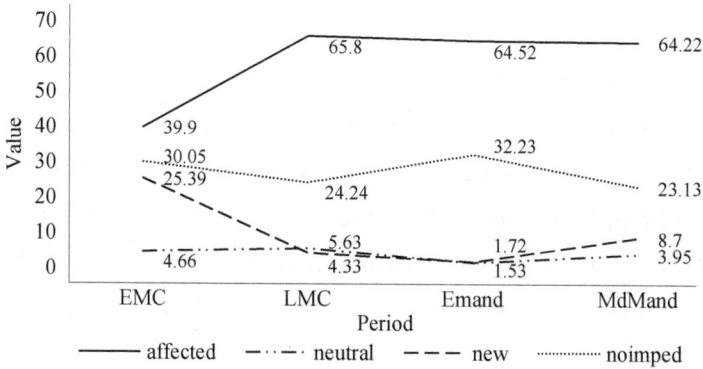

Figure 4.8 Diachronic variation along <functional change>

Moreover, variable change as such is indicative of the ongoing disruptive bias of the lexical item *pò*. In EMC, as long as the affected object is separated into parts, such a separation is categorized in terms of *pò,* no matter the separation is intended to create something new, to get rid of an impediment, or to affect the object's function. But in LMC, EMand, and MdMand, it is becoming more likely that only when the separation events involve separation and impairment, they are more likely to be categorized in terms of *pò*. Besides, in cases where objects are broken to reveal their inside, the separation of objects is also motivating the lexical categorization of *pò*. But such a categorization relationship is dwindling and accounts for a lesser proportion in the categorical system of *pò*.

Apart from material and function, the endstate is also a criterial variable in explaining the conceptualization variation of extensional *pò*. <Endstate> means the transition of an object from an intact state to a decomposed state. Three values are substantiated along with this variable, including *surface breaking, partial breaking*, and *breaking into pieces*. According to Figure 4.9, it is fairly clear that the value of *partial breaking* is playing an increasingly important role in the categorization of events of separation state change in the case of *pò*. *Partial breaking* increases from 46.63 to 81.82 and then levels off at the relative frequency of 69.86. In contrast, *piece breaking* decreases from 33.16 to 12.81

and is becoming less important in the categorical system of *pò*. *Surface breaking* is relatively stable, slightly dropping from 20.21 to 17.32. This suggests that the chance is higher in EMC than in MdMand that surface severance of an object is lexically categorized as *pò* instead of other lexical items. But in general, underlying the referential range of *pò* and at the variable of <endstate>, it is the change of *partial breaking* that contributes the most weight to the category member variation of *pò*. Although *surface breaking* and *fragmentary breaking* are also important in driving the categorization of events of separation state change, their importance is declining diachronically.

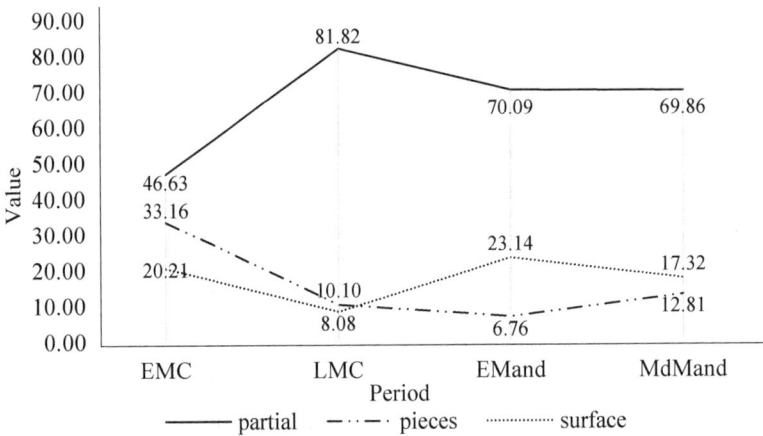

Figure 4.9 Diachronic variation along <endstate>

Overall, through tracing the three underlying variables of extensional *pò*, this study confirms that it is the underlying variable variation that drives the surface category member variation. The diachronic variation of the multiple underlying variables takes the form of variable value adjustment. Provided that one variable adjusts its level in the categorization process, the individual members resulting from the intersection of multiple variables will definitely change. But it should be noted that these variables are not necessarily easy to distinguish and are not necessarily present to consciousness in a clear and distinct fashion either. As such, exposing the underlying variables that motivate the specific category member variation is of great significance. Moving one step further, it is borne out that these variables do not motivate member variation in a parallel fashion but in an intersecting manner. The succeeding part explores how these variables cooperate in driving the category formation of *pò*.

4.2.3 Conceptual variable intersection

As revealed above, the categorization of events of separation state change, or the conceptualization of extensional *pò* is essentially a multivariate process. As such, the conceptualization of extensional *pò*, to a great extent hinges on the underlying multiple variables. This part explains how these multiple variables work in motivating the above-mentioned category member variation.

In the first place, conceptual variables inherent in the multivariate structure of prototypical lexical items do not motivate category member variation independently, but work together and determine category formation interactively. In other words, speakers unconsciously choose and intersect variables in their conceptualization process. Before venturing into the complexity of extensional *pò*, we first exemplify variable intersection. Figure 4.10 visualizes variable intersection in a simple fashion. The lines stand for the variables and the dots at intersections are category members thus arise. The lines colored in dark represent those primary variables and those in light represent those subsidiary variables. In the same vein, the dots in dark are prototypical category members while those in light are peripheral members. In consideration of the relationship between variables and members, it goes without doubt that prototypical members are always located at the intersection of weighted variable levels while peripheral members are represented by dots yielded from the intersection of subsidiary variable levels.

Returning to the complex multidimensional structure of *pò*, as noted above, *pò* is co-determined by three primary variables, namely MC, FC as well as ES. These three variables are measured in terms of specific values. The MCA plots in Figure 4.2 and Figure 4.3 have already demonstrated how the extensional range of *pò* is jointly determined by multiple conceptual variables. Figure 4.11

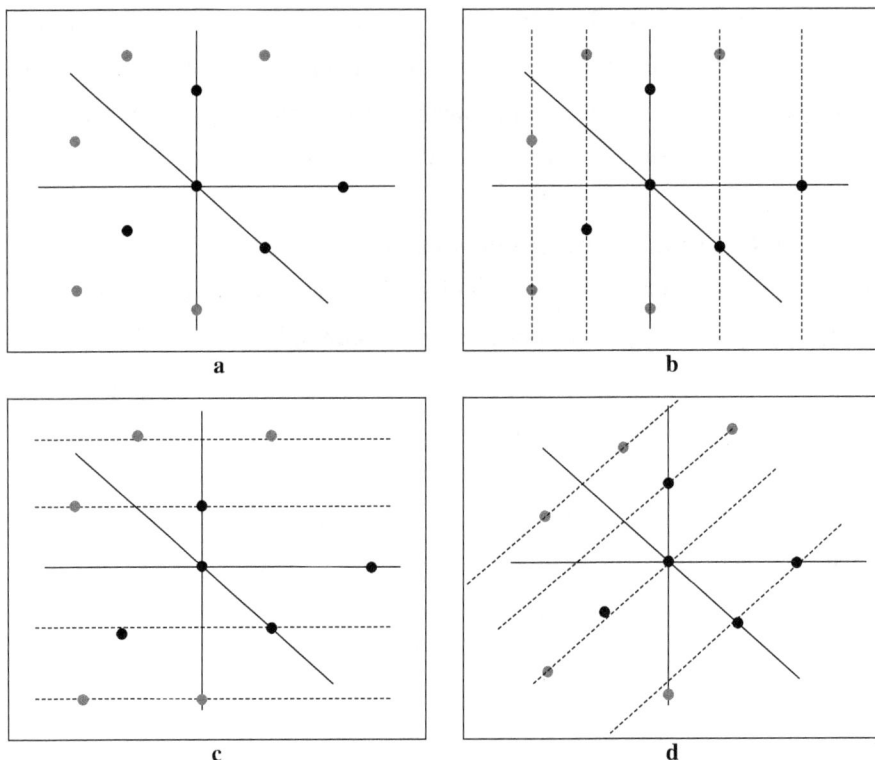

Figure 4.10 The multivariate semantic structure (Geeraerts 2007)

visualizes the extensional range of *pò* in terms of a multivariate template, in order to further expound that the extensional range of lexical items arises from the conceptual variable intersection. It shows the extensional range of *pò* at MdMand, with MC, FC and ES marked along with the height, length, and width of the rectangular. Prototypical members are shaded in black and nonprototypical members in grey. In this way, it is fairly clear that each extensional member is essentially located at the juncture of these three variables. For instance, *flex_affpar* appears as a joint point of *flexible*, *functionally affected*, and *partial breaking*. *Sti_noipar* shows up as a cross point of *stiff*, *no impediment*, and *partial breaking*. The same conjunction logic also goes to other referential members like *sti_affpar* and *fra_affpar*. Meanwhile, *fleshy*, *functionally affected*, and *partial breaking* are major conceptual variables in the conceptualization of *pò* at MdMand. As a result, *fles_affpar* shows up as the most prototypical member. The other prototypical members include *fles_affsur*, *sti_affpar*, and *sti_noipar*.

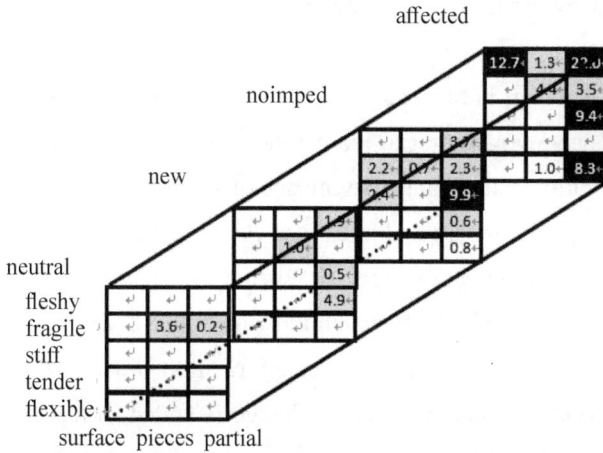

affected

noimped

		12.7	1.3	2?.J
		↵	4.4	3.5
			↵	9.4

new

		↵	↵	3.7	↵	↵	↵
		2.2	0.7	2.3	↵	1.0	8.3
		2.4	↵	9.9			

| | ↵ | ↵ | 1.5 | ↵ | .·· | 0.6 |
| | ↵ | 1.0 | ↵ | .·· | | 0.8 |

neutral

fleshy
fragile
stiff
tender
flexible

| | ↵ | 4.9 |
| ↵ | 3.6 | 0.2 |

surface pieces partial

Figure 4.11 The multivariate structure of *pò* in MdMand

Secondly, further considering the diachronic conceptual variation of extensional *pò*, it is easy to figure out that it is the underlying variable variation that motivates category member variation. For one thing, as long as the variable levels are adjusted and narrowed to a single variable level, category members arising from those deceased variable levels also fade away. To be specific, in the case of extensional *pò*, the variable levels of <material composition> confine themselves only to *fleshy* and *stiff* objects. Similarly, the values distributed along the variable of <functional change> zoom out from *affected*, *no impediment*, and *new* to only *affected*. The values measured on the variable of <endstate> shrink from *surface*, *pieces*, and *partial* to *surface* and *partial*. Attendant with these variable variations, category members arising from the junction of those obsolete variable values like *ten_newpar*, *fles_newpar*, *sti_noisur*, as well as *fles_noipar* recede from the conceptual range of *pò*. At the same time, the attentional focus on the variable levels of *fleshy*, *affected*, and *partial* gives rise to prototypical members like *fles_affpar*, *flex_affpar*.

Extending the variable intersection one step further, the referential range of extensional *pò* is inherently a flux continuum. On the basis of variable identification and variable level measurement, this continuum is segmented and organized by means of the concept of events of separation state change in human cognition and codified in terms of linguistic patterns like *pò*. Analytically speaking, in the prior conceptualization process, multiple variables are unconsciously evoked first to realize the segmentation and organization of events of separation state change. By means of segmentation, separation events are cut up from their forward and afterward events and form an integrated event unit. In virtue of organization, specific events of separation state change are prototypically organized in the human mind with both a definite core and a fuzzy boundary. After that, in the linguistic categorization process, the prototypical structure of events of separation state change is coded in terms of *pò*. But it should be noted that this prototypical structure is not constant. Along with the variable adjustment of events of separation state change, the conceptual organization of *pò* also varies.

Returning to the diachronic conceptual variation of *pò*, the diachronic specialization of *pò* reflects how variable adjustment drives the re-segmentation and reorganization of events of separation state change. In earlier stages, the three underlying continuous variables, with all their variable levels, fix the boundary of events of separation state change amid the flux continuum and linguistically categorized a great variety of events of separation state change as *pò*. But in later stages, the variable levels located on these variables are restricted respectively to *fleshy*, *functionally affected*, and *partial*. Such a variable adjustment re-segments the extensional range of lexical *pò*. As a result, the referential range of *pò* is confined to disruptive events of separation state change. Meanwhile, the conceptual range segment beyond that of *pò* does not return to the flux continuum but is further conceptualized and linguistically coded in terms of other lexical items such as *kāi*, *qiē*, and *suì*. For instance, in MdMand, events of separation state change like *ten_newpar*, *fles_newpar*, *sti_noisur* as well as *fles_noipar* drift beyond the range of lexical *pò* and are more likely to be categorized in terms of the onomasiological variants of *pò* such as *kāi* and *qiē*.

4.2.4 Interim summary

In sum, events of separation state change are part and parcel of the flux continuum of the natural world (Bowerman 2005; Majid et al. 2007a). It is based on attribute variable that human cognition and language segment this event type from the continuous flux and categorize it in terms of lexical items like *pò*. The conceptualization pattern variation associated with the referential range of lexical *pò* takes the form of conceptual re-segmentation or reorganization, namely, variable adjustment. In the earlier stages, three weighted variables and their variable levels contribute to the lexical categorization of variant events of separation state change as *pò*. To better store the segmented multiple variant events of separation state change, they are organized in the form of a prototype-based structure.

Across the four stages, the prototypical conceptual structure is not immune to cognitive-cultural changes, but adjusts its internal structure accordingly. By the period of MdMand, the three underlying variables adjust and restrict their values to *fleshy*, *functionally affected*, and *partial*. The prototypical structure of *pò* reorganizes its central core and peripheral boundary accordingly. In consequence, the referential range of lexical *pò* is restricted to disruptive events of separation state change. Those events of separation state change that move beyond the referential range of lexical *pò* are reorganized and incorporated by the referential range of other verbs such as *kāi* and *qiē*. In this sense, the conceptual range of events of separation state change is re-segmented and reorganized. Such conceptualization pattern variation demonstrates that human beings view and understand the natural world in a subjective and dynamic fashion.

4.3 Summary

In conclusion, this chapter captures the diachronic specialization trajectory of extensional *pò* based on its prototypically organized conceptual structure. As revealed above, the prototypical core of *pò* has undergone a narrowing trend and gradually restricts to the description of body part wounding in Mandarin. The peripheral boundary of *pò* flexibly adapts itself both to the internal structural adjustment and to the external cognitive-cultural evolution. As a result, the referential range of *pò* across the four stages gradually narrows down. The supporting framework for the prototype-based category structure is the attribute variable, including both perceptual and functional variables. The intersection of these variables constitutes the structure nodes, namely the category members. The category member variation is inherently driven by the reorganization of these underlying variables. Along with the conceptual variation of extensional *pò, pò* in its syntactic form has changed from a monomorphemic verb to a verb complement.

To get better insight into the conceptual reorganization of events of separation state change, the following chapter explores the conceptual competition between *pò* and its onomasiological variants in the categorization of events of separation state change.

CHAPTER 5

Diachronic conceptual boundary variation
of extensional *pò*, *qiē* and *kāi*

This chapter extends our study on the conceptual variation of one single verb (*pò*) to three near-synonymous verbs (*pò*, *qiē*, and *kāi*) whose conceptual relationship remains a controversial issue in previous studies (Levin 1993; Pye 1996; Majid et al. 2007a; Chen 2007; Croft 2015). Section 5.1 explores the conceptual boundary between these three keywords in ancient Chinese (EMC and LMC). Section 5.2 specifies their conceptual category variation in Mandarin Chinese (EMand and MdMand). Section 5.3 compares ancient Chinese and Mandarin Chinese and probes to the conceptual reorganization mechanism that motivates the conceptual boundary evolution.

5.1 Conceptual boundary between *pò*, *qiē* and *kāi* in ancient Chinese

As elaborated in Chapter 4, extensional *pò* has become specialized driven by the reorganization and readjustment of those variable levels along with multiple attribute variables. Nonetheless, the value of a word is not only determined entirely by its concept or meaning but is also determined by its comparable words [Saussure 1983(1916)]. Since previous studies have already posed the controversial issue of the conceptual relationship of *pò*, *qiē*, and *kāi*, this chapter further explores how these three semantically similar lexical items cooperate with each other in their categorization and segmentation of events of separation state change. In what follows, section 5.1.1 sets forth with the MCA visualization of the conceptual ranges of *pò*, *qiē*, and *kāi* in EMC and LMC. Then section 5.1.2 details the conceptual relationship among these three verbs in these two historical stages with specific examples. Section 5.1.3 goes on to an interim summary.

5.1.1 Research findings

To explore how boundaries of *pò*, *qiē*, and *kāi* change, we project their varying usages and their related variables onto MCA biplots. To reveal the conceptual relationship among these three verbs across four chronological stages, four MCA plots are drawn for detailed comparison. Each MCA plot visualizes the conceptual relationship among these three verbs in one particular chronological stage. Moreover, based on the four conceptual variables MC, FC, ES and SC considered in Chapter 4, we add additional conceptual variables to better demonstrate the conceptual boundary variation between *pò, qiē* and *kāi*. These conceptual variables include <initiation of force>, <locus predictability>, <change pattern>, <separation mode> and <reversibility>.

Figure 5.1 and Figure 5.2 are MCA biplots that show the conceptual boundary between these three keywords in EMC and LMC respectively. The first two dimensions of these two MCA biplots capture respectively 87% and 73.2% of the total variance (or inertia), thus being able to reflect the conceptual ranges of these three keywords (Greenacre 2007: Cha 11). Taking Figure 5.1 as an instance, as noted in the legend, dots within the streaky ellipse stand for the individual usages of *kāi*, dots within the grey ellipse for *pò* and dots within the blank ellipse for *qiē*. Those black squares represent the annotated variable levels. Those ellipses are 95% confidence ellipses drawn around individual usages of these three keywords. It should be noted that the confidence ellipse actually simulates the prototypical structure of the lexical category: the larger dot within the ellipse represents the centroid or prototypical core of the lexical category;

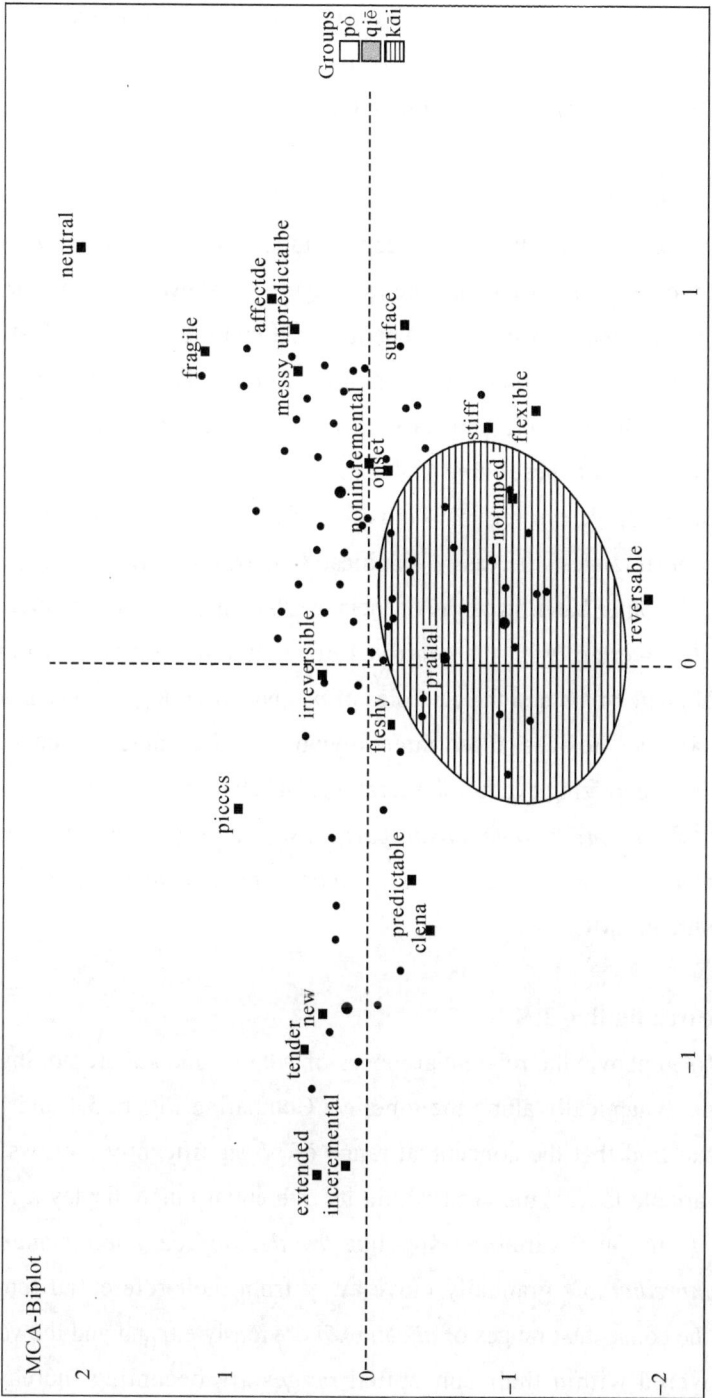

Figure 5.1 The MCA plot of *pò*, *qiē*, and *kāi* in EMC

those smaller dots at the boundary demonstrate the peripheral usages (Levshina 2015: Cha 19). A further comparison of the MCA biplot in EMC with that in LMC reveals the following significant findings.

Research finding 1:

It is more than clear that the conceptual ranges of *pò, qiē*, and *kāi* are to a great extent overlapped in ancient Chinese. Figure 5.1 shows that the conceptual ranges of these three keywords are superimposed upon each other in EMC. *Qiē* overlaps with *pò* in a relatively marginal area. *Kāi* greatly overlaps with *pò*, its centroid even falling on the boundary of *pò*. Figure 5.2 demonstrates how the conceptual ranges of these three keywords interact with each other in LMC. On the one hand, we can see that both *qiē* and *kāi* expand to a great extent in their conceptual ranges whereas *pò* significantly narrows down in its conceptual range. On the other hand, in terms of their overlapping areas, these three verbs significantly overlap, with the centroids of *pò* and *qiē* embraced within the conceptual range of *kāi* and the centroids of *pò* and *kāi* falling on the conceptual boundary of *qiē*. Besides, these three keywords share numerous conceptual variables in categorizing events of separation state change. For instance, variable levels like *fleshy, predictable, clean, partial, stiff*, and *noimped* are located at their intersection in EMC and *partial, nonincremental, flexible*, and *fleshy* lie in their juncture in LMC.

Research finding 2:

As noted above, the referential ranges of *pò, qiē*, and *kāi* are not invariant but change dynamically along the timeline. Comparing Figure 5.1 and Figure 5.2, we can find that the conceptual range of *pò* significantly narrows down and the variable levels embraced within its referential range display a marked decrease. Conceptual variable levels like *fragile, surface, nonincremental* as well as *unpredictable* gradually move away from their referential range. In contrast, the conceptual ranges of *qiē* and *kāi* obviously expand and the variable levels covered within their conceptual ranges are becoming increasingly

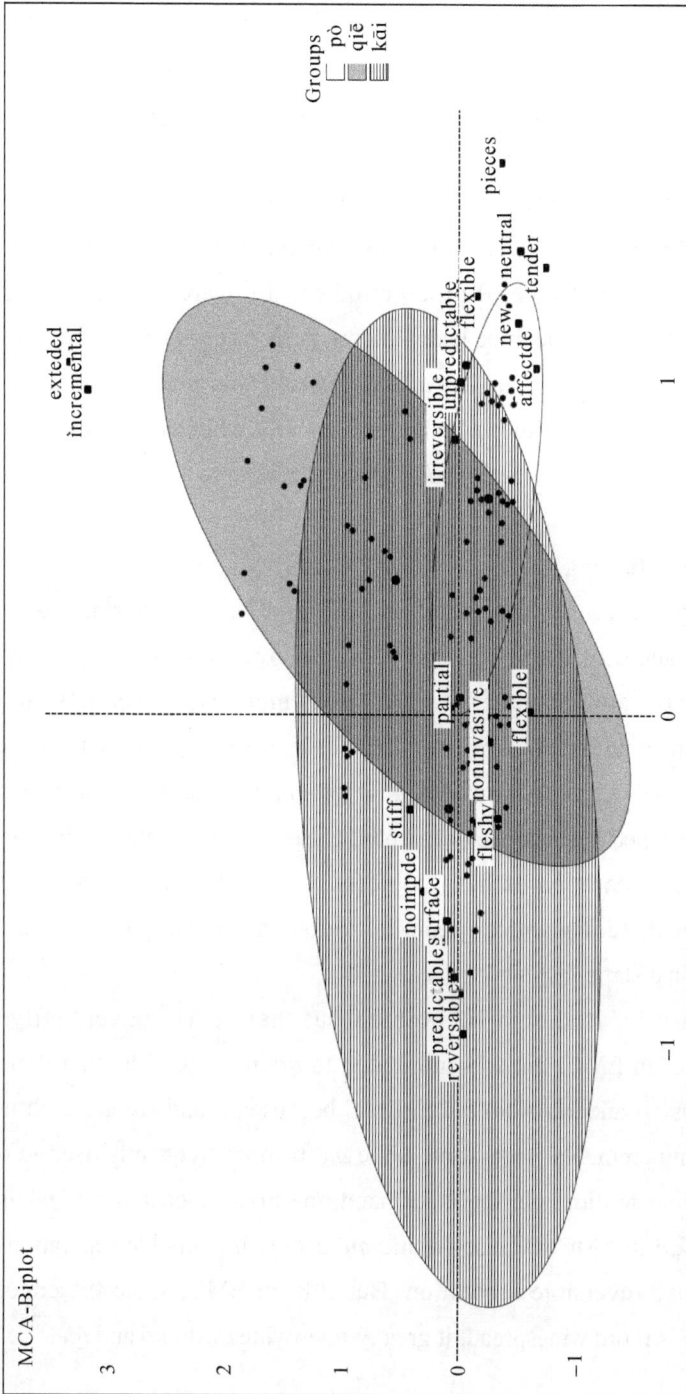

Figure 5.2 The MCA plot of *pò*, *qiē*, and *kāi* in LMC

numerous. Conceptual variable levels like *fleshy*, *partial*, and *irreversible* are further incorporated into the conceptual range of *qiē* and variable levels like *unpredictable*, *stiff*, *noimped*, and *surface*, etc. are further absorbed into the referential range of *kāi*.

This echoes our previous finding that the conceptual specialization of *pò* is correlated to its labor division with its near-synonyms in categorizing events of separation state change. By the period of LMC, apart from those shared variable levels among the three lexical items, *pò* is more approximate to variable levels like *unpredictable*, *fragile*, *affected*, *tender* and *neutral*, *qiē* is closer to *irreversible*, *pieces*, *new*, *extended* and *incremental* while *kāi* is more proximate to variable levels like *stiff*, *noimped*, *surface*, *predictable* and *reversable*.

Research finding 3:

Thirdly, despite the fact that *pò*, *qiē*, and *kāi* are overlapped in their conceptual ranges in both EMC and LMC, the overlapping areas among these three keywords are not static. In EMC, *pò* is more extensive, thus enclosing partial extensional usages of *qiē* and *kāi*. But in LMC, as *pò* narrows down, it only overlaps with *qiē* and *kāi* in a rather small range while *qiē* and *kāi* are greatly overlapped because they can both be used to refer to the nonincremental, onset, partial separation of fleshy objects. Such a diachronic change further verifies that these semantically similar verbs do not categorize the external experience in a static fashion.

Meanwhile, it should be pointed out that *pò* is conceptually more similar to *kāi* in EMC, but was more akin to *qiē* in LMC. The first dimension differentiates *pò* and *kāi* from *qiē* in EMC because *pò* and *kāi* are both used to describe nonincremental separation while *qiē* is more frequently used to denote incremental separation. On the other hand, the first-dimension sets *pò* and *qiē* apart from *kāi* in LMC because *pò* and *qiē* denote irreversible separation while *kāi* categorize reversible separation. But still, in LMC, since the conceptual range of *kāi* is more widespread, it greatly intertwines with *pò* and *qiē*.

5.1.2 Conceptual boundary variation

As mentioned above, there are no absolutely clear-cut conceptual boundaries between *pò*, *qiē*, and *kāi* in ancient Chinese. Rather, these three keywords are greatly overlapped in their referential ranges. But even so, these three verbs undergo diachronic changes in their referential ranges and as a result, their overlapping areas or conceptual boundaries vary accordingly.

To begin with, *pò*, *qiē*, and *kāi* carve up events of separation state change in an overlapping fashion in both EMC and LMC. But as these three verbs vary diachronically in their referential ranges, their overlapping areas also keep changing. For one thing, *pò* displays a fairly extensive referential range in EMC and encloses a wide range of variable levels. *Qiē* and *kāi* are partially intersected with *pò* in their categorization of events of separation state change. To be specific, *pò* overlaps with *qiē* in its description of the predictable clean separation of fleshy objects. For instance, as exemplified in (5.1), *pò* designates the slicing of animal flesh into pieces (5.1a) or the partial separation of fish (5.1b). Likewise, *qiē* also describes the fine cutting or the block cutting of meat (5.1c–5.1d). More importantly, no matter *pò* or *qiē* is used to denote the separation of meat, the locus of separation is predictable and the cross section of the separated flesh is clean. That is, whether *pò* or *qiē* is used to characterize the separation of fleshy objects, it is always possible to predict where exactly the animal flesh will disintegrate and the disintegrated cross section is always neat (Majid et al. 2007a; Essegby 2007). In the same vein, *pò* intersects *kāi* in characterizing the separation of stiff objects to get rid of impediments. For instance, the opening of a coffin or the instrument of punishment is denoted as *pò* (5.2a–5.2b). The opening of the bookcase as well as the opening of gate is described in terms of *kāi* (5.2c–5.2d). Whether *pò* or *kāi* is used, in such cases of opening separation, the affected objects are usually stiff in material composition and are separated to remove impediments so as to get access to the things within the affected objects (Bowerman 2005). For instance, the coffin is broken open so as to reach its inside and the book case is opened in order to get the book.

(5.1)

a. EMCpoe93: 用牛、羊、獐、鹿肉之精者⋯⋯**破**作片。

> Yòng niú, yáng, zhāng, lùròu zhī jīngzhě ... pò zuò piàn.

> With cow, sheep, roebuck, venison ZHI best … break into pieces

> "Cut the best beef, mutton, roebuck and venison into pieces."

b. EMCpoe100: 四**破**，於大釜煮之。

> Sì pò, yú dà fǔ zhǔ zhī.

> four break, LOC great pot boil it.

> "Break it into four parts and boil it in a big pot."

c. EMCqie12: 煮令熟，细**切**。

> Zhǔ lìng shú, xì qiē.

> boil make cooked, slice cut

> "Boil it cooked and then cut it into slices."

d. EMCqie5: 脔**切**羊肺一具。

> Luán qiē yáng fèi yījù.

> block cut sheep lung one-CL

> "Cut a lung of sheep into big blocks."

(5.2)

a. EMCpoe136: 辽西人见辽水中有浮棺，欲斫**破**之。

> Liáoxīrén jiàn Liáoshuǐ zhōng yǒu fú guān, yù zhuópò zhī.

> Liaoxi-people see Liao-water LOC have floating coffin, want saw-break it.

> "People in Liaoxi found a floating coffin in Liao water and wanted to hack it open."

b. EMCpoe164: 开其自新之路，一时**破**械遣之。

> kāi qí zì xīn zhī lù, yī shí pò xiè qiǎn zhī.

open his own new DE road, one time break instrument drive him

"Opened a new road for them and then released them by breaking the instrument of torture."

c. EMCkai23: 开匮得书，见公之功。

Kāi guì dé shū, jiàn gōng zhī gōng.

open box get book, see him DE contribution

"Opened the box, got the book and found his contribution."

d. EMCkai38: 开阖扇，通障塞。

Kāi hé shàn,　tōng zhàngsè.

open closed doors, clear obstruction.

"Opened the doors and cleared the obstruction."

In contrast, although the referential ranges of *pò, qiē* and *kāi* are still intertwined together in LMC, *pò* has narrowed down in its referential range and its overlapping areas with the other two verbs also shrink. As shown in Figure 5.2, the superimposition of *pò* with *qiē* and *kāi* is fairly limited in scope and there are no variable levels falling into this scope. This suggests that *pò, qiē*, and *kāi* are reorganized in their labor division in categorizing events of separation state change. In spite of this, *qiē* and *kāi* are significantly intertwined together and they share variable levels like *partial, nonincremental*, as well as *onset*. This is simply because both *qiē* and *kāi* are applicable for characterizing onset nonincremental partial separation. For instance, the cutting of bamboo and flesh described as *qiē* (5.3a–5.3b) and the opening of a door and a mouth denoted by *kāi* (5.3c–5.3d) are both carried out with onset initiation of force, and partially separated in a nonincremental mode (Talmy 2000b: 415; Croft 2015). Moreover, *qiē* and *kāi* form serial verb constructions in depicting the separation of animal hearts. As exemplified in (5.3e), *qiē* and *kāi* constitute the compound *qiē-kāi* and are both used to denote the clean separation of animal flesh. This further indicates that *qiē* and *kāi* can be used to describe similar separation scenarios.

(5.3)

a. LMCqie32: 古林之竹，劲而利，削为刀，割象皮如**切**芋。

    Gǔ lín zhī zhú, jìn ér lì, xuē wéi dāo, gē xiàng pí rú qiē yù

    old forest DE bamboo, tough and sharp, chop into knife, cut elephant fur like cut taro

    "Bamboo in the old forest is tough and sharp. When chopped into a knife, it can cut elephant fur as easily as cutting taro."

b. LMCqie18: 樊哙覆其盾于地，加彘盾上，拔剑**切**而啗之。

    Fánkuài fù qí dùn yú dì, jiā zhì dùn shàng, bá jiàn qiē ér dàn zhī.

    Fankuai put his shield LOC floor, put pork shield top, draw sword cut and chew it

    "Fankuai put his shield on the floor, and put the pork on top of it. He then cut the pork with his sword and chewed it."

c. LMCkai32: 尔后**开**门延敌，讫不复至。

    Ěrhòu kāi mén yán dí, qì bú fù zhì.

    then open door confront enemy, over not again back

    "Then they opened the door and fought their enemy, who will not come back again."

d. LMCkai628: 生即张目**开**口,若笑之容

    Shēng jí zhāng mù kāi kǒu, ruò xiào zhī róng.

    born then open eye open mouth, like laugh DE face

    "At birth, he opened his eyes and mouth, as if smiling."

e. LMCkai1145: 如饮食中鸡心猪心之属，**切开**可见。

    Rú yǐn shí zhōng jī xīn zhū xīn zhī shǔ, qiē kāi kě jiàn.

    like food LOC chicken heart pig heart and so on, cut open then see

    "Things like chicken heart and pig heart, when you cut them open, you can find they are empty inside."

Secondly, despite the fact that *pò*, *qiē*, and *kāi* are overlapped in EMC and LMC, their referential ranges keep changing across the two stages. Specifically speaking, *pò* functions as a generic verb in EMC and therefore encloses a great number of variable levels within its referential range (Chen 2007). It is used not only to describe the disintegration of fleshy objects (5.3a–5.3b) but also the partition of fragile and flexible objects (5.4a–5.4b), not only partial breaking but also surface breaking, not only function disruption but also the removing of impediments. Whereas in LMC, *pò* has become specialized and is more confined to describing the unpredictable, irreversible function disruption of fragile, flexible as well as fleshy objects. For instance, the shattering of fragile objects, the tearing of clothes as well as the wounding of body parts are likely to be categorized in terms of *pò* in LMC (5.4a–5.4c).

(5.4)

a. LMCpoe317: 亚父受玉斗，置之地，拔剑撞而**破**之。

> Yàfù shòu yù dǒu, zhì zhī dì,   bá jiàn zhuàng ér pò zhī.
>
> Yafu accept jade vessel, discard it ground, draw sword crash and break it
>
> "Yafu accepted the jade vessel, threw it on the ground and smashed it with a sword."

b. LMCpoe115: 幞头巾子露，衫**破**肚皮开。

> Fú tóujīnzǐ lù,   shān pò dùpí kāi.
>
> cover headscarf worn, shirt tear belly reveal
>
> "The headscarf was worn; the shirt was torn and revealed the belly."

c. LMCpoe133: 范惟一男，放鹰马惊，桑枝打**破**其脑。

> Fàn Wéi yī nán, fàng yīng mǎ jīng,   sāngzhī   dǎpò qí nǎo.
>
> Fan Wei one man, fly eagle horse frightened, mulberry-branch hit-break his head

"A man named Fan Wei frightened a horse by flying an eagle. His head was hit broken by the mulberry branch."

Accompanying the referential specialization of *pò* is the relative referential extension of *qiē* and *kāi*. Such a synchronic variation to a great extent indicates that those events of separation state change that are no longer categorized in terms of *pò* are more likely to be categorized by means of *qiē* and *kāi*. For instance, *pò* is once used to depict the partial separation of fleshy objects to create new uses in EMC, but such events of separation state change are more prominently characterized in terms of *qiē* in LMC (5.5a–5.5c). That is, *qiē* is not only used to describe the extended incremental fragmentary separation of fleshy objects in LMC but is also used to depict onset nonincremental partial separation of fleshy objects. Similarly, although *pò* and *kāi* are both employed for describing the surface separation of stiff objects in EMC, these events of separation state change are more prototypically categorized as *kāi* in LMC. As exemplified in (5.6a–5.6c), either the clean separation of gates or the messy separation of the brick furnace and canals are characterized in terms of *kāi*. Moreover, the opening of human body parts to get access to something is categorized as *kāi* (5.6d–5.6e) and the opening of flexible objects and the damage of clothes are also denoted as *kāi* (5.6f–5.6g). Further speaking, in the specialization process of *pò,* the conceptual range of events of separation state change is reorganized. *Qiē* and *kāi* incorporate those events of separation state change that are driven out of the referential range of *pò.*

(5.5)

a. LMCqie12: 哙既饮酒，拔剑**切**肉食之。

        Kuài jì yǐn jiǔ bá jiàn qiē ròu shí zhī.

        Kuài already drink wine draw sword cut pork eat it

        "Kuài, after drinking the wine, cut the pork to eat with his sword."

b. LMCqie38: 出兔肝，**切**以生鹿舌拌食之。

chū tù　gān, qiē yǐ shēng　lù shé　bàn shí zhī

out rabbit liver, cut with raw venison tongue mix eat it

"Took the rabbit liver out, cut it and mixed it with raw venison tongue to eat."

c. LMCqie20: 百姓共提击之，或**切**食其舌。

Bǎixìng gòng　tí jī　zhī, huò qiē shí qí　shé.

Public　together lift attack his head, or　cut eat his tongue

"The public attacked his head together, even cutting and eating his tongue."

(5.6)

a. LMCkai32: 尔后开门延**敌**。

Ěrhòu kāi mén yán　dí.

then open door fight enemy

"They then opened the door and fought against their enemy."

b. LMCkai113: 已来人户多于陵封内**开**掘烧砖窑灶。

Yǐ　lái rénhù duō yú líng-fēng　nèi kāijué shāo zhuān yáo zào.

already come people usually LOC memorial park inside open bake brick cave stove

"Many of those people who have already moved here usually built brick kins in the memorial park."

c. LMCkai332: 咸亨三年于岐州陈仓县东南**开**渠引渭水入原渠。

Xiánhēng sān nián yú　Qízhōu Chén Cāng xiàn dōngnán kāi qú　yǐn Wèi Shuǐ rù Yuán　Qú.

Xianheng third year LOC Qi state Chen Cang county southeast open canal lead Wei Water into Yuan Canal

"In the third year of Xianheng, he ordered people to open a canal in the southeastern part of Chen Cang county of Qi state and led Wei Water into the Yuan Canal."

d. LMCkai727: 刀划其腹**开**，以一卷之书，置于心腑。

Dāo huá qí fù kāi, yǐ yī juàn zhī shū, zhì yú xīnfǔ.

knife strike his belly open, with a-volume of book, put into heart

"His belly was cut open and a book volume was put on his heart."

e. LMCkai1647: 两个主管一齐用刑，都打得皮开肉绽，鲜血迸流。

Liǎng gè zhǔguǎn yīqí yòng xíng, dōu dǎ-dē pí kāi ròu zhàn, xiānxuè bèng-liú.

two CL chief-director together exert torture, both hit skin open flesh torn, blood run

"The two chief directors were put to torture together. They were both skin wounded, flesh torn and blood running."

f. LMCkai1618: 宇文绶接得书，展开看，读了词。

Yǔwén Shòu jiē dé shū, zhǎn kāi kàn, dú le cí.

Yuwen Shou accept the letter, unfold open see, read-LE the poem

"Yu Wenshou accepted the letter, unfolded it and read the poem."

g. LMCkai1615: 赶得汗流气喘，衣服拽开。

Gǎndē hàn liú qì chuǎn, yīfú zhuàikāi.

catch sweat run breath pant, clothes pull-open

"He tried to catch up but ended up sweating and breathing heavily with his clothes pulled open."

Thirdly, from a further examination of these three keywords in terms of their individual usages and variable levels, it can be found that the conceptual relationship between *pò*, *qiē*, and *kāi* has changed. As noted above, Figure 5.1 shows that *pò* and *kāi* are semantically more similar in EMC. The first dimension differentiates *qiē* from *pò* and *kāi*. *Pò* and *kāi* depict events of separation state change carried out with onset force and whose state change unfolds in a nonincremental manner. As exemplified in (5.7a–5.7d), the head and seeds are broken immediately when force is exerted (5.7a–5.7b) and the gate and mouth are open immediately once the force is applied (5.7c–5.7d). In contrast, *qiē* is responsible for characterizing events of separation state change that are initiated with extended force with their state change taking place incrementally. For instance, the slicing of a green onion and meat requires a sustained imposition of force and the slicing itself takes place incrementally (5.7e–5.7f).

(5.7)

a. EMCpoe129: 推一大石下，**破**其头。

        Tuī yī dà shí xià, pò qí tóu.

        push one big stone down, break his head

        "By pushing down a big stone, the person hurt his head."

b. EMCpoe1: 颜色虽白，啮**破**枯燥无膏润者，秕子也。

        Yánsè suī bái, nièpò kūzào wú gāorùn zhě, bǐzǐ yě.

        color although white, bite-break dry no wet DE, chaff

        "Although it is white, if it is dry when bit open, then it is chaff."

c. EMCkai34: 景阳乃**开**西和门。

        Jǐng Yáng nǎi kāi Xīhé mén.

        Jing Yang then open Xihe Gate

        "Jing Yang then opened Xihe Gate."

d. EMCkai21: 含气而生，**开**口而食。

        Hán qì ér sheng, kāi kǒu ér shí.

        contain air then born, open mouth to eat

        "They contain air when born and open mouth to eat."

e. EMCqie17: 细**切**葱白。

        xì qiē cōng bái.

        slice cut onion stalk

        "Cut the onion stalk into slices."

f. EMCqie65: 羊肉十斤，獐肉十斤，缕**切**之。

        Yángròu shí jīn, zhāngròu shí jīn, lǚ qiē zhī.

mutton ten kilos, roebuck ten kilos, fine cut it

"Fine cut ten kilos of mutton and ten kilos of roebuck."

But in LMC, *pò* is semantically more similar to *qiē* than to *kāi*. These three verbs form a conceptual continuum in their categorization of events of separation state change. To be specific, the first dimension sets *pò* and *qiē* apart from *kāi*. This to some extent partially affirms Rappaport Hovav and Levin's proposal (2001, 2005) that *cut* is a subtype of *break* as well as Majid et al's (2007a) finding that opening events are usually first distinguished from cutting and breaking. To be specific, the conceptual space of *kāi* falls on the negative end of the first dimension and denotes reversible separation while *pò* and *qiē* are located on the positive end and describe irreversible separation (Clark et al. 1995; Croft 2015). For instance, the opening of a gate and a mouth is reversible, because both a gate and a mouth could be closed again (5.8a–5.8b). But this is not the case for *pò* and *qiē*. Once human body parts or plants are parted, they cannot return to their integrated state anymore (5.8c–5.8d, 5.8e–5.8f). More exactly speaking, along the first dimension, we can find that *kāi* locates on the very left, *qiē* on the middle, and *pò* on the very right. *Kāi* describes reversible, nonincremetal, and predictable separation, *qiē* expresses irreversible, incremental (also nonincremental), and predictable separation while *pò* designates irreversible, nonincremental, and unpredictable separation. In view of this, it can be concluded that these three keywords constitute a conceptual continuum in their characterization of events of separation state change in LMC.

(5.8)

a. LMCkai32: 尔后开门延敌。

        Ěrhòu kāi mén yán dí.

        then open door fight enemy

        "They then opened the door and fought against their enemy."

b. LMCkai60: 等闲开口笑何人。

        děngxián kāi kǒu xiào hé rén

ordinary   open mouth laugh what people

"As ordinary people, what kind of people are you laughing at?"

c. LMCpoe80: 得奔走倒地，头**破**额裂。

děi bēn zǒu dǎo dì,   tóu pò   é   liè

need run walk fall ground, head break forehead crack

"They may run everywhere, fall over and break their forehead."

d. LMCpoe133: 桑枝打**破**其脑

sāngzhī   dǎpò   qí nǎo

mulberry-twig hit-break his head

"The mulberry twig hurt his head."

e. LMCqie28: 长女入厨**切**肉

zhǎngnǚ   rù   chú qiē ròu

elder daughter into kitchen cut meat

"The elder daughter went to the kitchen and cut the meat."

f. LMCqie44: 木杓头边镰**切**菜

mù   sháo tóu biān lián qiē cài

wooden spoon head part sickle cut vegetable

"Use sickle to cut the vegetables in the head part of a wooden spoon."

5.1.3 Interim summary

Generally speaking, lexical items constitute a subtype of linguistic structure that "represents a way of conceptualizing experience in the process of encoding it and expressing it in language" (Croft 1999: 77). The referential change of lexical items indicates that the experience they tend to verbalize also has undergone a diachronic change. This part shows that *pò* gets specialized and *qiē* and *kāi* become expanded in their referential ranges because those experience of separation they used to categorize in EMC are more likely to be reorganized and re-segmented by the period of LMC. Their labor division in categorizing events of separation state change are reorganized in LMC. Such a dynamic division of labor among these verbs is explicitly embodied in their conceptual boundary variation: the conceptual boundary between *pò, qiē*, and *kāi* changes from *qiē* and *kāi's* partial overlapping with *pò* to a side-by-side alignment along the first dimension. But it should be noted that despite the formation of conceptual continuum in LMC, *pò, qiē*, and *kāi* are still greatly overlapped in their referential ranges in these two ancient Chinese stages.

5.2 Conceptual boundary between *pò, qiē* and *kāi* in Mandarin Chinese

"In view of the changing environment and shifting concerns of language users, conceptual categories, and what count as members of these categories are liable to undergo modification over time" (Taylor 2002). Grounded in the bourgeoning social-cultural development since 1250s, the categorical members incorporated within *pò, qiē*, and *kāi* undergo further variation and therefore the conceptual boundary of these three keywords fluctuate accordingly. These three keywords become more specialized in their categorization of events of separation state change. Their conceptual boundary become increasingly discrete and the variable levels they are closely associated with are aggregated into independent groups. In the following sections, section 5.2.1 visualizes how these three verbs segment events of separation state change in Mandarin with MCA plots. Section 5.2.2 explains their conceptual boundary variation with specific examples. Section 5.2.3 summarizes the interim findings.

5.2.1 Research findings

Figures 5.3 and 5.4 are MCA plots that demonstrate conceptual ranges of *pò, qiē*, and *kāi* in EMand and MdMand respectively. The legend and plots are organized in the same way as in Figures 5.3 and 5.4, thus they are not introduced here. The first two dimensions respectively account for 81.6% and 80.6% of the total variance and thus are reliable for representing the conceptual variation of these three keywords. In the same way, 95% confidence ellipses are drawn to indicate their referential boundaries.

Research finding 1:

The conceptual boundaries between *pò*, *qiē*, and *kāi* become much more definite in Mandarin than in ancient Chinese. As shown in Figures 5.3 and 5.4, different from EMC and LMC, the overlapping areas gradually dwindle away in EMand and MdMand. In EMand, these three keywords overlap around a limited number of conceptual variables, like *flexible, nonincremental, partial*, and *onset*. In MdMand, their overlapping areas become even narrower. As shown in Figure 5.4, in MdMand, those multiple conceptual variables gather into three independent discrete groups. The conceptual centroid of each verb is closely attached to different groups of variable levels. To illustrate, *pò* locates more approximate to variable levels like *irreversible, messy, unpredictable, fragile*, and *affected*. Unlike *pò*, *qiē* is closely associated with variable levels such as *incremental, extended, tender*, and *new*. In contrast, the prototypical core of *kāi* is surrounded by a wider range of variable levels including *flexible, predictable, partial, nonincremental, predictable, reversible, surface, onset, noimped, clean*, and *fleshy*.

Research finding 2:

A closer scrutinization of the difference between EMand and MdMand finds that those shared variable levels are readjusted and are more attached to one of the three lexical categories. To be specific, *surface* is a shared variable level between *pò* and *kāi* in EMand, but as the surface opening of stiff objects to get access to their inside is more prototypically described as *kāi*, *surface* is finally enclosed within the referential range of *kāi* in MdMand. *Fleshy* is another variable level conjoining *pò* and *kāi*, because they both can be used to describe the separation of body parts, like the disintegration of a mouth, eyes, or a finger. By MdMand, it is further sucked into the conceptual range of *kāi* because *kāi*

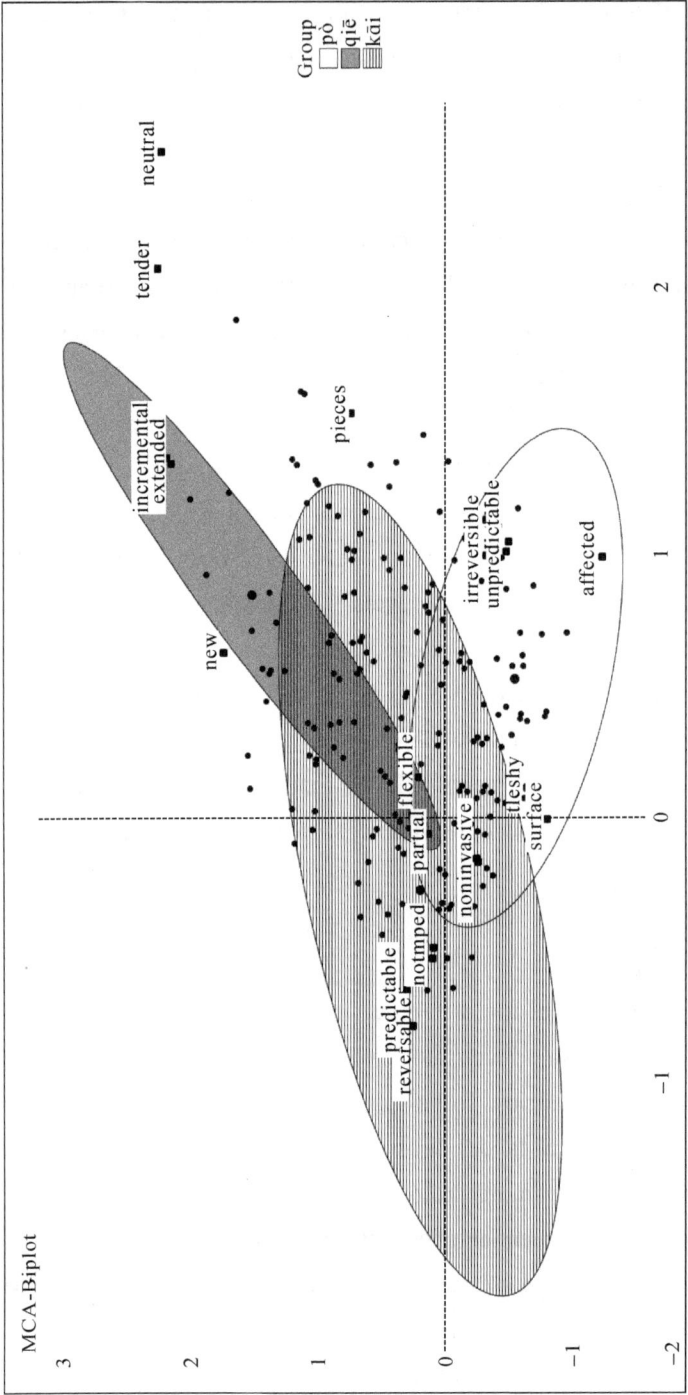

Figure 5.3 The MCA plot of *pò*, *qiē*, and *kāi* in EMand

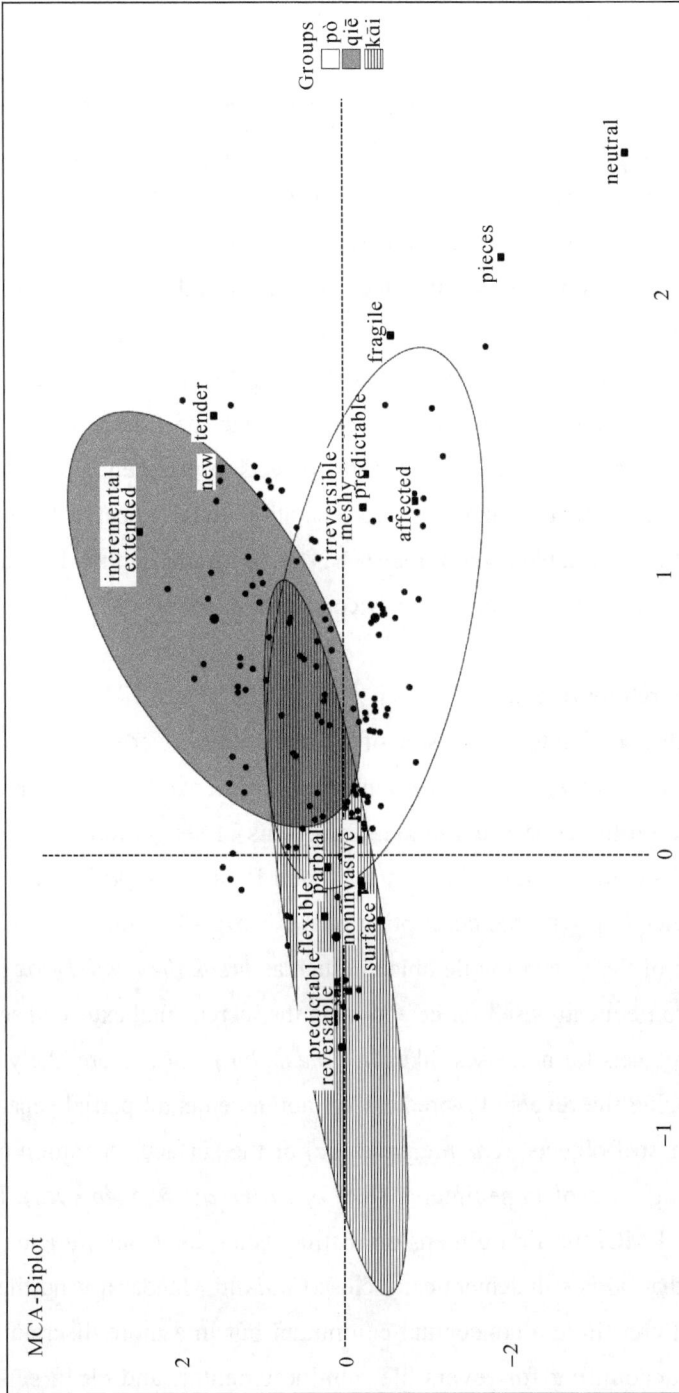

Figure 5.4 The MCA plot of *pò*, *qiē*, and *kāi* in MdMand

is prevalently used to denote the reversible separation of human body parts like opening eyes, opening a mouth, and opening hands. More importantly, such idiomatic expressions constitute a large proportion of the widespread usages of *kāi*. But it should be noted that *fleshy* is still an important conceptual variable within the referential range of *pò,* because *pò* is frequently used to denote the disruptive separation of body parts. As shown in Figure 5.5, when those idiomatic expressions of *kāi* are taken out, *fleshy* falls within the referential range of *pò.*

As for *pò* and *qiē*, their shared variable level is *pieces* in EMand, because they are both prototypically used to characterize the fragmentary slicing of tender objects and the shattering of fragile objects respectively. But in MdMand, there is a decreasing tendency of sliced separation in the conceptual range of *qiē*. As a result, the variable level of *pieces* has moved from the first quadrant to the fourth quadrant, which is more closely connected to *pò.*

Research finding 3:

Thirdly, coming to the division of labor, these three verbs are prototypically responsible for categorizing different events of separation state change and thus carve up the conceptual domain of events of separation state change in a neater fashion. As shown in Figure 5.3 and Figure 5.4, *pò* is comparatively more bounded up with the description of the irreversible, unpredictable messy separation of fleshy and fragile objects (such as *break the head, break the cup*); *qiē* is more frequently used for categorizing the incremental extended separation of tender objects for new uses (like *slice the melon*); *kāi* is more likely used for characterizing the reversible, predictable, nonincremental partial separation of flexible or stiff objects (*tear the envelope*) or the surface separation of fleshy objects to get rid of impediments (like *open the door*, *open eyes*). Besides, similar to LMC, the first dimension distinguishes *kāi* from *qiē* and *pò*. This suggests that *pò* is still semantically close to *qiē* in Mandarin. And these three verbs still constitute a conceptual continuum but in a more discrete fashion, with *kāi* accounting for reversible, nonincremental, and clean separation;

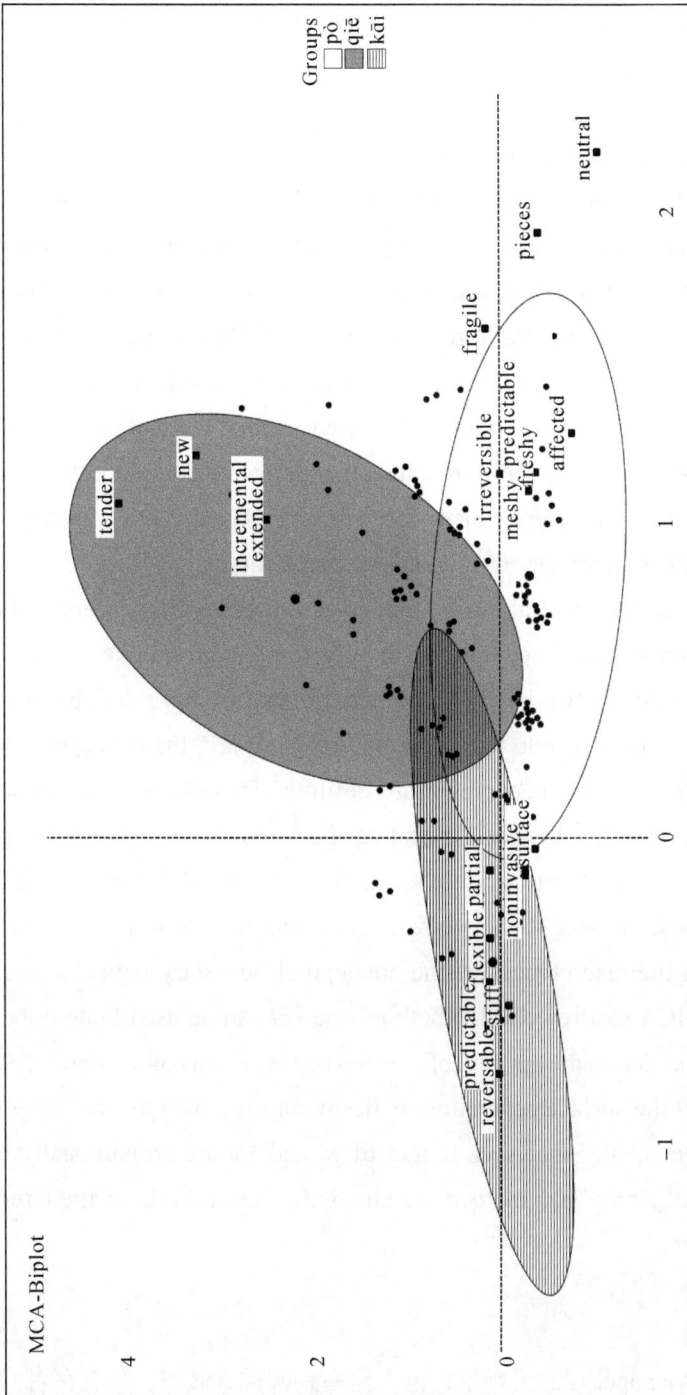

Figure 5.5 The MCA plot of *pò*, *qiē* and *kāi* in MdMand (without idiomatic expressions of *kāi*)

qiē for irreversible, incremental, clean separation and *pò* for irreversible, nonincremental, and messy separation.

5.2.2 Conceptual boundary variation

From ancient Chinese to Mandarin Chinese, the conceptual boundaries between *pò*, *qiē*, and *kāi* has finally evolved from conceptual overlapping to relative conceptual discreteness. Across the four targeted stages, conceptual discreteness begin to take form at the stage of EMand and by MdMand these three verbs are each responsible for categorizing different types of events of separation state change. Although those conceptual fluctuations that take place across EMand and MdMand are minor, it is through these minor fluctuations that the conceptual boundaries of these three verb classes have gradually changed from boundary overlapping to boundary discreteness.

First of all, speaking of *pò* and *kāi*, in EMand, the conceptual boundary between *pò* and *kāi* is contiguous around variable levels like *nonincremental*, *onset*, and *fleshy*. But by the stage of MdMand, as these variable levels have further incorporated into the referential range of *kāi*, the conceptual boundary between *pò* and *kāi* becomes more definite. This change indicates that the conceptual distance between lexical categories is associated with the grouping and ordering of certain variable levels (Langacker 1987: 150). To be specific, among these variable levels, *surface* and *fleshy* are two pronounced levels that constrain the discreteness of the conceptual boundary between *pò* and *kāi*. EMand MCA plot reveals that both *pò* and *kāi* can be used to describe surface separation, such as the opening of wooden objects like a coffin or box (5.9a–5.9d), as well as the surface separation of fleshy objects, such as the injury of body parts (5.9e–5.9h). Since such usages of *pò* and *kāi* are proportionally balanced in EMand, *fleshy* and *surface* are situated in the middle of their referential boundaries.

(5.9)

a. EMandpoe182: 天顺中，池人至南京柳林，**破棺**，犹有存者。

Tiānshùn zhōng, Chí rén zhì Nán Jīng liǔ   lín,   pò

guān,   yóu yǒu cún zhě.

Tianshun middle, Chi people to Nan Jing willow forest,

open coffin, still have survived person.

"In the middle of Tianshun period, people from Chi arrived

at Nan Jing willow forest. They opened the coffin and found

that there were some survivors inside."

b. EMandpoe1358: 以刀**破**箱，出衣物于庭中。

Yǐ dāo pò xiāng, chū yī wù yú tíng zhōng

with knife break box, out clothes in yard inside

"They opened the box with knife and took the clothes out

into the yard."

c. EMandkai10: 太尉便**开**了文匣。

Tài wèi biàn kāi le wén   xiá.

Taiwei then open LE document box

"Then Taiwei opened the document box."

d. EMandkai115: 便把箱儿打**开**，内中有十来包珠子。

Biàn bǎ xiāngér dǎkāi,   nèizhōng yǒu shí lái bāo zhūzī.

then BA box hit-open, inside   have ten some CL beads

"Then she opened the box and found there were around ten

packs of beads inside."

e. EMandpoe38: 那一日吃了一跌，额头上跌**破**了。

Nà yī rì chī le yī diē, étóu   shàng diēpò le.

that one day eat LE a fall, forehead LOC fall-hurt LE

"He fell down that day and hurt his forehead."

f. EMandpoe185: 芳脱下龙凤汗衫，咬**破**指尖，写了血诏。

Fāng tuō xià lóng fèng hànshān, yǎopò zhǐjiān,   xiě

le xuè zhào.

Fang take off dragon-phenix shirt,   bite-hurt finger-point,

write LE blood edict

"Fang took off his dragon-phenix shirt, bit his finger and

wrote a blood edict."

g. EMandkai141: 重责三十板子，打得皮开血喷。

    Zhòng zé sānshí bǎnzī, dǎ dē pí kāi xuè pēn.

    severe punish thirty boards, hit DE skin open blood running

    "He was punished with thirty severe boards, and his skin was open and his blood was running."

h. EMandkai1355: 常常打得皮开肉绽，头破血淋。

    Cháng cháng dǎ dē pí kāi ròu zhàn, tóu pò xuè lín.

    often hit skin open fleshy blossom, head hurt blood running

    "He was often hit with his skin opened, flesh blossomed, head hurt and blood running."

But differently, in MdMand, these two variable levels are finally encircled within the referential range of *kāi*. Specifically, the variable level *surface* is more closely attached to *kāi* because *kāi* is prototypically used to categorize irreversible surface separation of stiff objects in MdMand, like opening the box and opening the door. The variable level *fleshy* is enclosed within the referential range of *kāi* primarily, due to the proliferation of *kāi*'s being used to denote the reversible symmetrical separation of body parts like mouth, eyes, legs, and lips (5.10a–5.10d). Such compound expressions like *open mouth*, *open eyes*, *open arms*, and *open legs* are becoming idiomatic in MdMand. But it should be noted that if we go beyond these idiomatic expressions, the variable *fleshy* is actually within the prototypical range of *pò* (see Figure 5.5). In this sense, this finding is consistent with our previous conclusion that *pò* is more specialized in denoting the injury of fleshy body parts.

(5.10)

a. MdMandkai42: 韦女慢慢苏醒过来，天破晓时，已能开口说话。

    Wéi nǚ   màn màn sūxǐng guò lái, tiān pò xiǎo shí, yǐ   néng kāi kǒu shuōhuà

    Wei daughter slowly slowly wake-up DEIXIS, day break

light time, already can open mouth speak

"Wei's daughter slowly woke up. When it was dawn, she could already talk."

b. MdMandkai102: 道士让她睁开眼睛，看到自己已经到了一座很高的山峰上。

Dào shì ràng tā zhēngkāi yǎnjing, kàndào zìjǐ yǐjing dào le yī zuò hěn gāo de shānfēng shàng.

Taoist priest ask her open eyes, see herself already at LE one CL very high mountain LOC

"The Taoist priest asked her to open her eyes. She saw herself was already on a very high mountain."

c. MdMandkai568: 张开樱唇，衔起那枝玉簪。

Zhāng kāi yīng chún, xián qǐ nà zhī yù zān.

spread open cherry lips, pick up that CL jade clasp

"She opened her cherry lips and picked up that jade clasp with her mouth."

d. MdMandkai636: 北风大作，金兵在下风不能开目，大败而退。

Běi fēng dà zuò, Jīn bīng zài xià fēng bú-néng kāi mù, dà bài ér tuì.

North wind strongly blew, Jin soldiers at downwind cannot open eyes, utterly defeat and retreat

"The north wind was blowing strongly, soldiers of Jin who were downwind could not open their eyes and they were defeated utterly and retreated."

As for the conceptual relation between *pò* and *qiē*, it can be found that these two lexical categories are more closely related to each other in MdMand than they are in EMand. On the one hand, although the first dimension differentiates *kāi* from *pò* and *qiē* in both stages, EMand plot shows that these two lexical categories are to some extent intermediated by *kāi* in their conceptual distribution. On the other hand, MdMand plot reveals that the referential ranges of *pò* and *qiē* move a bit closer driven by their shared variable level *irreversible*. This indicates that *reversibility* assumes a higher structural weight in differentiating *pò* and *qiē* from *kāi*, consistent with previous findings on English *break*, *cut* and *open* (Croft 2012: 60, 2015). Specifically speaking, *pò* and *qiē* both categorize events of separation state change that cannot be reversed to their original status. Be this as it may, *pò* is also frequently used to describe reversible separation in EMand, like the opening of mouth to curse, the division of a ripple by fishhook as well as the disintegration of the cloud (5.11a–5.11c). Such events of separation state change, though categorized in terms of *pò,* are reversible in nature. As a result, although *pò* and *qiē* both prototypically describe irreversible separation, they are a bit parted from each other in conceptual spatial distribution. In MdMand, as those reversible usages of *pò* gradually fade away, *pò* and *qiē* are allocated closer to each other on the positive end of the first dimension.

(5.11)

a. EMandpoe593: 黄三太**破**口大骂道："刘士英你助纣为虐！"

    Huáng sān tài pò kǒu dà mà dào: "Liú Shìyīng nǐ zhù zhòu wéi nuè.

    Huang third wife open mouth great curse say: "Liu Shiying you help devil do vicious"

    "Mrs Huang yelled out an oath: Liu Shiying you dare help the devil do vicious things!"

b. EMandpoe42: 慢慢的将钩儿垂下水里去时，银丝钩**破**波纹。

    Mànmàn de jiāng gōuér chuí xià shuǐ lǐ qù shí, yín sī gōu pò bōwén

    slowly JIANG fishhook hang down water inside DEIXIS time, silver wire hook break ripple

    "When I handed down the fishhook into the water, the silver wire hook broke the ripple."

c. EMandpoe280: 云**破**月窥花好处。

Yún pò   yuè kuī huā hǎo chù.

cloud break moon peek flower good things

"When the cloud broke, the moon peeked at those nice flowers."

Besides, the variable level *pieces* is approximate to *qiē* in EMand but gradually moves to the vicinity of *pò* in MdMand. This is because a large amount of EMand data reveals that *qiē* is more frequently used to describe the slicing of objects into pieces than *pò* is. For instance, *qiē* is more often than not used to describe the shredding of vegetables such as bamboo shoots or meat and fish (5.12a–5.12b). But by the stage of MdMand, *pò* has surpassed *qiē* in its relative frequency in characterizing the smashing into pieces of objects like bones or porcelains (5.12c–5.12d).

(5.12)

a. EMandqie91: 青笋尖儿上头的尖儿。可要**切**成嫩条儿。

Qīng sǔn jiānér shàng tóu de jiān-ér. Kěyào qiē chéng nèn tiáo-ér.

endive sprout top   LOC   top, must cut into fresh slices

"This is the top of endive sprout. You must cut it into slices."

b. EMandqie227: 却又见左右将钓起的三尾鱼，**切**成细脍。

Què yòu jiàn zuǒ yòu jiāng diào qǐ de sān wěi yú, qiē chéng xì kuài.

but again see left right JIANG fish up three CL fish, cut into slice pieces

"But then he saw his attendants have cut the three fish into slice pieces."

c. MdMandpoe176: 一弹飞来，正中脑部，盖骨**破**碎。

Yī dàn fēi lái, zhèng zhòng nǎo bù, gàigǔ pòsuì.

a bullet fly DEIXIS, right middle brain part, skull break-smash

"A bullet shot right into his brain and his skull was smashed."

d. MdMandpoe237: 取出各种宝器，令相投击，……悉数**破碎**。

Qǔ chū gè zhǒng bǎo qì, lìng xiāng tóu jī, ... xīshù pò suì.

take out all kinds precious treasures, ask each throw attack, ... all break-smash

"He took out all kinds of precious treasures, and ordered them to throw them toward each other and smash them all."

In contrast to the observable variations between *pò* and *qiē* as well as between *pò* and *kāi*, the variations between *qiē* and *kāi* is relatively minor. The conceptual distance between their referential ranges is stable across EMand and MdMand. But their diachronic variation across LMC and EMand is rather significant. In LMC, even the conceptual centroid of *qiē* is enclosed within the referential range of *kāi*. This is because these two lexical categories overlap greatly in terms of conceptual variables like *partial, nonincremental, onset,* and *fleshy*. Both of them are predominantly used to describe the nonincremental, onset partial separation of fleshy objects, thus their prototypical cores are equally close to these conceptual variables. For instance, *qiē* describes the cutting of meat into parts and *kāi* depicts the opening of hand or mouth into parts (5.13a–5.13d). Differently, in Mandarin, as *qiē* is more frequently used to characterize the incremental and extended separation of tender objects for further use, the referential range of *qiē* gradually disassociate from that of *kāi*.

(5.13)

a. LMCqie18: 加彘盾上，拔剑**切**而啗之。

Jiā zhì dùn shàng, bá jiàn qiē ér dàn zhī.

put pork hock shield top, draw sword cut and chew it

"Put the pork hock on top of the shield, then cut it with his sword and chewed it."

b. LMCkai1145: 如饮食中鸡心猪心之属，**切**开可见。

Rú yǐn shí zhōng jī   xīn zhū xīn   zhī shǔ, qiē kāi kě jiàn.

like food LOC chicken heart pig heart and so on, cut open then see

"Things like chicken heart and pig heart, when you cut them open, you can find they are empty inside."

c. LMCkai39: 师展开两手而示。

Shī   zhǎnkāi liǎng shǒu ér shì.

master spread-open two hands and show

"The master spreads open his hand to show it."

d. LMCkai60: 等闲开口笑何人。

Děngxián kāi kǒu xiào hé rén.

ordinary open mouth laugh any people

"As ordinary people, what kind of people are you laughing at?"

5.2.3 Interim summary

Generally speaking, the conceptual boundaries between *pò*, *qiē* and *kāi* finally come into a discrete and stabilized stage in Mandarin Chinese. By this stage, the division of labor among these three verb classes in segmenting and categorizing events of separation state change has become more discrete. Each of them has formed their own prototypical structure with their prototypical usages at the core. More importantly, the individual usages and variable levels that fall within their prototypical core demonstrate maximum discriminability (Rosch 1973). That is, prototypical members of these three verbs are those that are maximally different from their near-synonymous lexical categories on the same level of linguistic contrast. Meanwhile, the stability of these three verbs in categorizing events of separation state change does not indicate rigidity. The flexible categorization of their shared conceptual members suggests that these three verbs are flexibly evolving in their characterization of events of separation state change.

5.3 Conceptual boundary variation between ancient Chinese and Mandarin Chinese

Concepts can be ordered and grouped in various ways and be determined to lie at a different distance from one another (Langacker 1987: 150). On account of the conceptual modulations that occurred in ancient Chinese and Mandarin Chinese, it goes without saying that the conceptual domain of events of separation state change is restructured and the distance between its referential members are reordered in the Chinese language. Since 5.1 and 5.2 have covered those detailed conceptual adjustments, this part zooms out to the big picture of conceptual boundary variation. 5.3.1 talks about the conceptual boundary variation between the three keywords. 5.3.2 explores the cognitive mechanisms that motivate the conceptual boundary variation. 5.3.3 is an interim summary.

5.3.1 Conceptual boundary variation

From ancient Chinese to Mandarin Chinese, conceptual boundaries between the three verb classes has changed from an overlapping pattern to a discrete pattern. Conceptual overlapping suggests that the same experience can be verbalized in terms of varied lexical categories, showing synchronic variation. Such a synchronic variation is the source of diachronic change (Geeraerts 1997: 6; Croft 2010). Conceptual discreteness, on the contrary, demonstrates that lexical categories are prototypically structured for the categorization of particular event types and that such prototypically structured categories are maximally different from other lexical categories at the same level (Rosch 1973).

Firstly, speaking of conceptual overlapping, it is stated that overlapping areas constitute the most sensitive areas where synchronic variation resides and prove to be the areas that are most likely to undergo conceptual reorganization and diachronic change (Kronenfeld and Rundblad 2003; Geeraerts 1997:127; Croft 2010). From a closer examination of the referential ranges of these three verb classes, it is easy to find that diachronic variations take place primarily at the overlapping areas. Across the four historical stages, three pronounced overlapping areas are worth mentioning, namely the overlapping areas between *pò* and *qiē,* between *pò* and *kāi*, and between *qiē* and *kāi.* The diachronic development of these three verb classes in categorizing events of separation state change is inherently the conceptual reorganization of these three overlapping areas.

Specifically speaking, in the first overlapping area, both *pò* and *qiē* are alternatively used for the characterization of the cutting of meat, fruit, or vegetables into slices. As exemplified in (5.14a–5.14d), *pò* behaves exactly in the same way as *qiē* and is also used to refer to the slicing of meat and skull in a precise and clean manner. Similarly, in the second overlapping area, *pò* and *kāi* are exchangeable in describing events of separating impediments. Taking the opening up of a coffin as an example, the breaking up of a coffin to show its inside is encoded either as *pò* or *kāi* in EMC (5.15a and 5.15c). Likewise, the excavation of a tomb is also simultaneously described in terms of both *pò* and *kāi* in ancient Chinese (5.15b and 5.15d). But it should be noted that although *pò* is used similarly to *kāi, pò* does not necessarily indicate clean separation. When a coffin or tomb is "*pò*", the coffin or tomb is more likely opened in a forceful way and ends up being destroyed. In this sense, *pò* is conceptually similar to *kāi* but in a marked fashion. Another evidence for this proposal is the opening of one's mouth. As exemplified in (5.15e) and (5.15f), opening one's mouth to curse is described in terms of *pò* while opening one's mouth to talk is denoted by means of *kāi*. The third overlapping area shows that both *qiē* and *kāi* can be used to describe the onset partial separation of fleshy objects. As Example (5.16) demonstrates, either *qiē* or *kāi* can be used to describe the separation of animal flesh or human mouth (5.16a–5.16b). More importantly, *qiē* and *kāi* can be compounded together to denote the process of cutting one's clothes into parts

(5.16c).

    (5.14)

a.LMCqie7: 山药也，炊熟，片**切**，渍以生蜜。

        Shānyáo yě, chuī shú, piàn qiē, zì yǐ shēng mì.

        Chinese yam, cooked, slice cut, soak with raw honey.

        "The Chinese yam can first be cooked, then cut into slices, and finally soaked with raw honey."

b.EMandqie2: 带肋条的就好。大片**切**著。

        Dài lèi-tiáo dē jiù hǎo. Dà piàn qiē zhuó.

        With rib   DE is good. Large slice cut.

        "Pork with rib is good. Cut it into large slices."

c. EMCpoe93: 用牛、羊、獐、鹿肉之精者……**破**作片。

        Yòng niú, yáng, zhāng,   lùròu zhī jīngzhě…pò zuò piàn.

        With cow, sheep, roebuck, venison   ZHI   best… break into pieces

        "Cut the best beef, mutton, roebuck and venison into pieces."

d. LMCpoe440: 及明，果坠在床下，遂**破**为六片，零置瓦沟中。

        Jí míng,   guǒ zhuì zài chuáng xià, suì pò wéi liù piàn, líng   zhì wǎgōu zhōng.

        By tomorrow, expect fell LOC bed under, then break into six parts, casually throw ditch in.

        "The next day, as expected, the skull had fallen under the bed, so he broke it into six parts and threw it away into the ditch."

    (5.15)

a. MdMandpoe746: **破**其棺，棺中有人。

        Pò qí guān, guān zhōng yǒu rén

open that coffin, coffin inside have person

"He opened the coffin and found a person inside."

b. LMCpoe135: 决潴沱河水绕城，**破**一古墓。

Jué hùtuó hé shuǐ rào chéng, pò yī gǔ mù.

Burst Hutuo river water surround city, open an ancient tomb.

"Water from Hutuo River was made to surround the city and broke through an ancient tomb."

c. LMCkai618: 敦不信，开棺无尸。

Dūn bú xìn,   kāi guān wú shī.

Dun NEG believe, open coffin no corpse.

"Refusing to believe it, Dun opened the coffin and found no corpse."

d. LMCkai679: 众人即开墓，视遍身之骨。

Zhòng rén jí kāi mù,   shì   biàn shēn zhī gǔ.

All people then open tomb, check all over ZHI bones.

"The crowd opened the tomb and checked bones all over the body."

e. EMandpoe480: 沙龙**破**口大骂，所有十一家猎户俱是他一人承当。

Shālóng pò kǒu dà   mà, suǒyǒu shíyī jiā lièhù jù shì tā yī rén chéngdān.

Shalong open mouth angrily curse, all   eleven CL hunter all are he one person responsible.

"Shalong angrily cursed that he was responsible for all those eleven hunters."

f. LMCkai1079: 今世文人才士，开口便说国家利害。

Jīn   shì wénréncáishì,   kāi kǒu biàn shuō guójiā lì hài.

Today world knowledgeable people, open mouth then talk country gains losses.

"Those knowledgeable people in the world today always talk about the gains and losses of government policies."

(5.16)

a. LMCqie12: 唅既饮酒拔剑**切**肉食之。

Kuài jì yǐn jiǔ bá jiàn qiē ròu shí zhī.

Kuai then drink wine draw sword cut pork eat it

"Kuai then drank wine and cut the pork to eat with his sword."

b. LMCkai921: 拗**开**其口，灌之即活。

Niùkāi qí kǒu, guàn zhī jí huó.

Bend-open his mouth, fill it then alive

"If bent open his mouth and let him drink the medicine, and he came to life."

c. MdMandqie22: 衣服已被**切开**一个尺长的大口子。

Yīfú yǐ bèi qiēkāi yī gè chǐ cháng de dà kǒuzī.

clothes already BEI cut-open one-CL-chi long DE big opening

"The clothes has been cut apart with a one-inch-long opening."

In sum, it goes without saying that the existence of synchronic onomasiological variants apparently violates the isomorphism principle of "one form, one meaning" (Geeraerts 1997: 2). It is redundant and a waste of lexical resources to name the same specific event in terms of two different lexical categories (Evans and Green 2006: 756), and to represent the marked use of a lexical category with another lexical category (like *pò* for *kāi*). To attribute the reasons that give rise to such synchronic variations, we speculate that the innovative extention of the uses of *pò* from its etymological origin (shattering of stones) to describing cutting and opening separations constitute one important reason that leads to the coincidences with the extant usages of *qiē* and *kāi*. In this sense, innovation is the major source for variation. But since events of separation state change are events of higher-codability, synchronic variation, especially lexical variation, is transient and will finally give way to diachronic stability (Croft 2010). Further speaking, conceptual overlapping will gradually be readjusted and replaced by conceptual discreteness in the linguistic pursuit of expressive economy.

In substitution of conceptual overlapping, conceptual discreteness represents a diachronically stable stage where events of separation state change are segmented more definitely and represented by lexical categories of maximal discriminability (Rosch 1973). At this stage, the three verb classes are discrete in their division of labor and are each responsible for categorizing different events of separation state change. Meanwhile, they are internally structured, conforming both to the isomorphism principle and the prototypical principle. In this way, the Chinese language achieves its end of expressive economy in representing events of separation state change (Geeraerts 1997: 124).

For one thing, the three verb classes are used, following the isomorphism principle in Mandarin, to categorize only one particular type of events of separation state change. There is no way to find cases where *pò* is used to describe cutting and opening separation. For instance, in Mandarin, *pò* is only applicable for referring to breaking events rather than the opening of objects. As shown in the minimal pair in (5.17), when a book is *pò*, the book is torn into parts (5.17a) while when the book is *kāi*, it is open (5.17b). Likewise, the collocation of *pò* with a wooden case indicates that the case is broken down into parts (5.17c). In contrast, the co-occurrence of *kāi* with a wooden case denotes the opening up of the cover of the case (5.17d). Likewise, in describing the separation of fleshy body parts or tender objects, *pò* only lends itself to denote the disruptive disintegration of body parts (5.18a) and the coarse partition of fruit or vegetable with hands (5.18b). The fine cutting of meat is, however, more likely delineated in terms of *qiē* (5.18c and 5.18d).

(5.17)

a. EMandpoe109: 遂扯**破**其书，重责小军二十，赶出府门而去。

　　　　　Suì　chěpò　qí shū, zhòng zé xiǎo-jūn　èrshí, gǎn

　　　　　chū　fǔmén érqù.

therefore tear-break the letter, severely punish minor-soldier twenty, chase out mansion away

"Therefore, he tore the letter, punished the minor soldier severely with twenty sticks and chased him out of the mansion."

b. EMandkai3153: 等到天黑回来，他把这本书摊**开**。

Děng dào tiān hēi huí lái, tā bǎ zhè běn shū tānkāi.

wait until sky dark come back, he BA this CL book unfold-open.

"When it was getting dark, he came back and opened the book."

c. MdMandpoe278: 这箱子没有钥匙，无论如何不能开，除了将箱子打**破**。

Zhè xiāngzī méiyǒu yàoshì, wúlùn rúhé bù néng kāi, chúlē jiāng xiāngzī dǎpò.

this case without key, no matter how cannot open, except JIANG case hit-break.

"Without key, we cannot open this case with whatever methods, except by breaking it open."

d.MdMandkai14：偷偷打**开**箱子一看，箱子里装的都是金银珠宝。

Tōu-tōu dǎkāi xiāngzī yī kàn, xiāngzī lǐ zhuāng dē dōu shì jīnyínzhūbǎo.

Stealthily open box a look, box inside fill all is gold, silver and jewelry

"He opened the box stealthily to have a look, and found it was full of gold, silver and jewelry."

(5.18)

a. EMandpoe38: 那一日吃了一跌，额头上跌**破**了。

Nà yī rì chī lē yī diē, étóu shàng diēpò le.

that one day fall down, forehead LOC fall-hurt LE.

"He fell down that day and hurt his forehead."

b. MdMandpoe24: 葱切段，姜拍**破**。

　　　　　　Cōng　qiē duàn, jiāng pāi　pò.

　　　　　　green-onion cut parts, ginger pound break.

　　　　　　"Cut the green onion into parts and pound the ginger into pieces."

c. MdMandqie3: 一副心肝，由客取置杯前，用匕首**切**好薄片。

　　　　　　Yī fù xīn gān,　　yóu kè qǔ　　zhì bēi qián, yòng bǐshǒu qiè hǎo bó piàn

　　　　　　a pair of heart liver, with guest bring　to cup front,　with knife　cut into thin slices

　　　　　　"The guest brought a pair of heart and liver to the front of the cup and cut them into slices with a knife."

d. MdMandqie76: 法正拿着这块肉给**切**薄了。

　　　　　　Fǎ Zhèng ná　zhe　zhè kuài　ròu gěi　qiē　bó le.

　　　　　　Fa Zheng hold ZHE this piece meat cause cut slice LE

　　　　　　"Fa Zheng held this piece of meat up and cut it into slices."

Admittedly, constrained by the isomorphism principle, the three verb classes are each responsible for the categorization of breaking, cutting, and opening events of separation state change. But it should be noted that the isomorphism principle only applies to prototypical categories as a whole, not to any specific categorical members. Prototypical principle precedes isomorphism principle (Geeraerts 1997: 124). As the MdMand MCA plot demonstrates, *pò*, *qiē*, and *kāi* are prototypically structured, with their central members at the prototypical core and noncentral members at the referential edge. Specifically speaking, *pò* prototypically categorizes the irreversible messy separation of fleshy objects with the purpose to disrupt their function. *Qiē* prototypically represents the incremental separation of tender objects with extended force with an intention to create new use. *Kāi* prototypically characterizes the reversible nonincremental separation of stiff objects in the surface with onset force aiming to get rid of impediments. With such prototypical structures, these three lexical categories demonstrate maximum discriminability, greatly different from each other in their prototypical core (Rosch 1973).

But even so, their referential edges are still contiguous and they are still bordered with each other at their referential edges. Their contiguous distribution is especially demonstrated with their compound usages. For instance, *pò-kāi* shows that the messy functional partition of vegetables is located at the periphery of *pò* and *kāi* (5.19a). *Qiē-kāi* indicates that the no-impediment clean severance of chicken is situated at the edge of *qiē* and *kāi* (5.19b). *Qiē-pò* demonstrates that the messy cutting of animal body parts stands at the juncture between *qiē* and *pò* (5.19c). In this way, the prototypical structured lexical categories are iconic to the continuous flux of physical experience.

(5.19)

a. MdMandpoe35: 用刀顺白菜中间**破**开，取出菜心留用。

        Yòng dāo shùn báicài zhōngjiān pòkāi, qǔ chū cài xīn liú yòng.

        with knife along cabbage middle break-open, take out cabbage core later use

        "Break the cabbage open in the middle with a knife and take the stem out for later use."

b. MdMandqie25: 邢老安人将毛挦得干净，又用刀将鸡肉一块一块地**切开**。

        Xíng lǎo-ān rén jiāng máo xián dē gānjìng, yòu yòng dāo jiāng jīròu yī kuài yī one kuài dē qiēkāi.

        Xing old woman JIANG feather pick clean, also with knife JIANG chicken one piece piece cut-open

        "Mrs. Xing picked all the chicken feather and cut the chicken open into pieces."

c. EMandpoe121: 将猪心**切破**，取热血调药。

        Jiāng zhū xīn qiēpò, qǔ rè xuè tiáo yào.

        make pork heart cut-open, get hot blood make medicine.

"Cut the pork heart open and get blood out to make medicine."

Apart from that, prototypicality is an additional restriction on the operation of the isomorphic principle (Geeraerts 1997: 132). This is because the conceptual system and lexical items are incongruous in the sense that conceptual system is analog and infinite while lexical items are digital (Carey 2009: 8). To resolve this incongruity, conceptual systems are linguistically organized based on a prototypically-based structure. The prototypical core of lexical categories indicates their salient reference and the contiguity of their conceptual boundary suggests that lexical categories are inherently continuous. In this way, lexical categories though discrete are iconic to their represented conceptual systems.

Moreover, it should be noted that the syntactic form of these three lexical items also has undergone a diachronic change. *Pò* and *kāi* are more likely to appear as verb complements in the form of V+*pò* and V+*kāi* and denote the result of the action. In contrast, *qiē* is more frequently used as the action verb with its result denoted by the complements either in the form of a preposition phrase or a simple adjective. As mentioned above, such syntactic variations seem to be correlated to the conceptual variations of these three lexical items. And such a correlation is left for future research.

5.3.2 Cognitive mechanisms

Linguistic organization of concepts is acknowledged to be a fundamental task of language in cognitive linguistics (Langacker 1987; Croft and Cruse 2004). As a linguistic category, verbs are conceived to organize the continuous flux of events or experiences (Langacker 2008: 104). The linguistic organization is not diachronically stable, the development of social-culture and the change of expressive needs would give rise to linguistic reorganization (Croft and Cruse 2004: 92-93). The present study reveals that the conceptual boundary variation of *pò*, *qiē*, and *kāi* is inherently motivated by the linguistic reorganization of the conceptual domain of events of separation state change at two levels: variable coordination and prototypical structure.

To start with, conceptual domains are not organized arbitrarily, but by virtue of multiple dimensions (variables) (Langacker 1987: 150-152). For instance, the color domain is resolvable into the three variables of brightness, hue, and saturation. Likewise, conceptual domains like separation is also structured of variables like <material composition>, <functional change> and <change pattern> etc. But the difference is that the organization of natural domains like color is relatively stable while semantic domains like separation are subject to reorganization through the evolution of language. The linguistic reorganization of semantic domains is essentially the readjustment of those multiple variables that configure them. Specifically speaking, despite the fact that the conceptual domain of events of separation state change appears to be only loosely coherent, several variables figure in its conception as a network, including <material composition>, <functional change>, <endstate>, <reversibility>, <change pattern>, <initiation of force>, <separation mode> and <locus predictability>. The coordination of these multiple variables configures this conceptual domain, and those specific separation events are located at the coordinates of several crisscrossing variables (Langacker 1987: 152; Geeraerts 2007). Breaking, cutting, and opening separations are three conceptual potentials that are found to be organized and grouped within this conceptual domain. They are formed of numerous specific separation events which are coordinates of the multivariate space.

In ancient Chinese, breaking separation covers a wide range of the coordinates of the multivariate space of separation, ranging from fragile to tender and stiff objects, from function disruption to new function and removing impediment, from reversible to irreversible, from messy to clean, to name a few. Cutting and opening separations are respectively structured up of a smaller part of the multivariate space. Cutting separation encloses the coordination of variable levels like *tender* and *fleshy objects*, *new function*, *pieces*, *irreversible*, *incremental*, *extended force*, *clean* and *predictable*. Opening separation incorporates the combination of variable levels like stiff objects, remove impediment, partial, reversible, nonincremental, onset force, clean and predictable. In view of this, cutting and opening separations are partially overlapped with breaking separation. Nonetheless, as the multivariates of breaking, cutting and opening separations are reorganized in the development of language, breaking separation shrinks to fragile and fleshy objects, function disruption, pieces and surface, irreversible, nonincremental, onset force, messy and unpredictable. Cutting separation maintains its referential range to the incremental clean shredding of tender or fleshy objects with extended force. Opening separation minorly enlarges its space to include the reversible partial separation of flexible objects. Consequently, these three lexical categories get increasingly discrete in their segmentation of the conceptual domain of separation. They lie at a different conceptual distance from one another within the separation domain.

Accompanying the multivariate reorganization of the separation domain, the prototypical structure of the three lexical categories *pò*, *qiē*, and *kāi* are also reorganized. At the variable level, specific events of separation state change are coordinates of those multiple variables and are enclosed into one of these three separation types based on their variable levels. At the level of prototypical structure, those specific events of separation state change are further organized into a prototypical structure following principles like family resemblance and typicality gradience (Rosch 1975, 1978). To be specific, in Mandarin Chinese, the prototypical core of *pò* is occupied by the surface wounding of body parts, and at its referential edge are the fragmentary separation of fragile objects, the partial separation of flexible objects, as well as the fragmentary separation of stiff objects. The prototypical core of *qiē* is possessed by the incremental separation of meat, fruit and vegetables and its referential edge is surrounded by the partial separation of fruit and the surface cutting of stiff objects etc. At the prototypical core of *kāi* is the surface opening of stiff objects while at its boundary are the surface opening of meat, fruit or flexible objects. In a nutshell, these three lexical categories each form their own prototypical structure in Mandarin. But this is not the case in ancient Chinese. These three lexical categories overlap together in ancient Chinese. Although they each have their own prototypical core, the prototypical cores of *qiē* and *kāi* are enclosed within the referential range of *pò*. That is, there was one main prototypical structure in the conceptual domain of separation. And it is the breaking of fragile objects that is located at the prototypical core, whereas the cutting of tender objects and the opening of stiff objects are noncentral members at the nonprototypical area. In sum, comparing the conceptual structure of separation in Mandarin Chinese with that in ancient Chinese, it is self-explanatory that the prototypical structure is reorganized.

Apart from the above two levels of conceptual reorganization, social-cultural development and expressive needs are the embodied motivations for the reorganization of the conceptual domain of events of separation state change. Social-cultural development emphasizes the social-cultural background of language (Traugott and Dasher 2002: xi; Geeraerts 2006: vi; Bybee 2010: 204), and here refers particularly to the advancement of instruments and the refined design of objects. In ancient time, there is a lack of instruments for the separation of stiff objects (like case) and tender objects (like fruit), therefore these objects are often broken up in a coarse manner with hands. In contrast, in modern time, cases are usually designed to be locked and opened with keys, and fruit is separated with special knives. Due to such social-cultural development in the carrying out of events of separation state change, the linguistic organization of separation events is adjusted accordingly. *Pò* is employed for categorizing messy separation events while *kāi* and *qiē* are used for categorizing finer separations. Along with social-cultural development, the expressive need is another unneglectable motivation that highlights the communicative function of language (Geeraerts 1997: 105; Evans and Green 2006: 759). As long as objects are separated in different ways, there is a necessity to linguistically categorize separation events in a finer-grained fashion. When the particular way of linguistically categorizing events of separation state change is repeated enough, it turns into a conventionalized way of packaging those concepts for speaking and "thinking for speaking" (Slobin 1996; Bybee 2010: 219). For instance, *kāi* is a conventional way for characterizing the reversible clean separation of particularly designed separable objects like door, window, and teapot.

5.3.3 Interim summary

In sum, the conceptual boundaries between *pò*, *qiē*, and *kāi* have changed significantly from conceptual overlapping to conceptual discreteness. In this process, the linguistic segmentation and categorization of events of separation state change have been reorganized from both the variable level and the structural level. Variable level reorganization takes the form of value adjustment. Structural level reorganization manifests itself as the prototypical range adjustment. Reorganization and adjustment at these two levels are embodied in the development of social-culture and the change of expressive needs.

5.4 Summary

Our corpus-based multivariate study on the referential ranges of Chinese break, cut, and open verbs corroborates that these three semantically similar verbs categorize and segment events of separation state change in a diachronically dynamic fashion. Their conceptual boundaries change from being overlapped to becoming increasingly clear cut. The cognitive mechanism that operates underlying their conceptual boundary variation is conceptual reorganization. That is, it is the reorganization of those multiple conceptual variables underlying the conceptual system of events of separation state change that accounts for these conceptual changes. Further speaking, driven by social-cultural development as well as speaker expressive need, available lexical items are reorganized in their segmentation and categorization of the conceptual system of events of separation state change. We leave it to future work to investigate the conceptual division between *pò* and other near-synonymous verbs like *duàn*, *liè*, *suì*, and *làn*. Moreover, the correlation between conceptual variation and syntactic change of *pò*, *qiē*, and *kāi* also remains to be explored.

CHAPTER 6

Diachronic conceptual variation of intensional *pò*

In chapters 4 and 5, we have restricted our attention to extensional usages of break verbs, both from word to usage (semasiology) and from usage to word (onomasiology) (Geeraerts 1997: 17, 2006: 77). Those extensional usages are subsumed under the individual reading of physical disintegration. On this basis, this chapter turns to intensional readings of the break verb *pò* and aims to unravel the cross-domain correspondence between its extensional usages and intensional readings. As mentioned in Chapter 3, we intend to prove that intensional readings always take their starting-point in the extensional subsets. Therefore, we can always keep track of the extensional origins of intensional readings. To this end, this chapter first summarizes the intensional readings of *pò* across the four established chronological stages in section 6.1. Then the structural parallelism between intensional readings and extensional references is elaborated in section 6.2. Finally, the appearance and disappearance of intensional *pò* in relation to extensional *pò* are discussed in section 6.3.

6.1 Intensional readings of *pò*

In addition to the intensional reading of physical disintegration, another fifteen major intensional readings are captured from the dataset of 5,619 intensional examples. As shown in Table 6.1, the application domain of *pò* has shifted away from the physical domain of separation to more abstract domains like war, cognition, rule, consumption as well as emotional and temporal state. To set the stage for cross-domain comparison in 6.2 and 6.3, this part first elaborates these fifteen intensional readings and their close semantic relationship by taking into account their specific examples from the diachronic corpus CCL. Although this study is not aimed at explicating the metaphoric and metonymic relations involved in semantic extension and semantic change (Sweetser 1990; Heine et al. 1991; Hopper and Traugott 2003\1993), such conceptual relations are inevitably mentioned in elaborating the semantic extension of *pò*. As such, following categorical metaphor (Goossen 1990; Heine et al. 1991), the fifteen intensional readings are classified into six metaphorical categories, including relational change, cognitive change, possessive change, observance change, emotional change and temporal change. Such a wide range of application domains fully demonstrates the referential power and reading malleability of the lexical item *pò* (Robert 2008).

Table 6.1 Intensional readings of *pò*

Domain	Label	Example	Definitional gloss	Frequency
Relational	A	(1)	to win against sb/sth in a war, competition etc.	2,369
	B	(2)	to take control of a place or building using force	1,307
	C	(3)	to damage sb/sth so badly that it no longer exists	801
	D	(4)	to succeed	48
Cognitive	E	(5)	to discover sth that is not easy to see, hear etc.	297
	F	(6)	to make sb know sth that previously could not be seen	258
	G	(7)	to get rid of irritation, doubt or hatred etc.	68
	H	(8a-b)	to know what someone or something means	42
	I	(8c-d)	to tell sb about sth in a way that makes it easy to understand	33
Possessive	J	(9a-b)	to pay money for sth or particular purpose	173
	K	(9c-d)	to spend time doing sth	6

Continued

Observance	L	(10)	to go against a law or an agreement	116
Emotional	M	(11a-b)	to scare	44
	N	(11c-d)	to change from one state to a different state	37
Temporal	O	(12)	to start happening or existing	20

6.1.1 Relational change

Relational change constitutes the first salient application domain of *pò*. In this domain, the given context of war contributes to the intensional value of *pò*. *Pò* is pervasively used to designate the defeating of the adversary, the controlling of a country or city, the destroying of blockage, and the success of armies or leaders. Relational change resides in the transition from the friendly and equal relationship between two sides of a war to hostile and unequal relations. Intensional readings that fall into this domain account for more than 80% of the total intensional usages of *pò*. As shown in Table 4.1, these intensional readings include "to win against" (A), "to take control" (B), "to damage" (C), and "to succeed" (D). These four readings are closely related, with the latter reading entailing the former one(s). The last reading is enclosed within an idiom that is frequently used to describe warfare.

Specifically speaking, *pò* is most predominantly used to denote the winning against of sb/sth in a war or a competition. With regard to sb, *pò* is widely used to denote the defeat of a general or an armed force (Xu 2005). For instance, *pò* is applicable for describing Liu Bang's triumph over Xiang Yu (6.1a), Tian Shan's overcoming of the armed force of Yan (6.1b) as well as Gongsun Zan's winning against the rebels of Huangjin (6.1c). With regard to sth, the instrument metonymically represents the people who use the instrument (Evans and Green 2006: 317-318). In this case, the leader and army are metonymically represented by their martial style and military *zhènfǎ*. And usages of *pò* accommodate such metonymic representation. As in (6.1d), a broadsword and a double-baston stand for the fighters who use these armaments, and the vanquishing of the double-baston by broadsword represents broadsword's defeating of the double-baston.

Likewise, *zhènfǎ* is a military tactic preferentially employed in ancient wars, which is inherently an irregular transformation of army formation. As such, the overcoming of a *zhènfǎ* means disorganizing the formation and defeating the leader who makes use of this *zhènfǎ* (6.1e).

(6.1)

a. EMCpoi173: 西汉五年**破**项羽，即皇帝位，都长安。

    Xi Hàn wǔ nián   pò   Xiàng Yǔ, jí huáng dì wèi, dū Cháng ān.

    West Han fifth year defeat Xiang Yu, inherit emperor, capital Chang'an

    "When he defeated Xiang Yu in the fifth year of West Han, he became the emperor and set his capital in Chang'an."

b. EMCpoi95: 田单守即墨之城，**破**燕兵，复齐墟。

    Tián Shàn shǒu Jímò zhī chéng, pò Yàn bīng, fù Qí xū.

    Tian Shan guard Jimo city,   defeat Yan soldiers, restore Qi wasteland

    "Tian Shan guarded Ji Mo city, defeated Yan soldiers and restored Qi."

c. EMCpoi402: 公孙瓒击青州黄巾贼，大**破**之。

    Gōngsūn Zàn jī Qīng Zhōu Huáng Jīn zéi, dà pò zhī.

    Gongsun Zan attack Qing Zhou Huang Jin enemy, utterly attack them

    "Gongsun Zan attacked Qing Zhou Huang Jin enemy and defeated them utterly."

d. EMandpoi511: 刀棍并举，胜老者单刀**破**双棍。

    Dāo gùn bìng jǔ, shèng lǎo zhě dān dāo pò shuāng gùn.

    sword baston both raise, Sheng old man broadsword attack double baston

"With both sword and baston raised, Sheng defeated double baston with broadsword."

e. EMandpoi744: 两教圣人率诸门人共**破**万仙阵。

Liang jiào shèng rén shuài zhū mén rén gòng pò wàn xiān zhèn.

Two sect leaders lead all group people together attack Wanxian Zhen

"Leaders of the two religious sects led all their followers and defeated Wanxian Zhen."

Following "to win against", "to take control" is the second widespread usage of *pò*. This intensional reading entails the defeating of an army and at the same time indicates a further taking control of the country or city. In other words, "to take control" is the result of "to win against". Only when one has defeated his opponent, can he take control of the country or city owned by his opponent. Further speaking, these two intensional readings demonstrate a metonymic transfer from cause to result. For instance, when the four-country alliance overcame Zhao, they took over the territory of Zhao (6.2a). When the country Song was defeated, its territory was partitioned and controlled by its enemies (6.2b). Similarly, when cities were attacked, they turned out to be under the control of the adversary (6.2c–6.2d).

(6.2)

a. EMCpoi104: 约曰，四国为一，以攻赵，**破**赵而四分其地。

Yuē yuē, sì guó wéi yī, yǐ gōng Zhào, pò Zhào ér sì fēn qí dì.

covenant said, four countries to one, to attack Zhao, defeat Zhao and four separate its land

"The covenant said, combine the four countries into one to attack Zhao and separate its land into four parts."

b. EMandpoi1658: 后大喜曰："汝主刘钧若肯同心**破**宋……"

Hòu dà xǐ yuē: "rǔ zhǔ Liú Jūn ruò kěn tóng xīn pò
sòng …"

Empress great happy said: "your master Liu Jun if like one
heart attack Song …"

"The empress happily said: 'If your master Liu Jun would
like to attack Song together …'"

c. EMandpoi40: 宋朝差宋江等兵马前来厮杀，连**破**两个城池。

Sòng cháo chāi Sòng Jiāng děng bīng mǎ qián lái sī
shā, lián

pò liǎng gè chéng chí.

Song dynasty assign Song Jiang etc soldier horse come
DEIXIS fight, continuously

attack two CL cities

"Song assigned soldiers led by Song Jiang to fight and they
attacked two cities successively."

d. EMandpoi1565: 引曹操**破**我冀州⋯⋯！

Yǐn Cáo Cāo pò wǒ Jì Zhōu …!

lead Cao Cao attack our Ji Zhou …!

"Attract Cao Cao to attack Ji Zhou …!"

Another result of "to win against" or more generally of war is the
destruction of residence, home, and buildings, the harm of people, and life,
as well as the eradication of alliance and regime. All these happenings are
subsumed under the third reading of *pò*, "to damage sb/sth so badly that he/she/
it no longer exists or works". For instance, when countries or cities have gone
through fighting, countries and cities would be ruined (6.3a–6.3b), homes would
be destroyed (6.3c) and people would be slaughtered (6.3d). All such destructive
events are described with *pò*. Moreover, *pò* is also used to denote the ending of
alliance and the disruption of moral principles (6.3e–6.3f).

(6.3)

a. EMandpoi1057: 今须一败，不至于国**破**邦亡。

        Jīn xū yī bài, bú zhì yú guó pò bāng wáng.

        today need one defeat, not lead to country destroyed country lost

        "Being defeated once will not cause our country being destroyed and taken over."

b. EMCpoi483: 于是一郡**破**残，死伤过半……

        Yú shì yī jùn pò   cán,   sǐ shāng guò bàn ...

        hence one county destroyed damaged, casualty more half ...

        "Hence a country was destroyed and there was more than half casualty."

c. LMCpoi27: 无赖险獠，崔家**破**家。

        Wú-lài-xiǎn-liáo, Cuī jiā pò jiā.

        rascal,   Cui family destroy home

        "Being a rascal, the Cui family was destroyed."

d. LMCpoi963: 天生此妖，以**破**残百姓。

        Tiān   shēng cǐ yāo, yǐ pòcán bǎixìng.

        God give birth to this monster, to destroy public

        "God gave birth to this monster and he destroyed and ruined the public."

e. EMCpoi120: 张仪为秦**破**纵连横……

        Zhāng Yí wèi Qín pò   zòng lián héng ...

        Zhang Yi for Qin destroy vertical unite horizontal

        "Zhang Yi helped Qin to destroy vertical cooperation and realize horizontal cooperation."

f. EMCpoi210: 辩慧则**破**正道。

        Biàn huì   zé pò zhèng dào.

        debate intelligent then destroy righteous

        "Those who are intelligent and good at debating usually destroy the righteous."

The last reading in this domain is closely associated with a frequently used idiom. And *pò* receives its intensional readings "to succeed" from the derived meanings of this idiom (Geeraerts 2002). In this idiom, *pò* cooccurs with bamboo and constitutes the idiom *shì-rú-pò-zhú* (6.4a–6.4b). And this idiom literally describes the splitting of bamboos. The metaphorical reading "being successful all the time" is constructed based on the encyclopedic knowledge that when bamboos are broken on the very top with swords, they split quickly down to their ends. In other words, it is in terms of this cultural imagery of bamboo splitting that the idiom *shì-rú-pò-zhú* in its composite form is metaphorically used to describe the irresistible force of an army in fighting against its enemies and obtains the derived reading "being successful all the time".

(6.4)

a. EMandpoi1873: 一路关隘无阻，势如**破**竹。

Yī lù guānài wú zǔ,   shì   rú   pò   zhú.

all way passes no hinderance, power like break bamboo

"There were neither passes nor hinderance all the way, so they went across as powerful as   breaking bamboos."

b. MdMandpoi1028: 带病领兵势如**破**竹，一直杀至夏都。

Dài bìng lǐng bīng shì rú pò zhú, yī zhí shā zhì Xià dū.

with illness lead soldier powerful like split bamboos, all kill to Xia capital

"He was ill but led soldiers and fought to the capital of Xia with an imposing manner like splitting bamboos."

6.1.2 Cognitive change

The second intensional domain of *pò* is cognitive change, referring to the cognitive knowledge change of speakers or addressees in their understanding or recognition of theories, ideas, schemes, or events. Altogether five intensional readings are summed up in this domain. The first and last two readings are actually two contrastive pairs of cognitive change. The first pair includes "to discover or notice sth" (E) and "to make sth known to sb" (F). The third reading designates the discarding of cognitive or emotional feelings like irritation, hatred, or doubt (G). The second pair composes "to know what sb or sth means" (H) and "to tell sb what sth means" (I).

To illustrate, the first intentional reading of *pò* denotes one's discovery or notice of sth that is not easy to see or hear, like human intention, enemy's tricks, and someone's deception. When these intangible and abstract objects are discovered, one's cognitive state changes from confusion to clearness. For instance, *pò* is used to describe the emperor's mother's discovery of his intention to keep the two beauties, namely, Empress dowager Xiang's seeing through of a trick (6.5a), and someone's detection of a scheme (6.5b–6.5c). Moreover, one's completely seeing through of the vanity of worldly affairs is also designated as *pò* (6.5d). The second intensional reading is metonymically contiguous to the first reading in a cause-effect relation (Piersman and Geerearts 2006). The transfer of *pò* from naming "seeing through" to naming "revealing" is based on the semantic contiguity between these two readings (Geereaerts 1997: 86). In this second reading, *pò* denotes revealing schemes, secrets, or cases that people previously could not see or understand. For instance, by asking people to plug their noses, Jin Touhu made the incense scheme known to everyone (6.6a). By the same token, *pò* also designates the disclosure of a doubting point, the exposure of someone's secret identity as well as the uncovering of the covert process of a theft (6.6b–6.6d).

(6.5)

a. MdMandpoi50: 及徽宗嗣位，向太后早窥**破**徽宗之意……

        Jí Huīzōng sì wèi, Xiàng tài hòu zǎo kuī pò Huī zōng zhī yì ...

        When Hui-emperor take throne, Xiang empress dowager early see through Hui emperor DE intention ...

"When emperor Hui took the throne, empress dowager Xiang saw through his intention ..."

b. EMandpoi1852: 个人打发来到此处私访，叫我张大哥识**破**了机关。

Gèrén dǎfā láidào cǐchù sī fǎng, jiào wǒ zhāng dà gē shí-pò le   jīguān.

Personal assign come here private visit, make my Zhang big brother see through LE tricks

"He came here to have a private visit but his tricks were seen through by my big brother Zhang."

c. MdMandpoi1282: 因此赵高李斯的诡谋，终未被人窥**破**。

Yīn-cǐ   Zhào Gāo Lǐ Sī de guǐmóu, zhōng wèi bèi rén kuī pò.

Therefore Zhao Gao Li Si DE tricks, finally not BEI people see through

"Therefore Zhao Gao and Li Si's tricks were not seen through by anyone in the end."

d. MdMandpoi1431: 她因看**破**世情，入了空门。

Tā yīn   kàn pò   shìqíng, rù le kōngmén.

she because see through secular, into LE Buddhism

"She went to become a nun, because she saw through the world."

(6.6)

a. EMandpoi1034: 金头虎喊道："闻不着药的可堵鼻子！"一句话说**破**了五路薰香计。

Jīn tóu hǔ hǎn dào: "wén bú zháo yào de kě dǔ bí zī !" Yī jù huà shuō pò le wǔ lù xūn xiāng jì.

Jin Touhu yell say: "smell not medicine can plug nose!" One sentence reveal Wulu incense trick

"Jin Touhu yelled and said: "plug your nose if you cannot smell the medicine". By saying this he revealed the Wulu incense trick."

b. MdMandpoi220: 说**破**疑团，使人醒目。

    Shuō   pò   yítuán, shǐ rén   xǐng mù.

    speak break doubt, make people wake eyes

    "When he cleared up the doubt, everybody was awake."

c. EMandpoi17: 冒得官一见他守着众人揭**破**他的底细⋯⋯

    Mào Déguān yī jiàn tā shǒu-zhe zhòng-rén jiēpò tā-de dǐxì ...

    Mao Deguan once see he   with   public uncover his secrets

    …

    "Mao Deguan saw him uncovering his secrets in front of people."

d. EMandpoi1372: ⋯⋯盗案立**破**。

    ... dào àn   lì   pò.

    ... theft case immediately solve

    "... solve the theft case immediately."

The third intensional reading that indicates cognitive change is getting rid of distress, irritation, or doubt. When these interruptive thoughts are erased from mind, one's cognitive state changes from worried or irritated to easy and relaxed. But different from the disposal of the rotted part of an apple, such cognitive removal is much more abstract. As shown in example (6.7a), *pò* is used to describe the expelling of irritation by means of intelligence. When irritation is driven away, one's cognitive state changes from irritated to relaxed and easy. Similarly, in (6.7b–6.7d), *pò* is extended to denote the getting rid of annoyance, disturbance as well as hatred. When these disturbing cognitive states are thrown off, one's cognitive mood becomes cheerful and light-hearted.

(6.7)

a. EMCpoi21: 傥不以智慧照**破**烦恼⋯⋯

    Tǎng bù yǐ zhì huì zhào pò fán nǎo ...

if not with intelligence dispel annoyance

"If we do not dispel annoyance with intelligence ..."

b. EMCpoi46: 但事迹原委，亦可以消愁**破**闷。

Dàn shì jì yuán wěi, yì kě yǐ xiāo chóu pò mèn.

With event beginning to end, also can resolve anxiety dispel annoyance

"When you get clear of the event from its beginning to the end, you can resolve anxiety and dispel annoyance."

c. EMCpoi30: ……将**破**碎纷扰。

... jiang pò suì fēnrǎo.

will break annoyance

"will get rid of annoyance."

d. EMCpoi45: 是后中原士夫，深为子孙忧，恨入心髓，牢不可**破**。

Shì hòu Zhōng Yuán shì fu, shēn wéi zǐ sūn yōu, hèn rù xīn suǐ, láo bù kě pò.

This after central plains social officials, deep for offspring worry, hate into heart, strong cannot break

"After this, social-officials of central plains are very worried about their offspring. They hate the proposers so deep in their heart that nothing can break that hatred."

The fourth and fifth readings also display a metonymic cause-effect relation, one denoting "to know what someone or something means" and the other designating "to tell sb about sth in a way that makes it easy to understand". With the fourth reading, *pò* expresses one's realization or understanding of ideas, theories, or purposes. For instance, the leader's realization of the situation he is facing up to is encoded as the compound *xǐng-pò* (6.8a). *Xǐng* and *pò* are synonyms, indicating reflection and realization. Likewise, the understanding of someone's intention or purpose is designated as *jiě-pò* (6.8b). *Jiě* is also synonymous with *pò,* showing one's understanding of something. With the fifth reading, *pò* means explaining something difficult in an easy way, like elaborating the existence of Taoism (6.8c) and explaining someone's opinion and comment on certain events (6.8d).

(6.8)

a. EMandpoi1172: 主上省**破**，诛灭群奸……

　　　　　　Zhǔshàng xǐng pò, zhūmiè qún jiān ...

　　　　　　Emperor realize break, kill all evil-counselors

　　　　　　"The emperor came to realize the truth, and killed all those evil counselors."

b. MdMandpoi165: 那些人也不解**破**他的用意，向四散分开。

　　　　　　Nàxiē rén yě bù jiěpò tā-de yòngyì, xiàng sì sàn fēnkāi.

　　　　　　those people also not understand his intention, toward all-direction apart

　　　　　　"Those people cannot understand his intention and they scattered apart to all directions."

c. LMCpoi35: 白云为你点**破**。

　　　　　　Bái Yún wéi nǐ diǎn pò.

　　　　　　Bai Yun for you point break

　　　　　　"Bai Yun unraveled everything for you."

d. EMandpoi718: 今蒙恩爹指**破**，真是极口赞颂，心尽力竭的了。

　　　　　　Jīn méng ēn diē zhǐ pò, zhēn shì jí kǒu zàn sòng, xīn jìn lì jié de le.

　　　　　　today indebt father point break, really is great praise, heart die strength over DE LE

　　　　　　"I am very grateful for my father's whole-heart revealing and reminding."

6.1.3 Possessive change

The third intensional domain of *pò* is concerned with possessive change, namely using something available on hand to exchange for something in need.

Things on hand range from money to time and things to be exchanged for include goods and events. For instance, *pò* can be used to describe scenarios when people pay money to buy goods, or hire killers for assassination. Officials spend public money in order to buy groceries in the market (6.9a). Similarly, people may pay killers to help assassinate a personal enemy (6.9b).

Visible materials like money can further extend to invisible objects like time. As shown in (6.9c) and (6.9d), *pò* is also used to denote cases when people spend time going somewhere or doing something. For instance, in (6.9c), *pò* denotes the scenario when Chongbo spent half a day visiting his wife. Likewise, (6.9d) *pò* describes the case when people spent two days making clothes for someone.

(6.9)

a. LMCpoi120: 又重**破**官钱买······杂物。

> Yòu chóng pò guān qián mǎi ... zá wù.
>
> again spend public money buy... miscellany
>
> "Again he spent public money to buy those market miscellany."

b. EMandpoi683: 舅太爷须得**破**些钱财，小的托他行刺。

> Jiù tài yé   xū děi pò   xiē qiáncái, xiǎo de tuō tā
>
> xín cì.
>
> uncle great-grandfather need spend some money,   I ask him assassinate
>
> "You may need to spend some money so that I can hire him for assassination."

c. MdMandpoi867: 此刻离夫人所居不过里余。崇伯何妨即去一转，再来督师，不过**破**费半日功夫。

> Cǐ kè lí fū rén suǒ jū bú guò lǐ yú. Chóngbó hé fáng jí qù yī zhuàn, zài lái dū shī, bú guò pò fèi bàn rì gōng fu.
>
> now from Madam living less than a mile. Chongbo why not go to look, then come to office, less than spend half day time

"It's only a mile away from Madam's living place. Chongbo can go and have a look and then come back to the office. It will only take half a day."

d. EMandpoi1827: 既是有了棉花合布，这做是不难的，我**破**二日工夫，拿到家里，与他做了送来罢。

Jì shì yǒu le mián huā hé bù, zhè zuò shì bù nán de, wǒ pò èr rì gōng fū, ná dào jiā lǐ, yǔ tā zuò le sòng lái bà.

Since have cotton and cloth, this do is not difficult, I spend two days time, take home, for him do send DEXIS

"Since you have cotton and cloth, this will not be difficult to make. I can spend two days working on this at home and then send it back to him."

6.1.4 Observance change

In its fourth intensional domain of observance change, *pò* denotes going against or violating rules, laws, or agreements. It should be noted that violating the law does not mean that the law is destroyed but the efficacy of the law is affected. In other words, what is changed is not the law itself, but the executive force of the law.

As Example (6.10a) shows, *pò* is used to describe the violation of the commandment of staying away from women. Although the binding effect of this commandment is breached, the commandment itself is still there. Similarly, the violation of government law is also denoted as *pò*, and although the law is attenuated in its restrictive force, its specific rules are always constant (6.10b). The observance of law further extends to daily rules. As shown in (6.10c), "*pò-lǐ*" is a frequently used expression in Mandarin, denoting the violation of a daily rule. The rule itself still remains intact. What changes is the efficacy of the rule.

(6.10)

a. EMandpoi12: 吾被你赚骗，使我**破**了色戒，堕于地狱。

Wú bèi nǐ zhuànpiàn, shǐ wǒ pò le sèjiè, duò   yú

dìyù.

I BEI you deceive, make me break LE lust, degenerate into hell

"I was deceived by you and made to break the sexual percept and thus degenerated into the hell."

b. MdMandpoi1742: 安能**破**朝廷之法耶?

An néng pò cháo tíng zhī fǎ yé?

how can break court DE law

"How come you break court law?"

c. EMandpoi552: 我竟**破**个例给你通个信儿去。

Wǒ jìng   pò gè lì gěi nǐ tōng gè xì-ér   qù.

I unexpectedly break a rule for you send a message DEIXIS

"I broke the rule and sent a message for you."

6.1.5 Emotional change

The fifth intensional domain is related to emotional change. In this extended domain, *pò* describes one's emotional change from one state to another. The first reading is derived from a frequently used compound *pò-dǎn*. In this compound, *pò* literally describes the breaking of the guts of soldiers or leaders. But in the derived meaning, the word "guts" is used metonymically to refer to one's courage based on the imagery that inner organs are conceptualized as loci of emotions (Kraska-Szlenk 2014). In this sense, if one's guts is broken, then one's courage is agitated and one's emotional state changes from composed to scared. For instance, the princes become too scared to provide any good idea (6.11a), and the ministers are scared because their emperor is in danger (6.11b).

In the second reading, *pò* is directly used to describe one's facial expression changing from one emotional mood to another. For instance, *pò* describes the concubine's emotional change from crying to laughing in example (6.11c). It denotes the emperor's affectional change from annoyance to delight in example (6.11d).

(6.11)

    a. EMCpoi485: 则大诸侯之有异心者，**破胆**而不敢谋。

        Zé dà zhū hóu zhī yǒu   yì xīn zhě,   pò dǎn ér   bù gǎn móu.

        then big dukes DE have rebelling intention, break gut and not dare plan

        "Those dukes who have an intention to rebel dare not to plan this."

    b. EMCpoi491: 圣躬蹈危，臣下**破胆**。

        Shèng gōng dǎo wēi, chén xià pò dǎn.

        emperor endangered, subject break gut

        "The emperor was endangered and I felt scared."

    c. MdMandpoi157: 各姬妾等**破**涕为笑，又在老袁前说长论短。

        Gè jī qiè děng pò tì wéi xiào, yòu zài lǎo yuán qián shuō cháng lùn duǎn.

        every concubine break cry to laugh, again in elder Yuan LOC gossip

        "Every concubine changed from crying to laughing and gossiped again in front of elder Yuan."

    d. MdMandpoi627: 虽在极懊恨的当儿，也往往**破**颜为之一笑。

        Suī zài jí ào hèn de dāng ér, yě wǎng wǎng pò yán wéi zhī yī xiào.

        although in great hatred, also often break face for this a laugh

        "Although he was in great hatred but he would change facial expression to laugh."

6.1.6 Temporal change

The final intensional domain is extended to the temporal sphere where *pò* is used to designate the beginning of a new temporal stage. As noted in the previous studies (Heine et al. 1991), the metaphorical transfer from the physical spatial domain to the temporal domain is a prevailing directionality in the process of semantic extension. Although physical separation refers to the specific partition or disintegration of concrete objects, such semantic specificity has been completely emptied of in the temporal domain. In this domain, *pò* simply designates the entering into another new time period or a new time taking place of an old time. As shown in example (6.12a), the beginning of a new day is described as breaking a new day. In (6.12b), *pò* denotes the getting rid of darkness, which represents the beginning of a new day. Likewise, *pò* can also describe the starting of a new month.

(6.12)

　a. EMandpoi1008: **破**天亮时，李中堂便委了委员来敬代拈香。

　　　　　　　Pò tiān liàng shí, Lǐ Zhōngtáng biàn wěi le wěi yuán lái jìng dài niān xiāng.

　　　　　　　break dark time, Li chancellor then assign member DEIXIS respect with incense

　　　　　　　"When it was dawn, chancellor Li assigned member to show respect with an incense on behalf of him."

　b. MdMandpoi178: 天将**破**晓，太后才回寝宫歇息……

　　　　　　　Tiān jiāng pò xiǎo, tài hòu cái huí qǐn gōng xiē xi ...

　　　　　　　day will break dark, empress dowager go back to bedchamber rest ...

　　　　　　　"By dawn, empress dowager went back to rest in her bedchamber ..."

6.1.7　Interim summary

To sum up, the source concept of *pò* refers to the elementary human experience of object separation. Serving as the reference point, this concrete physical domain has transferred to six abstract application domains, and the intensional reading of *pò* has switched from physical separation to abstract readings accordingly. The cognitive principle underlying this semantic extension process is the "principle of the exploitation of old means for novel functions" (Werner and Kaplan 1963: 403; Heine et al. 1991), namely, employing the existing form *pò* to refer to new concepts. The channel bridging the existing form and new concepts is the physical experience of object integrity change. With this conceptual channel, relational, cognitive, emotional as well as temporal changes are also denoted as *pò*. Moreover, the semantic specificity of *pò* is gradually sifted out and what remains intact is the semantic core of "state change". Further speaking, it is the physical separation that gives access to abstract separations and stage change, and the old term *pò* is adapted to new realities or new concepts (Robert 2008).

Concerning the cause for such semantic transfer, it is the desire to meet the unfulfilled communicative needs that drive the intensional extension of *pò*. For instance, it can be envisaged that there are no adequate linguistic designations to describe the winning against of enemies. Since war is fleshed out with physical object separation, *pò* stands out as the most accessible lexical form to describe the winning against of enemies. In this sense, there are direct motivations for picking up *pò* to denote the above elaborated six intensional domains. In what follows, the cross-domain correspondence between the physical usages and intensional readings of *pò* is detailed.

6.2 Correspondence between intensional readings and extensional references

As revealed in Chapter 4, the referential range of *pò* is fairly broad in ancient Chinese, including not only disruptive separation, but also new function separation and impediment removal separation. Tracing the semantic development of *pò*, this section brings to sight three lineages of the evolution of the intensional readings of *pò* and demonstrates how intensional readings develop in response to their extensional references. The three semantic lineages stem from three types of extensional usages. Figure 6.1 formulates semantic extensions of *pò* in terms of a top-down diagram, starting from the three extensional usages of separation, continuing with intensional readings of increasing abstractness, and ending with the most abstract readings. In what follows, we explain how intensional readings of *pò* evolve along these three lineages.

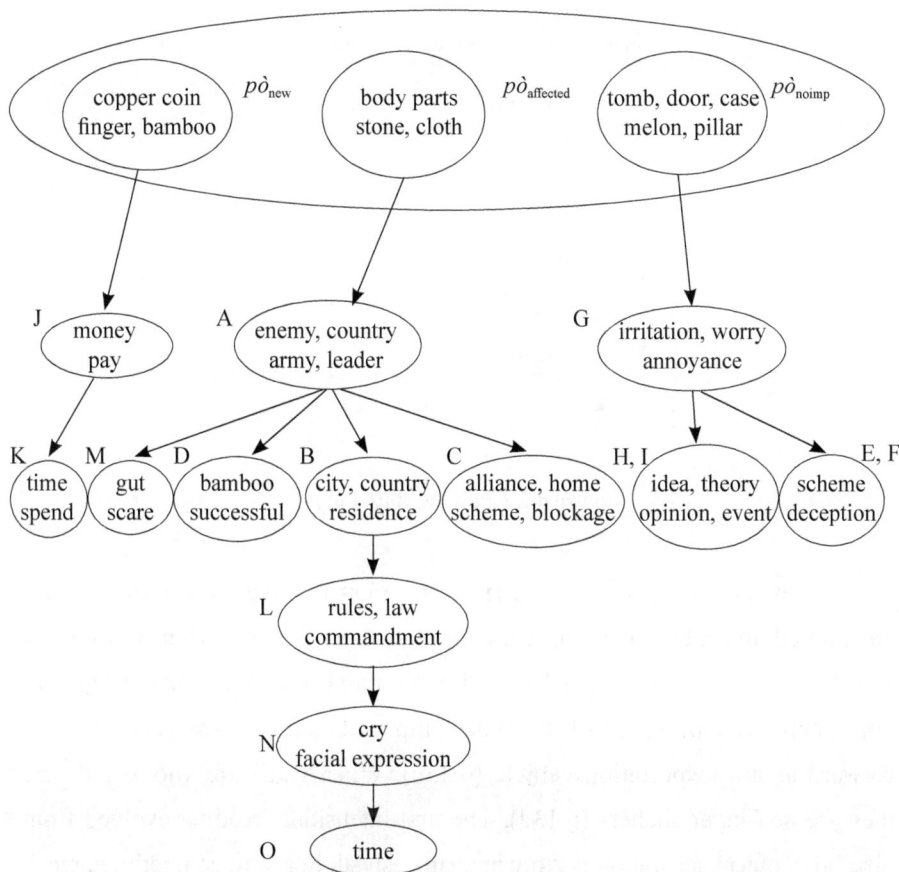

Figure 6.1 Semantic extensions of *pò*

6.2.1 Semantic lineage of disruptive separation

First and foremost, eight of the fourteen intensional readings of *pò* are developed along the lineage of disruptive separation. There exists a close extensional association between intensional readings like "to win against", "to take over", "to succeed" etc. and the extensional usages like "to separate objects like stones, body parts or cloth with their function being disrupted". This extensional line is the longest among the three and constitutes the most important developing line of *pò*. The intensional readings along this semantic lineage display a metonymy-metaphor chain shift (Robert 2008) as follows:

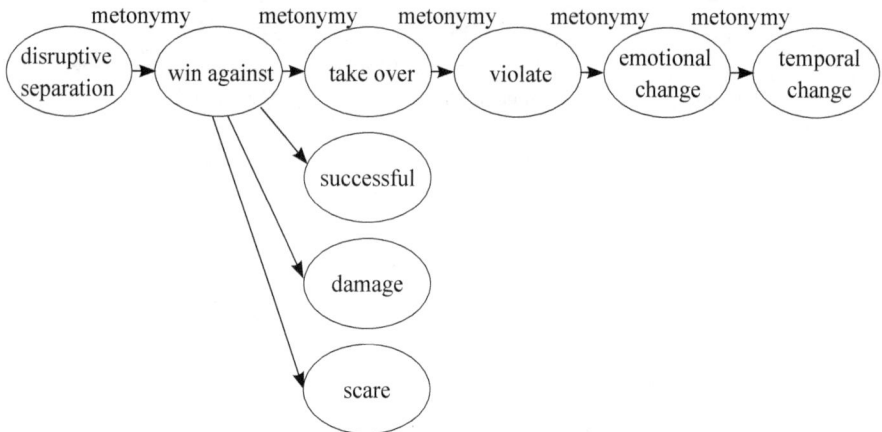

Figure 6.2 Chaining shift 1 of *pò*

To be specific, disruptive separation refers to cases where objects are partitioned and their functions are disrupted. For instance, when vessels are smashed, they can no longer be used as containers (6.13a). When legs are hurt, people cannot walk (6.13b). When ships are damaged, they cannot move forward as a transportation vehicle (6.13c). When walls are knocked down, they are no longer shelters (6.13d). The first intensional reading evolved from disruptive object separation is "to win against sb/sth in a war, competition, etc.". The emergence of this reading first should be attributed to the "part for whole" relation, or more exactly "characteristic for entity" (Piersman and Geeraerts 2006). In ancient China, war is characterized by the smashing of the stones of city walls and fortress. The smashing of these defense structures usually symbolizes the conquering of the city or the country. As such a characteristic of stone smashing is highly consistent with the etymological usage of *pò*, *pò* is metonymically used to stand for winning the war. Moving further from this "characteristic for entity" relation, *pò* is believed to be the most easily accessible lexical item that speakers can retrieve from their mental lexicon to describe war scenarios (Harmon and Kapatsinski 2017). For one thing, war is usually replete with the destruction of walls, disintegration of instruments, and partition of body parts. For another, *pò* is pervasively used to describe such concrete separations, thus it is readily employed to describe the more general war affair, which is represented with these separation events, such as the winning against of enemies, armies, and leaders.

(6.13)

a. EMCpoe68: 取水实于大盎中，盎**破**水流地。

　　　　　Qǔ shuǐ shí yú dà àng zhōng, àng pò shuǐ liú dì.

　　　　　get water put into big vat, vat break water run ground

　　　　　"Put water into the big vat, when the vat broke, water ran to the ground."

b. EMCpoe192: 剖人心，**破**人胫。

　　　　　Pōu　rén　xīn, pò　rén　jìng.

　　　　　dissect human heart, break human leg

　　　　　"They dissected the hearts and broke shins of people."

c. LMCpoe370: 海中遇风，舟**破**坠水。

　　　　　Hǎi zhōng yù　　fēng, zhōu pò　zhuì shuǐ.

　　　　　sea middle encounter wind, boat break fall water

　　　　　"The boat was damaged in the storm and fell into the water."

d. LMCpoe421: 妻贫儿幼，遭暴风雨，墙宇**破**坏。

　　　　　Qī pín ér yòu,　zāo　bào fēng yǔ, qiáng yǔ pò　huài.

　　　　　wife poor kids young, encounter storm rain,　wall　break destroy

　　　　　"His wife was poor and kids were young. They encountered a storm and their wall broke."

Upon this intensional reading of "to win against", four intensional readings which describe the result of war come into being. Further speaking, the intensional reading "to win against" bears a "cause for effect" metonymic relation with the four intentional readings "to take over", "to scare", "to succeed" and "to destroy schemes" (Norrick 1981: 87; Piersman and Geeraerts 2006). The first result is taking control of the cities or even countries of the opponent. It is a natural result for the winners to take over their opponents' cities or countries. In this way, *pò* in this reading entails the defeat of enemies and denotes the taking over of their cities or countries. The second result is the soldier's being scared which is denoted by means of the compound *pò-dǎn* (break-guts). The third result is the success of the winning country, represented in terms of the idiom *pò-zhú-zhī-shì* (break-bamboo-force). These two idiomatic expressions are pervasively used in the genre of ancient Chinese wars. The compound employs the separation of the body part "guts" to describe emotional scare and the idiom draws on the breaking feature of bamboos to describe the overwhelming force of armies. The fourth result is the destruction of alliance, schemes as well as blockages during wars. This intensional reading indicates that winning a war includes not only fighting on the battle field but also the contest between politicians.

Following the lineage of "to take over", more intensional readings of increasing metaphorical abstractness develop. In other words, different from the above-mentioned metonymic relations, this intensional reading of "to take over" metaphorically shifts from the domain of war to more abstract domains (Langacker 1987: 379; Heine et al. 1991; Evans and Green 2006: 310). The first intensional reading resulting from the metaphorical shift is the eleventh reading "to go against the law". In the reading of "to take over", the belonging of cities or countries is ignored. Analogously, in the reading of "to go against the law", the existence and efficacy of laws, commandments, and rules are disregarded. But different from "to take over", the violation of laws and rules does not entail any destruction. When laws, commandments, and rules are violated, they are still in existence. The behaviors that should be taken following the law are superseded by behaviors going against the law. Continuing the abstraction of "to take over", *pò* further extends to the emotional domain and temporal domain. In the emotional change domain, *pò* denotes "to change from one state to another". This reading indicates the replacement of a facial expression with a different one, like changing from crying to laughing. In the temporal domain, *pò* designates "to start happening". In analogy to "to go against the law", "to start happening" indicates the substitution of one temporal period with a different temporal period, like the day substituting the night.

6.2.2 Semantic lineage of impediment removal separation

The second developing lineage originates from impediment removal separation. In this type of separation event, objects are separated or opened on the surface so as to reveal their interior. For instance, plants are skinned off to show their inner part (6.14a) and tombs are excavated to disclose the treasures buried inside (6.14b). Intensional readings that extend from this separation event include "to get rid of irritation, doubt and hatred, etc.", "to notice sth", "to make sth known to sb", "to know what someone or something means", as well as "to tell sb about sth". The metaphorical extension from impediment removal separation to readings related to cognitive change is a cross-domain transfer from the physical domain to the cognitive domain (Kraska-Szlenk 2014). Chaining shift 2 demonstrates the metaphorical and metonymic relationship among these intensional readings.

To be specific, the first reading that extends from impediment removal events is "to get rid of irritation, doubt and hatred etc.". Clearly, in this intentional reading, irritation, doubt, and hatred are impediments that hinder people from being relaxed and happy. Thus, after getting rid of these annoying emotions, one's mood will become easy and pleased. As noted above, the other four readings constitute two cause-result pairs. The first pair is "to notice sth" and "to make sth known to sb". These two readings are related to the "seeing through" and "revealing" of abstract objects which are not easy to see or notice, like schemes, tricks, and cases. For instance, in analogy to removing impediments, seeing through enemies' scheme involves clearing away the

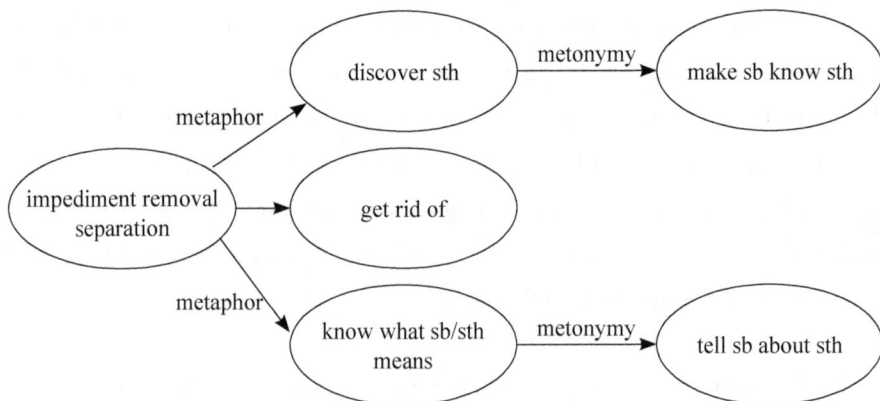

Figure 6.3 Chaining shift 2 of *pò*

surface disguise of deception (6.14c). Likewise, solving a theft includes sorting out the clues and evidence and bringing to light the process of stealing (6.14d). The second cause-result pair is concerned with understanding and explaining ideas and theories. As we know, ideas and theories cannot be understood without first figuring out the surface meaning and then the essential meaning. In this sense, this intensional reading pair is also derived from the impediment removal separation. As shown in (6.14e), understanding someone's intention requires first getting clear of his recent behaviors and his attention focus in the particular context and then predicting his purpose for showing up. In the same way, to explain what a sentence means, one needs to first make clear the literal reading encoded by each word and then further interpret the entailment or implication that goes beyond words (6.14f).

(6.14)

a. EMCpoe112: **破**其外青皮，得白心，即莂藤。

　　　　Pò qí wài　qīng pí, dé bái xīn,　jí Kēténg.

　　　　break its outside green skin, get white core, namely Keteng.

　　　　"Break its green skin and get the white core which is called Keteng."

b. LMCpoe445: 县官云："此古器，当是**破**家得之。"

Xiàn guān yún: "cǐ gǔ qì, dāng shì pò zhǒng dé zhī.

county official said: this ancient appliance, must be break tomb obtain it

"The official said: 'this ancient appliance must have been obtained by breaking the tomb.'"

c. EMandpoi351: 不料计未成而敌已识**破**……

Bú liào jì wèi chéng ér dí yǐ shí pò ...

not expect trick is not successful but enemy already see through…

"Unexpectedly, the trick has not been successfully employed but is already seen through by the enemy…"

d. EMandpoi452: 冒大人船上失窃东西，限捕快三天替我**破案**。

Mào dà rén chuán shàng shī qiè dōngxī, xiàn bǔkuài sān tiān tì wǒ pò àn.

Mao official boat LOC   lose things, give constable three days for me solve case

"Official Mao lost something on his boat. You must solve the case within three days."

e. MdMandpoi165: 那些人也不解**破**他的用意，向四散分开。

Nà−xiē rén yě bù jiěpò tāde yòngyì, xiàng sì sàn fēnkāi.

those people also not understand his intention, toward four directions separate

"Those people did not understand his intention and separate toward all the directions."

f. EMandpoi756: 你瞧瞧老娘娘这签上怎么说的？给**破**说**破**说呢！

Nǐ qiáo qiáo lǎo niáng niáng zhè qiān shàng zěnme shuōde? gěi pò shuō pò shuō ne!

you look look old empress this sticker LOC how say give me explain explain

"Look what is said on this old empress sticker and tell me the truth."

6.2.3 Semantic lineage of new function separation

The third extensional lineage is a shorter one, with two intensional readings "to spend money for goods, services or particular purposes" and "to spend time doing sth". These two intensional readings are metaphorically associated with each other as shown in chaining shift 3.

Chaining shift 3

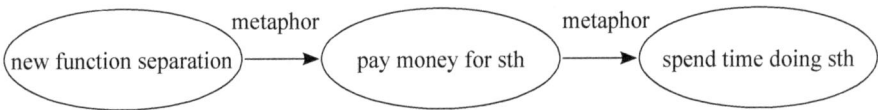

Figure 6.4 Chaining shift 3 of *pò*

By new function separation, it means that objects are separated to bring about further use. For instance, the white gourd can be emptied in the center and dried to make a gourd ladle (6.15a). A tree can be cut into parts and made into walking sticks (6.15b). Musical instruments with fifty strings can be separated into two different instruments each with twenty-five strings (6.15c). Heavy coins from ancient times can be recast to lighter ones (6.15d). Generalizing from these four extensional usages, it is not uneasy to conclude that physical objects can be separated and made use of to create different objects. Moreover, fewer physical objects like large bills can also be "separated" to get small changes. It is a social custom that if we want to change a large bill into small change, we need to spend some money and such an experience is described as *pò-qián* (break money). Metaphorically extending from these extensional usages, *pò* is abstractly used to denote paying something to get something else. For instance, *pò* describes paying money to get a house, and spending time staying with someone (6.15e–6.15f). All these said, the objects we have on hand abstract away from well-delineated physical objects like gourd, trees, instruments, and coins to less-delineated nonphysical objects like time. Similarly, the objects we intend to get access to metaphorically extend from concrete objects like gourd dipper, stick, musical instrument, and house to more abstract objects like accompany.

(6.15)

a. EMCpoe3: 二十日出，黄色好，**破**以为瓢。

   Èr shí rì chū, huán sè hǎo, pò yǐwéi piáo.

   twenty days out, yellow good, break into ladle

   "It comes out in twenty days. Yellow one is good and you can break it into a ladle."

b. EMCpoe80: 十年，中四**破**为杖，一根直二十文。

   Shí nián, zhōng sì pò wéi zhàng, yī gēn zhí èr shí wén.

   ten years, middle four break into stick, one CL worth twenty cents

   "In ten years, you can break it into four parts in the middle and make it sticks. Each stick is worth twenty cents."

c. LMCpoe62: 黄帝使素女鼓瑟……乃**破**为二十五弦……

   Huáng dì shǐ Sùnǚ gǔ sè … nǎi pò wéi èr shí wǔ xián…

   Huang Di ask Sunv play Se … then break it into twenty-five strings

   "Huang Di asked Sunv to play Se … then broke it into twenty-five strings."

d. LMCpoe56: 故盗铸者**破**重钱以为轻钱。

   Gù dào zhù zhě pò zhòng qián yǐ wéi qīng qián.

   thus stealthily cast person break heavy money to make light money

   "Thus those people who used to cast stealthily, broke the heavy money and made it into lighter money."

e. EMandpoi788: 等着狮子街那里，替你**破**几两银子买所房子。

   Děng zhē shī zi jiē nà lǐ, tì nǐ pò jǐ liǎng yín zi

mǎi suǒ fáng zi.

wait   Lion street over there, help you spend several CL money buy CL house

"Wait and see, I will spend money to buy you a house on Lion street."

f. MdMandpoi 839: 女学生又掉过脸去，周正勋无奈，只得打算**破**工夫跟她几日。

Nǔ xué shēng yòu diào guò liǎn qù, Zhōu Zhèngxūn wú nài, zhǐ dé dǎ suàn pò gōng fu gēn tā jǐ rì.

female student again turn back face DEIXIS, Zhou Zhengxun helpless, only can plan spend time stay with her several days

"The female student turned back her face again. Zhou Zhengxun felt helpless and could only spent several days with her."

6.3 Grammaticalization at semantic–syntactic interface

Based on the above semantic extension tendency of *pò*, it can be predicted that *pò* has undergone a process of grammaticalization. This section further investigates the grammaticalization of *pò* both at the semantic level and the syntactic level. Section 6.3.1 reveals that specific readings anchored objectively in extralinguistic situations gradually transfers to readings grounded in the speaker's subjective cognitive understanding and emotional change (Hopper 1991). Section 6.3.2 demonstrates that the syntactic status of *pò* as a predicate verb has been gradually reassigned to a less prime category of complement (Traugott and König 1991). In spite of such semantic and syntactic changes, this study asserts that *pò* is still in its incipient stage of grammaticalization because its multiple semantic variants coexist in Mandarin and its verb form has not completely grammaticalized into a verb suffix.

6.3.1 Grammaticalization at the semantic level

At the semantic level, semantic readings of *pò* have gradually transferred from concrete separation grounded in extralinguistic experience to abstract separation grounded in subjective experience with an increasing degree of speaker involvement. This indicates that the semantic readings of *pò* become more subjective and grammaticalized. But the widespread coexistence of concrete and abstract readings evinces that *pò* is still in its early stage of grammaticalization. Taking the lineage of disruptive separation as an example, it displays an obvious abstraction trend at levels of the Agent who initiates force, and the Figural entity which undergoes a change as well as the Results of the change.

To be specific, in physical separation events, the Agent is usually a volitional person and the Figural entity is a qualitative and configurational physical object. The agentive person initiates force intentionally or unintentionally upon the physical object and gives rise to the object's disintegration into parts. Parallel with physical object separation, the Agent in war relational event is a country, an army, or a leader and the Figural entity is a country, an army, or a leader on the opposite side. The two sides' fighting against each other results in one side's victory and the other side's defeat. What are separated in this scenario include city walls, blockages, residences, and body parts of soldiers and common people. Besides the result of winning or losing the war, the other result is that the country or city of the loser is taken over or incorporated into the territory of the winner.

Different from physical separation and war fighting, the Agent in possessive change event is a volitional person. The Figural entity is money or time. The Agent gives up his possession of money or time to exchange for property or accompany. In cognitive change, an Agent is a person who knows or understands some tricks or theory. The Figural entity is the cognitive state of the patient or the patient's understanding of the tricks or theory. The Agent causes the patient's cognitive state change from unknown to known by explaining or revealing the tricks or theory. In observance change event, the Agent is also a volitional person, and the Figural entity is an abstract rule, law, or commandment. The Agent may bring the rule or law into nullity if he or she violates the rule or the law. But what is disrupted is the efficacy of the rule (or law) while the rule (or law) itself still exists. In emotional change events, there is no Agent, the volitional person is the Experiencer who experiences emotional change. He or she has no control over his or her emotional mood. It is the external stimulus that causes his or her facial expression to change. In temporal change events, there is neither Agent nor Experiencer. The elapse of time should be an objective natural phenomenon, but is subjectively described the substitution of one time period with another.

Table 6.2[①] **Semantic abstraction of *pò***

Event type	Agent	Figural entity	Result
physical separation	person	physical object	partition
relational change	leader, army	leader, army, country, city	win or lose; take over
cognitive change	person	cognitive state	cognitive state change
possessive change	person	money, time	house, accompany
observance change	person	rule, law, commandment	violation
emotional change	(person/experiencer)	facial expression	facial expression change
temporal change	(time period)	(time period)	time change

Generally speaking, as summarized in Table 6.2, the semantic content of *pò* becomes impoverished by and by, yet what remains unchanged is the topological image-schema of state change. But such impoverishment does not mean that *pò* has grammaticalized into a pragmatic marker. It just indicates that the concrete, spatial domain of reading embedded in this image-schema is replaced by more abstract and more subjective readings (Sweetser 1988; Traugott and König 1991). For instance, although emotional change is an uncontrollable personal

---

① Since there is no Agent in emotional change and neither Agent nor Figural entity in temporal change, the semantic roles that seem to correspond to Agent and Figural entity are bracketed.

experience, it is embedded into the "Agent causes Figural entity to separate" schema of *pò*. Likewise, despite the fact that time goes by naturally without human involvement, temporal change is subjectively conceived as time period replacement.

6.3.2 Grammaticalization at the syntactic level

At the syntactic level, the syntactic status of *pò* undergoes de-categorization (Hopper 1991). *Pò* is relegated from the syntactic position of predicate verb to verb subordinate complement. In ancient Chinese, *pò* is predominantly used as a monosyllabic predicate verb with independent reading. For instance, in (6.16a–6.16b), *pò* functions as the predicate verb and denotes winning against enemies or taking over countries or cities. Moreover, as a verb, *pò* is modified by degree adverbials like *dà* (severely) and frequency adverbials like *lǚ* and *dié* (frequently) (6.16c–6.16f). But in stark contrast, Mandarin Chinese reveals that *pò* is more frequently used in resultative constructions and its reading is dependent on the local construction (Traugott and König 1991). Specifically, as a verb complement, it usually denotes the completion of the actions encoded by its preceding verbs. For instance, in (6.17a–6.17b), *pò* compounds with verbs like *xí* and *gōng*. These two verbs both mean "attack" and *pò* designates the successful completion of attacking. Likewise, in (6.17c–6.17d), *pò* collocates with verbs like *shí* (recognize) and *kàn* (see). These perception verbs denote mental analysis of something and *pò* complements the verbs with the reading of effectuation. For instance, *kàn* only means "see" while *kàn-pò* means "see through". In spite of such syntactic de-categorization, it is inappropriate to conclude that *pò* has grammaticalized into a verb suffix (Sun 1999). But to the extent that *pò* has been reassigned into a less prime category of verb complement, it can be concluded that *pò* has undergone grammaticalization at least at its incipient stage. Meanwhile, its lexical reading also has generalized from a specific process to only the general reading of "finish" or "completion". In this sense, the grammaticalization of *pò* resembles that of aspectual markers (Xu 2001; Hu 2005). But different from aspectual markers, *pò* denotes specific readings, although these readings are dependent on its collocated verbs.

(6.16)

a. EMCpoi75: 武王将素甲三千领，战一日，**破**纣之国。

    Wǔ wáng jiàng sù jiǎ sān-qiān lǐng, zhàn yī rì, pò Zhòu zhī guó.

    Wu king lead basic weapon three-thousand CL, fight one day, break Zhou DE country

    "King Wu led three thousand soldiers who were armed with three-thousand weapons, fought for one day and finally took over the country of Zhou."

b. LMCpoi351: 及董卓**破**京师，收其美人，焚其堂馆。

    Jí Dǒng Zhuó pò Jingshī, shōu qí měi rén, fén qí tángguǎn.

    when Dong Zhuo took over capital, received its beautiful women, fired its mansions

    "When Dong Zhuo broke the capital city, he took over all those beautiful women and fired the mansions."

c. EMCpoi88: 齐因起兵击魏，大**破**之马陵。

    Qí yīn qǐ bīng jī Wèi, dà pò zhī Mǎ Líng.

    Qi because assign soldiers attack Wei, utterly break it Ma Ling

    "Qi declared war against Wei and broke it in Ma Ling."

d. EMCpoi106: 秦攻赵于长平，大**破**之，引兵而归。

    Qín gōng Zhào yú Cháng Píng, dà pò zhī, yǐn bīng ér guī.

    Qin attack Zhao at Chang Ping, utterly broke it, lead soldiers and back

    "Qin attacked Zhao at Chang Ping, utterly broke it and then led soldiers back."

e. EMandpoi503: 晞屡**破**强寇，雄名甚盛。

Xī lǚ pò qiáng kòu, xióng míng shèn shèng.

Xi often break strong enemy, great reputation very popular

"Xi broke the strong enemies all the time and won a very good reputation."

f. MdMandpoi640: 自出兵河北，迭**破**群盗······

Zì chū bīng Hé Běi, dié pò qún dào ...

since lead soldiers He Bei, often broke group thieves

"He led soldiers to attack He Bei and broke group thieves several times."

(6.17)

a. MdMandpoi2: 袭**破**桂林、郁林、思恩。

Xí pò Guì Lín, Yù Lín, Sī En.

attack break Gui Lin, Yu Lin, Si En

"Attacked and took over cities like Gui Lin, Yu Lin and Si En."

b. MdMandpoi42: 我们不论王全斌到与不到，且设计攻**破**此寨。

Wǒ men bú lùn Wáng Quánbīn dào yǔ bú dào, qiě shèjì gōngpò cǐ zhài

we not mention Wang Quanbin come and not come, and devise plan attack this fastness

"No matter Wang Quanbin come or not, we should devise a plan to attack this fastness."

c. MdMandpoi69: 索性被警察识**破**了，纠众来拿我。

Suǒ xìng bèi jingchá shí pò le, jiū zhòng lái ná wǒ.

simply BEI police see through-LE, ask public DEIXIS catch me

"The worst thing is nothing more than I am seen through by the police and he asks people to arrest me."

d. MdMandpoi101: 此番刘英谋为不轨，早被一个人看**破**情形。

Cǐ fān Liú Yīng móu wéi bù guǐ, zǎo bèi yī gè rén kàn

pò qíngxíng.

this time Liu Ying plot do not legal, early BEI a CL person see through situation

"When Liu Ying plotted to do things illegal this time, he was seen through by a person."

To get a better understanding of the grammaticalization of *pò*, we collect different collocation patterns of *pò* across the four chronological stages. These collocation patterns include *pò*+NP, NP+*pò*, *pò*+V and V+*pò*. *Pò*+NP refers to the pattern in which *pò* is used as a monosyllabic predicate verb (6.18a–6.18b). NP+*pò* shows the pattern when *pò* appears in the intransitive structure (6.18c–6.18d). *Pò*+V is the compounded pattern of *pò* and other verbs in which *pò* stays in the first verb position (6.18e–6.18f). V+*pò* is a resultative construction that emerges from the co-occurrence of *pò* with a widespread range of verbs. In such cases, *pò* functions as the complement of verbs (6.18g–6.18h). Table 6.3 and Table 6.4 demonstrate the diachronic distribution of these four *pò* constructions in their extensional and intentional usages respectively. Figure 6.5 and Figure 6.6 are their corresponding bar charts, from which we can get a clearer picture of the developing trend of these four construction patterns.

(6.18)

a. MdMandpoe1022: 他从金蛋中**破**壳而出……

    Tā cóng jīn dàn zhōng pò ké ér chū ...

    he from golden egg inside break shell and out ...

    "He broke the shell and came out from the golden egg ..."

b. MdMandpoi1031: 有一次，竟以五百人**破**伪抚王的十三万之众于扬州地方。

    Yǒu yī cì, jìng yǐ wǔ bǎi rén pò wěi fǔ wáng de shí sān wàn zhī zhòng yú Yángzhōu dì fang.

    have one time, unexpectedly with five-hundred people break pseudo Fu King DE one hundred and thirty thousand population at Yang Zhou

"Once, he fought against the one hundred and thirty thousand soldiers of pseudo King Fu with only five hundred people at Yang Zhou."

c. LMCpoe366: 忽爆作巨声，头已**破**矣。

Hū   bào zuò jù shēng,   tóu yǐ   pò yǐ.

suddenly explode loud sound, head already wound

"There was a sudden explosion with a loud sound and his head was wounded already."

d. MdMandpoi29: 至江宁城**破**……

Zhì Jiāng Níng chéng pò ...

when Jiang Ning city break ...

"When the city Jiang Ning was broken ..."

e. EMandpoe388: 拿两只鸡来杀了，**破**洗了。

ná liǎng zhī jī   lái   shā le, pò xǐ le.

take two CL chicken DEIXIS kill-LE, cut wash-LE

"He took two chicken here, killed it and then cut it open and washed it."

f. MdMandpoi802: 然后此之隐患，所关甚大，即令限三日内**破**获。

Rán hòu cǐ zhī yǐn huàn, suǒ guān shèn dà,   jí lìng xiàn sān   rì nèi   pò huò.

then this hidden trouble, related most important, then constrain three days within uncover

"The hidden troubles were related to most important things, so he asked people to uncover it within three days."

g. MdMandpoe498: 碎石块溅在白亮的腮帮子上，崩**破**了十几处。

Suì shí kuài jiàn zài bái liàng de sāi bāng zi shàng, bēng pò le shí jǐ chù.

smashed stone splash LOC Bai Liang DE cheek, break LE ten some places

"The smashed stones splashed on Bai Liang's cheek and

broke more than ten parts of his cheek."

h. MdMandpoi858: 一路行去，并未被人察破，但无意中却露出**破**绽来。

Yī lù xíng qù, bìng wèi bèi rén chá pò, dàn wúyì
zhōng què lùchū pòzhàn lái.

all way walk DEIXIS, and not BEI people see through, but
unintentionally middle but reveal identity secret DEIXIS

"He was not seen through by anyone all the way and
unintentionally revealed his identity."

Table 6.3 Extensional usages of *pò*

Patterns	EMC Frequency	Ratio	LMC Frequency	Ratio	EMand Frequency	Ratio	MdMand Frequency	Ratio
pò+NP	114	0.59	233	0.34	433	0.29	261	0.21
NP+*pò*	25	0.13	217	0.31	286	0.19	185	0.15
pò+V	37	0.19	37	0.05	48	0.03	274	0.22
V+ *pò*	17	0.09	206	0.3	740	0.49	513	0.42
Total	193	1	693	1	1507	1	1233	1

Table 6.4 Intensional usages of *pò*

Patterns	EMC Frequency	Ratio	LMC Frequency	Ratio	EMand Frequency	Ratio	MdMand Frequency	Ratio
pò+NP	245	0.56	1134	0.66	1079	0.57	683	0.43
NP+ *pò*	103	0.23	148	0.09	240	0.13	212	0.13
pò+V	61	0.14	121	0.07	121	0.06	167	0.1
V+*pò*	30	0.07	326	0.19	468	0.25	529	0.33
Total	439	1	1730	1	1908	1	1591	1

A first glance at these two charts finds that monosyllabic usages of *pò*+NP
decrease significantly. On the contrary, its resultative construction V+*pò* shows
a pronounced increasing trend. Such opposite developing trends indicate that
pò is less often used as a verb to denote the process of causing something
to separate than as a complement to denote the completion of actions. To be

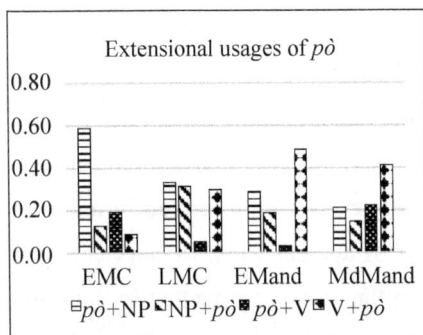

Figure 6.5 Extensional usages of *pò*

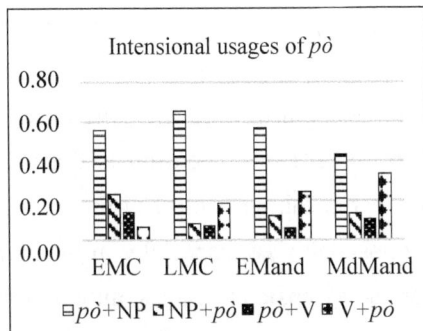

Figure 6.6 Intensional usages of *pò*

specific, although in ancient Chinese *pò* is frequently used as a predicate verb, it appears more often as a complement in the form of V+*pò* in Mandarin Chinese. It seems that all kinds of verbs which lead to a certain result can collocate with *pò* in a given scenario. For instance, Mandarin Chinese has V+*pò* forms like *kē-pò* (knock-break), *shuāi-pò* (throw-break), *hǎn-pò* (yell-break), *tī-pò* (kick-break), *chá-pò* (observe-break), *kàn-pò* (see-break), etc. Meanwhile, the disyllabic form *pò*+V also shows the verbal usages of *pò*, but this structure is constrained in range. In both ancient Chinese and Mandarin Chinese, we can only find a limited number of *pò*+V such as *pò*-huài (break-ruin), *pò*-chú (break-remove), *pò*-kuì (break-burst), *pò*-jiě (break-solve), *pò*-miè (break-eliminate), and *pò*-luàn (break-disturb). NP+*pò* shows the intransitive use of *pò* in which *pò* only denotes a general result of breaking. This form is also limited in frequency, thus is not further elaborated. Generally speaking, *pò* has changed from a verb to a verb complement. This finding is consistent with prior syntactic studies (Xu 2001; Hu 2005) and also testifies to our statement that *pò* has undergone grammaticalization at least at its incipient stage.

A further scrutinization of these two charts reveals that the grammaticalization of *pò* shows a register-based variation (Hopper 1991), particularly in terms of the collocational structure of *pò*+NP. Specifically speaking, the descending trend in the usage of *pò*+NP is less significant in the intensional domain than in the extensional domain. From the intensional usages of *pò,* it is still possible to catch hold of a great number of *pò*+NP forms. Needless to say, in ancient Chinese, *pò*+NP is widely used in descriptions of conquering armies, destroying cities as well as overcoming military tactics. What needs our attention is that even in Mandarin Chinese, the winning against or taking control of the opposite country is still described in terms of monosyllabic *pò*, especially in the narration of ancient wars. In stark contrast, for the extensional usages, although monosyllabic *pò* is prevalent in denoting object separation in ancient Chinese. It is confined to a very limited number of idiomatic patterns like *pò-tǔ-ér-chū* (break-soil-and-out), *pò-mén-ér-rù* (break-door-and-in), *pò-ké-ér-chū* (break-shell-and-out) in Mandarin. Such differences suggest that there are register-based variations in the grammaticalization of lexical items. In this case, the grammaticalization of *pò* mainly takes place in denoting the physical separation of objects but is rather restricted in denoting the winning against or taking over of cities or countries. To corroborate this finding, further cross-domain studies should be conducted in the future.

6.4 Diachronic conceptual variation trajectory of intensional *pò*

To sum up the historical development of intensional *pò*, Figure 6.7 charts the diachronic trajectory and the semantic interaction of the multiple readings of *pò*. The emergence and disappearance of various readings of *pò* fully illustrate that the huge gulf between synchrony and diachrony envisaged by Saussure can be closed (Weinreich, Labov and Herzog 1968: 120; Croft 2006). Synchrony reflects diachronic semantic change and diachrony within synchrony equals variation (Geeraerts 1997: 6). This part further explicates the evolution of *pò* upon a fuller picture of its diachronic trajectory.

Firstly, the diachronic trajectory thoroughly displays the referential pathway of each intensional reading. Motivated with explicit extensional origins, various readings of *pò* emerge in succession across the four chronological stages. Some readings are stabilized all through the four stages, some die out in later stages, some crop up in a certain stage and disappear in the subsequent stage, and others come into being in very recent times. To be specific, the physical reading "to separate an object to disrupt its function" and four of its five derived readings "to win against" (A), "to take over" (B), "to damage" (C), "to scare" (M) came into being as early as in West Han and maintained a fairly smooth developing trend all along the later stages. The exception is that the idiomatic reading of "to succeed" (D), although cropped up in the Tang and Song dynasties, became stabilized only after the Ming dynasty. Among the three readings extended from "to take over" (B), "to go against" (L) and "to change from one state to another state" (N) showed up in the Six Dynasties and are still widely used in Mandarin. In contrast, "to start happening" (O) did not crop up until the Song dynasty, died out between five dynasties and the Ming dynasty, and came into being again in the Ming dynasty. The physical reading of "to separate an object to remove impediment" showed up in East Han and gradually disappeared after the Qing dynasty. The intensional readings derived from this lineage include "to get rid of" (G) and the two cause-result pairs. Among them, "to get rid of" (G) existed in parallel with its physical reading, appearing from Eastern Han and disappearing after Qing. Among the two extended cause-result pairs, "to tell sb about sth" (I) and "to know what sb/sth means" (H) respectively came into being in the Six Dynasties and the Tang dynasty, but both died out after Qing. Although "to make sb know" (F) and "to discover sth" (E) did not appear until the Song dynasty, they have remained popular readings of *pò* until now. The third physical reading "to separate objects to make new use" emerged in Six Dynasties and faded away after Qing. Its extended reading "to pay money for sth" (J) appeared also in the Six Dynasties and is still in use in Mandarin. The further extended reading "to spend time doing sth" (K) sprang up in the Ming dynasty and remains the intensional reading of *pò* in Mandarin.

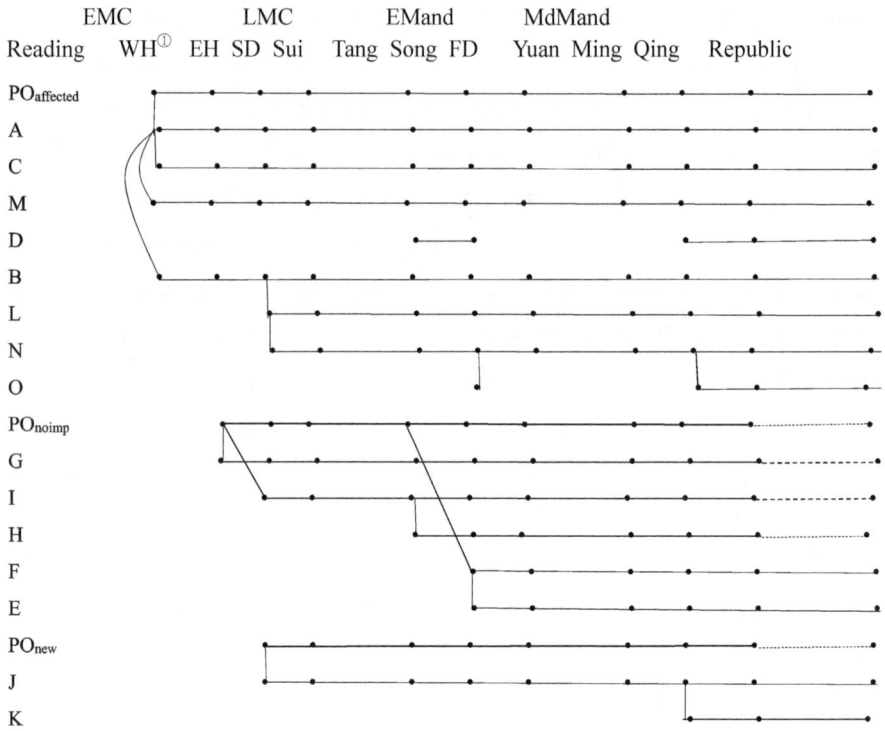

Figure 6.7 The diachronic trajectory of *pò*

Secondly, these multiple extensional readings of *pò* demonstrate the strong referential power and conceptual adaptability of lexical items (Robert 2008). Despite the dying out of certain extensional origins, the demotivated intensional readings can still survive. As shown in Figure 6.7, the physical reading "to separate objects to remove impediment" fails to subsist in Mandarin, but two of its intensional readings "to discover sth" (E) and "to make sb know" (F) turn out to become two important readings of *pò*. Similarly, although the physical reading "to separate objects for further use" faded away after the Qing dynasty, its extended readings like "to pay money for sth" and "spend time doing sth" are still widespread in Mandarin. On the one hand, such diachronic development verifies our finding in Chapter 4 that the extensional usages of *pò* gradually narrow down to "to separate objects to disrupt their function". On the

---

① WH stands for Western Han, EH for Eastern Han, SD for Six Dynasties, FD for Five Dynasties.

other hand, the emergence and subsistence of the multiple intensional readings of *pò* demonstrate that there exists a cross-domain correspondence between extensional references and intensional readings. Intensional readings always arise from their extensional usages and even when the extensional usages have died out, these intensional readings might still subsist. One important reason for their subsistence should be attribute to their firm ground in social-cultural development. For instance, the emergence and subsistence of intensional readings like E (to discover sth), F (to make sb know sth), H (to know what sb means), and I (to explain) are to a great extent grounded in the flourishment of Buddhism particularly in the Six Dynasties, the Tang as well as the Song dynasty. These intensional readings are especially constrained to the Buddhist scriptures. Only after the Ming dynasty, these readings gradually have broken away from scriptures and have been widely used in general texts. Likewise, although "to go against law or commandment" (L) arose from the intensional reading "to take over" (B), it first appeared in Buddhist scripture in the Six Dynasties and designated the violation of religious disciplines or commandments. In later stages, this intensional reading further extended to the violation of rules, laws, and stipulations.

Finally, the diachronic trajectory of *pò* to some extent reveals the cognitive evolution of human beings and records the social development of human society. Further speaking, language is a historical entity, and its change and variation are closely tied to human cognition and social-cultural development (Traugott and Dasher 2002: xi; Wong 2008; Geeraerts 2018). The Chinese character *pò*, in its etymon, refers to the breaking of stones. Such a pictograph origin already showcases the cognitive and cultural motivations in the employment of this word to designate "to separate object". Moreover, this word is extended to denote the separation of a wider range of objects and varied types of separation, thus giving rise to the differential extensional usages of *pò*. Then driven by cognitive mechanisms like metaphor and metonymy, and motivated by social-cultural backgrounds like war and Buddhism, the intentional readings of *pò* further extend from physical separation to abstract separations such as defeating the enemy country, taking over cities, violating commandments, and seeing through tricks. This extensional process fully shows that lexical items are subject to deformation and variation in the context of social-cultural changes. In this extensional process, the semantic content of *pò* is sifted out by and by and only the semantic core of state change remains. Generally speaking, the trend of language evolution reflected in the semantic change of *pò* reveals that language is the cumulative result of purposeful human activities restricted by the environmental conditions. Language change encompasses shared human cognition and socially distributed knowledge.

6.5 Summary

In general, the intensional readings of *pò* evolve in systematic ways across time. The diachronic semantic development of *pò* across the physical and metaphorical domains verifies our hypothesis that the intensional readings of lexical items always have their extensional origins. The multiple intensional readings of *pò* on the one hand demonstrate the malleability of language in adapting to differential scenarios or contexts and on the other hand reveal that diachronic variations are regulated by mechanisms of metaphor and metonymy. In addition, it is proved that semantic extension and grammaticalization can be coalesced into one continuum. Semantic extension feeds grammaticalization. In this case of *pò,* although its intensional readings have abstracted away from physical separation to emotional and temporal changes, it is still at the incipient stage of grammaticalization.

CHAPTER 7

Conclusions

This study explores conceptual variations of Chinese break verbs under the theoretical framework of DPS. It extends beyond previous synchronic extra-typological studies by further bringing into view a diachronic intra-typological perspective on conceptual variation. This chapter wraps up this study first with its general conclusions sketched in section 7.1. Then a tentative model of diachronic conceptual variation is proposed in section 7.2. Implications of this study are presented in section 7.3. Limitations that need to be further addressed in future studies are pointed out in section 7.4. Finally, directions for future studies are put forward in section 7.5.

7.1 General conclusions

To conclude this study, this section first summarizes the diachronic conceptual variation of break verbs in terms of their diachronic pathways and the underlying cognitive mechanisms respectively in section 7.1.1 and section 7.1.2. Then our proposed revisions on the theoretical framework of DPS are elaborated in section 7.1.3.

7.1.1 Diachronic conceptual variation pathways

Firstly, speaking of extensional *pò*, the conceptual range of extensional *pò* demonstrates a diachronic specialization pathway across the four historical stages of EMC, LMC, EMand, and MdMand. Its prototypical core moves away from conceptual variables like *tender*, *new*, and *pieces* toward *fleshy* and *affected*. Its conceptual range narrows down from denoting varying events of separation state change to only describing disruptive events of separation state change. Specifically, in EMC, it is broad in conceptual range and applicable to denoting the partition of tender and fleshy objects (like fruit, vegetables, fish, and beef) for new use, the disintegration of stiff objects (like door, wall) to get rid of impediments as well as the wounding or injury of body parts. In LMC, it gives up the depiction of the separation of tender or fleshy objects for further use and constrained itself only to the description of body part injury and separating stiff objects to remove impediments. In EMand, its conceptual range further narrows down and is limited only to the disruptive separation of fleshy objects and flexible objects. By MdMand, it further readjusts its conceptual range at its conceptual boundary and includes the disruptive separation, of a wider range of objects like fragile, stiff, tender, flexible as well as fleshy objects.

This finding supports Winters' (1987) argument that when enough changes have occurred in the categorical structure, the core meaning will also change and so does the prototypicality. It also suggests that Geeraerts' (1997) proposal that prototypical centers of lexical items are always stable should be revised. This is because prototypical centers of lexical items are not absolutely but relatively stable. As the conceptual ranges of lexical items vary across time, their prototypical centers adjust to the variation accordingly.

Secondly, conceptual boundaries between *pò, qiē*, and *kāi* display an increasingly clear-cut pathway. From EMC to MdMand, conceptual boundaries between these three keywords have changed from conceptual overlapping to conceptual discreteness. In EMC, extensional *pò* is broad in its conceptual range and extensional *qiē* and *kāi* are partially overlapped with it. From EMC to LMC, the conceptual boundaries between *pò, qiē* and *kāi* change from *qiē* and *kāi*'s partial overlapping with *pò* to a side-by-side alignment along the first dimension because some conceptual variable levels like *new, noimp, clean* and *reversible* are further absorbed into the referential ranges of *qiē* and *kāi*. In EMand, their conceptual boundaries become rather clear-cut compared with those in EMC and LMC, but conceptual ranges of *pò* and *kāi* are still contiguous around variable levels like *nonincremental, onset, fleshy*. Nonetheless, in MdMand, as these variable levels are further incorporated into the referential range of *kāi*, the conceptual boundary between *pò* and *kāi* becomes even more definite. At this stage, the division of labor of these three verbs in segmenting and categorizing events of separation state change becomes more stabilized. Each of them has formed their own prototypical structure with their prototypical usages at the core. The individual usages and variable levels that fall within their prototypical cores demonstrate maximum discriminability (Rosch 1973).

In contrast to previous synchronic studies (Levin and Rappaport Hovav 1995, 2008; Pye et al. 1996; Majid et al. 2007a, 2007b; Croft 2012, 2015), this finding reveals that conceptual boundaries between *pò, qiē*, and *kāi* should be viewed from a dynamic perspective and a diachronic one. These three lexical items are not stable in their conceptual ranges and thus their conceptual boundaries do not remain constant. With this finding, controversies on the classification of these three lexical items are resolved and their dynamic conceptual boundaries are visualized. *Pò* and *kāi* are similar in their conceptual ranges in EMC, *pò* and *qiē* become more similar in LMC and EMand, but they are each responsible for categorizing different events of separation state change in MdMand. Further, cross-linguistic comparison of event categorization is significant, because it reveals typological universals. But it should be highlighted that the diachronic exploration of event categorization is equally important, because it reveals human cognitive development.

Finally, intensional *pò* exhibits an expansion pathway. It has expanded from the physical state change domain to six abstract state change domains, including relational change, cognitive change, possessive change, observance change, emotional change as well as temporal change. In this process, intensional *pò* displays fifteen intensional readings. These readings arise along three diachronic lineages. Along the first lineage, intensional *pò* develops from denoting separating objects for a new use to spending time working on something and spending money to buy something. The second lineage is the longest and the most important developing line. Along this lineage, intensional *pò* evolves from disintegrating stones, instruments, and body parts, to winning against enemy, to taking over cities or countries, to breaking up rules and laws, to changing emotions, and further to changing time. Along the third lineage, intensional *pò* extends from expressing separating objects to removing impediments, to getting rid of irritation and worries, to explaining a theory, and to disclosing schemes. Moreover, in its intensional expansion, intensional *pò* becomes increasingly impoverished in its semantic core. What remains unchanged is the topological image-schema of state change. Such impoverishment, however, does not indicate that *pò* has grammaticalized into a pragmatic marker. It just evinces that the concrete, physical domain of reading embedded in this image-schema is replaced by a more abstract and more subjective domain of readings (Sweetser 1988; Traugott and König 1991).

The significance of this finding resides in its demonstration of the operationalization of bringing together extensional usages and intensional readings in accounting for semantic change. Previous studies on semantic change (Hopper 1991; Jiang 2005, 2006; Dong 2009) overly emphasize the transition from one semantic sense to another but overlook the extensional origin of each intensional reading, let alone the multiple extensional origins of different intensional readings. Moreover, this finding also shows the importance of taking into consideration the collocating arguments of the verb. As demonstrated in previous studies (Jia and Wu 2015), the semantic change of a verb is disclosed by its agent, patient, theme.

Moving beyond the above-mentioned research findings and research advancements, the correlation between conceptual variation and syntactic change is also worth mentioning at this stage. In terms of syntactic change, previous studies have already revealed that *pò* has changed from a monomorphemic verb to a verb complement (Xu 2001; Hu 2005). The formation of V+*pò* is motivated by the cognitive mechanism of reanalysis (Xu 2001). As for conceptual variation, this study shows that the conceptual range of *pò* has undergone a specialization trajectory. *Pò* has changed from denoting all kinds of events of separation state change to only denoting disruptive events of separation state change. Such a specialization trajectory is motivated by the cognitive mechanism of reorganization. Based on further reflection on the correlation between syntactic change and conceptual variation, we would like to propose it is the reorganization of the conceptual range that gives rise to the reanalysis of the syntactic pattern. That is, when *pò* is specialized to denoting disruptive separation, its syntactic pattern is synchronically more likely to take the form of V+*pò*. This proposal is also applicable to *qiē* and *kāi*. The specialization of *qiē* and *kāi* is also accompanied by their syntactic changes. The credibility of this proposal waits for further discussion and verification.

7.1.2　Cognitive mechanisms

As for the underlying cognitive mechanisms, this study proposes that the conceptual specialization of *pò* and the conceptual boundary variation between *pò, qiē,* and *kāi* are driven by the cognitive mechanism of reorganization. It is the reorganization of those multiple conceptual variables underlying the conceptual system of events of separation state change that accounts for the conceptual specialization of *pò* and the conceptual boundary variation between *pò, qiē* and *kāi*. Although this mechanism is mentioned in previous studies (Langacker 1987; Geeraerts 1997), it has not been explicitly verified in empirical research. In this sense, this study contributes an empirical verification for the operation of reorganization.

Driven by this cognitive mechanism, extensional *pò* has gradually narrowed down in its conceptual range. In EMC, it is sensitive neither to the perceptual nor to the functional variable. As long as the affected object is separated, the events are categorized as *pò*. But in later stages, the underlying conceptual variables of events of separation state change reorganize their matrix combination. Those events of separation state change categorized in terms of *pò* are gradually reduced to the variable value of *fleshy* along with the material composition variable, to the variable value of *functionally affected* along with the functional change variable, and to the variable value of *partial* along with the endstate variable. As a result, extensional *pò* becomes more susceptible to variable levels of *fleshy*, *partial*, and *functionally affected*. Only those separation events that involve body part wounding are more likely to be categorized in terms of *pò*.

In the same vein, driven by the mechanism of reorganization, *pò*, *qiē*, and *kāi* keep adjusting their labor division in categorizing events of separation state change. Overlapping areas among these three keywords are the most sensitive areas subject to reorganization. In EMC, conceptual variables enclosed within *pò* and *qiē*'s overlapping area include *fleshy*, *predictable* and *clean*, and those within *pò* and *kāi*'s overlapping area include *partial* and *noimped*. But along the timeline, the underlying conceptual variables keep moving and adjusting. In LMC, conceptual variables within the above-mentioned overlapping areas have dispersed. But a new overlapping area between *qiē* and *kāi* come into being, incorporating variable levels like *nonincremental*, *onset*, *partial*, *fleshy*, and *flexible*. In EMand, both *pò* and *qiē* intersect with *kāi*, and their overlapping areas incorporate variable levels like *flexible*, *partial*, *nonincremental*, and *onset*. In MdMand, conceptual variables within the overlapping areas have scattered. The underlying conceptual variables are further reorganized and form three independent clusters. In consequence, *pò*, *qiē*, and *kāi* are each responsible for denoting prototypically different events of separation state change.

The mechanisms that drive intensional development are mainly metaphor and metonomy. The following three chaining shifts demonstrate how intensional readings are derived from different extensional usages. For one thing, metaphor and metonomy are two overwhelming mechanisms that motivate the rise of intensional readings. With regard to metaphor, it is the schematic relation of similarity that promotes the semantic extension from, for instance, emotional change to temporal change and from paying money for sth to spending time doing sth. As for metonomy, it is the schematic relation of contiguity that makes it possible to realize the semantic extension from disruptive physical separation to winning against the enemy and taking over countries. For another, intensional *pò* is becoming increasingly impoverished in its semantic core. Its syntactic function has changed from a predicate verb to a verb complement and its semantic function has changed from encoding both action and result to only denoting result. In this sense, *pò* is undergoing a process of grammaticalization at its incipient stage. It is still specific in its extensional reference but is becoming increasingly abstract in its intensional readings. In addition, in terms of the corresponding relation between extensional references and intensional readings, on the one hand, it is always possible to trace the extensional origins of intensional readings and on the other hand, it is manifest that intensional readings develop relatively independently in its further evolution.

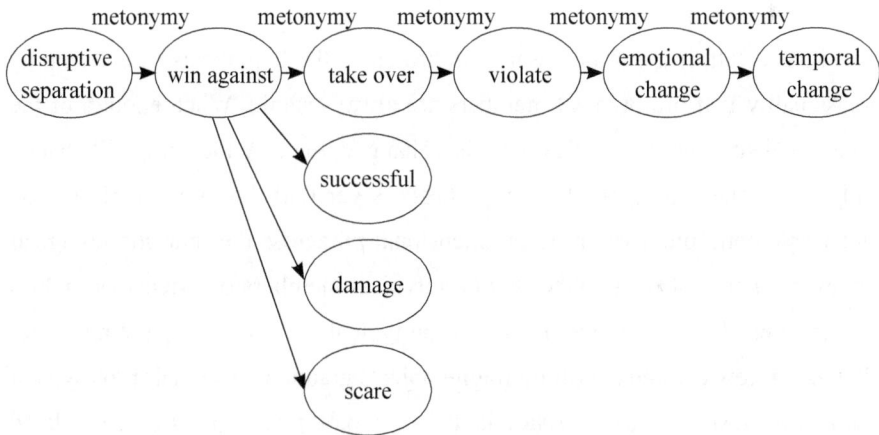

Figure 7.1　Chaining shift 1 of *pò*

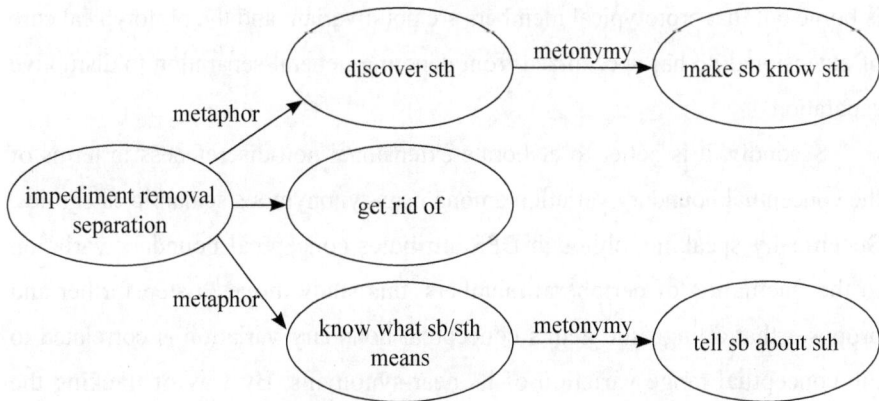

Figure 7.2　Chaining shift 2 of *pò*

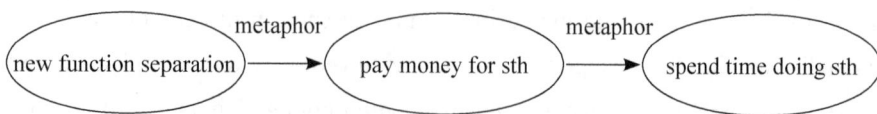

Figure 7.3 Chaining shift 3 of *pò*

7.1.3 Proposed revisions of DPS

This study frames itself under the theoretical framework of DPS. Its argument starts with the extensional and intensional hypotheses that DPS argues for. But these hypotheses are not accepted as they are. They are further revised and corroborated with those extensional and intentional studies conducted in Chapters 4, 5, and 6.

First of all, it is not necessarily indicated in the hypothesis of extensional non-equality that prototypical members are always stable. When enough of the categorical structure of a lexical item has changed, the core meaning will change and so will the prototype. This hypothesis is verified through examining the diachronic conceptual variation of extensional *pò* across the four chronological stages in Chapter 4. It is found that prototypical members of extensional *pò* do not remain stable all the time. Instead, prototypical usages like separating tender objects for new use and smashing fragile objects gradually lose their prototypical status from EMC to LMC. What take up the prototypical core is usages related to the disruptive separation of body parts in EMand and MdMand. In this way, it is borne out that prototypical members are not invariant and the prototypical core of extensional *pò* has specialized from denoting general separation to disruptive separation.

Secondly, it is better to elaborate extensional non-discreteness in terms of the conceptual boundary variation among near-synonymous semantic categories. Specifically speaking, although DPS attributes conceptual boundary variation to the fluctuation of peripheral members, this study moves a step further and proposes that a linguistic item's conceptual boundary variation is correlated to the conceptual range variation of its near-synonyms. By way of tracking the conceptual boundaries between extensional *pò*, *qiē*, and *kāi* in Chapter 5, it is proved that lexical items of the same lexical field cooperate with each other in their categorization of a corresponding conceptual field. The conceptual variation of any lexical item is correlated to and will give rise to adjustment in its labor division with other lexical items in characterizing a certain conceptual field.

Finally, the intensional hypotheses framed within DPS emphasize the clustered structure and encyclopedic nature of intensional readings. This study states that intensional non-equality and non-discreteness should also pay attention to the cross-domain correspondence between extensional references and intensional readings. It is always possible to figure out the extensional origins of the intensional readings of a lexical item. Even when their extensional usages have faded away, the intensional readings will still subsist and can be further extended to give rise to novel intensional readings. For instance, the rise of those multiple intensional readings of *pò* always originate from its extensional usages. Three diachronic lineages along which intensional readings of *pò* develop are delineated. In this intensional evolution process, although some of the extensional usages of *pò* have died out, those intensional readings they give rise to are maintained all along.

7.2 A tentative model of diachronic conceptual variation

In terms of the three case studies on the extensional and intensional conceptual variations of break verbs, this study proposes a tentative spatial model for diachronic conceptual variation. This model is proposed to instruct our future study on the lexical field of BREAK verbs. In what follows, section 7.2.1 provides a general picture of this spatial model. Section 7.2.2 details its working principles.

7.2.1 A model of diachronic conceptual variation

As shown in Figure 7.4, this multivariate model is a twin-track model.

It captures both extensional and intensional conceptual variations. The extensional level encompasses all the extensional usages subsumed under one single intensional reading. In contrast, the intensional level embraces all the rest multiple intensional readings. To explore the diachronic development of a linguistic item, both its extensional level and intensional level should be taken into account.

With regard to the extensional level, linguistic items are thoroughly explored in terms of their extensional usages. These extensional usages are inherently network nodes at the juncture of numerous conceptual variables and their level is composed of different variable levels. As formulated in Figure 7.4, A, F, M, P, and G are underlying variables that drive the formation of numerous extensional usages. For instance, A1F1M1P1G1 constitutes one extensional usage and A1F1M2P2G2 forms another one. For one thing, the extensional range of linguistic items are made up of extensional usages which are conceptually organized by means of a prototypical structure. Prototypical extensional usages are located at the prototypical center and nonprototypical extensional usages at the boundary. For another, linguistic items of the same lexical field usually categorize a certain conceptual field. Therefore, it is usual to find linguistic items each responsible for characterizing a different segment of their shared conceptual field. For instance, as displayed in Figure 7.4, W^a and W^b are two conceptually intersected linguistic items. They have their own prototypical structures and each characterizes a different portion of their shared conceptual field. But it should be noted that such labor division among linguistic items is dynamic, because when the prototypical structure of any linguistic item changes, its conceptual relation will change concomitantly. For instance, when W^a narrows down its prototypical structure, W^b may expand its prototypical structure so as to adapt to their labor division change.

In parallel with the extensional level, intensional readings of linguistic items are also prototypically organized. Along with extensional development, intensional readings are also dynamically evolving. On the one hand, the two parallel levels are not independent but closely related. It is always possible to

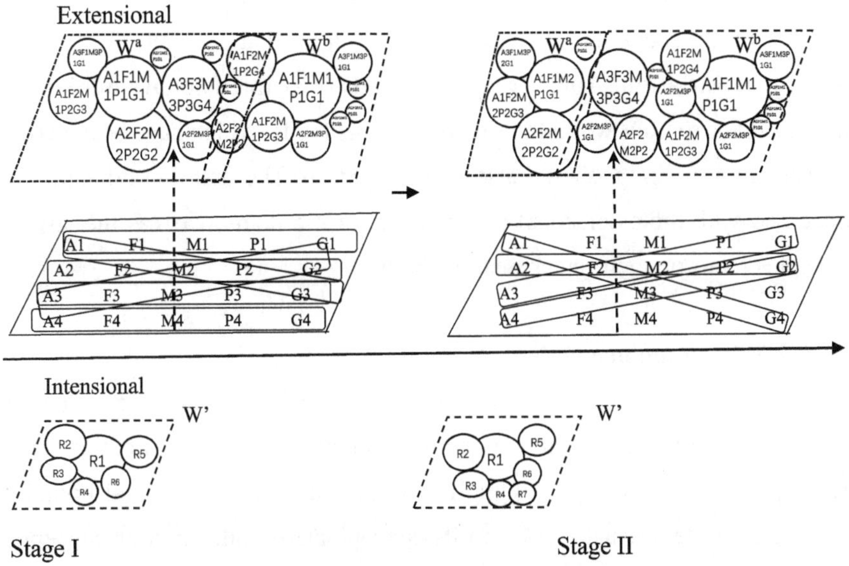

Figure 7.4 A multivariate model of diachronic conceptual variation

trace the extensional origins of the intensional readings. On the other hand, the diachronic development of intensional readings is relatively independent of its corresponding extensional evolution. The disappearance of extensional usages does not necessarily give rise to the fading away of their corresponding intensional readings. The emergence of certain extensional usages does not always result in the coming into being of novel intensional readings. For instance, despite the conceptual specialization of W^a in its extensional usages, its intensional readings remain stable across the two chronological stages (comparing W' in stage I and stage II). To be further, intensional readings are born out of extensional usages, it is not reasonable to talk about intensional readings without mentioning their extensional counterparts. But when these intensional readings become stabilized enough, they develop along their own track without being influenced by the conceptual narrowing or expanding of their extensional usages. Moreover, some intensional readings are further extended readings from the existing intensional readings. In such cases, intensional readings of linguistic items expand in their own right (like the emergence of R7)

253

without giving rise to any change in the extensional usages.

Generally speaking, this study proposes a unified account of diachronic conceptual variation. Apart from the extensional-intensional double-track elaborated above, four working principles of this model which have been verified in Chapters 4, 5, and 6 should also be summed up. The first two principles are concerned with the extensional usages of linguistic items whereas the last two principles focus on their intensional readings.

7.2.2 Working principles

The first principle is "conceptual adjustment". This principle involves either the realignment of the conceptual boundary or the rectification of the prototypical center. The narrowing or expansion at the conceptual boundary of a linguistic item usually leads to its conceptual specialization or conceptual expansion. The rectification of the prototypical center nonetheless gives rise to more pronounced variations, like the prototypical center shift from one prototypical member to another, or even conceptual shift from one physical domain to another. In chapter 4, we conducted an in-depth study on the prototypical categorical structure of *pò*. Through tracing extensional usages of *pò* across four chronological stages, we revealed that the prototypical core of *pò* has narrowed down from all kinds of separation to only disruptive separation. The conceptual boundary of *pò* also fluctuate flexibly with some peripheral members dying out and others coming into being. Apart from conceptual adjustment at the level of referential members, conceptual adjustment at the level of underlying conceptual variables is also worth mentioning. As demonstrated in Chapter 4, the referential specialization of *pò* is to a great extent motivated by the realignment of the intersection of conceptual variables like <functional change>, <material composition> and <endstate>, etc. This is because referential members are nodes at the intersection of different variable levels. With the dying out of some variable levels like new function, fragile objects, and breaking into pieces, referential members that have arisen from their combination also disappear.

"Conceptual reorganization" works as the second principle. The conceptual base for this working principle is the conceptual field. The terms "organization" and "reorganization" refer to the segmentation or re-segmentation of a particular conceptual field. Specifically speaking, semantically similar linguistic items or linguistic items of the same lexical field are identified as linguistic instruments for segmenting and organizing a particular conceptual field. The referential range of each linguistic item is inherently part of the conceptual field. As a result, the conceptual variation of any linguistic item will give rise to the reorganization of the conceptual field. Chapter 5 expounds in detail how three lexical items *pò*, *qiē*, and *kāi* is located the conceptual field of events of separation state change across the four chronological stages. In EMC, *pò* is fairly extensive in its referential range. *Qiē* and *kāi* are partially overlapped with *pò*. The prototypical core of *kāi* locates at the conceptual boundary of *pò*. But after decades of conceptual reorganization, in MdMand, the prototypical core and conceptual boundary of these three lexical items are distant from each other. Their division of labor in categorizing the conceptual field of separation becomes clearer. Generally speaking, language serves as an instrument for organizing our conceptualization of the physical world. Linguistic items are not studied as if they are autonomous, but as reflections of the conceptual organization (Geeraerts 1997: 7). Despite the fact that linguistic items remain stable in their formal structures, as conceptual containers, their conceptual structures do not remain static but are dynamically evolving across varying historical stages.

"Conceptual alignment" between extensional usages and intensional readings is another important principle in the exploration of semantic change and conceptual variation. Chapter 6 details how fifteen intensional readings of *pò* are derived from its numerous extensional usages. The alignment relationship between the extensional usages and its fifteen intensional readings manifests itself in two aspects. For one thing, whether in its extensional usages or intensional readings, *pò* is uniformly used to describe a change from one state to another. The extensional usages characterize physical state change, whereas intensional readings describe relational change, cognitive change, possessive change, observance change, emotional change as well as temporal change. Moreover, conceptual alignment between the extensional usages and intensional readings also resides in their functional parallels. That is why intensional readings of *pò* display three evolution lineages. For instance, in the first lineage, the extensional usages denote the separation of objects for further use. Correspondingly, the intensional readings denote spending money to get something or spending time working on something.

"Conceptual independence" is another principle concerning the parallel relationship between extensional usages and intensional readings. This principle indicates that although intensional readings are derived from extensional usages, their further evolution and development are not necessarily constrained by their extensional usages. As discussed in Chapter 6, among the fifteen intensional readings of *pò*, it is found that three of them are directly connected with the extensional usages, and nine of them are further extensions from these three intensional readings. And another three display a further grammaticalization trend from stage change to emotional and temporal change. Taking the second lineage as an instance, from extensional usages of *pò* like smashing stones, tearing clothes, and wounding body, develops the extensional reading of winning against the enemy, army, or a leader. Further, on the basis of this intensional reading, there appear more intensional readings like "to take control", "to damage", "to succeed", and "to become scared". These four intensional readings denote the consequence of winning against the opponent. Moreover, along with the intensional reading of "to take control", more schematic readings like "to go against the law", "to change emotional state" and "to start happening" gradually show up. These three intensional readings are far more abstract and more independent of the extensional usages of *pò*. These readings in fact indicate that *pò* is undergoing a process of grammaticalization, becoming increasingly impoverished. In this way, the intensional readings of *pò* are becoming more and more independent of their extensional usages.

7.3 Implications

This study stems from the controversial issue of whether there exist clear-cut conceptual boundaries among verbs like break, cut, and open. Correspondingly, the first implication of this diachronic study also lies in the aspect of conceptual boundary investigation. Admittedly, in previous investigations on boundary variation (Guerssel et al. 1985; Levin and Rappaport Hovav 1995, 2008; Bohnemeyer et al. 2007; Majid et al. 2007a, 2007b), the typological approach is a top priority. But this does not mean the cross-linguistic comparison is the only approach applicable to lexical category boundary exploration. This study suggests that a corpus-based diachronic approach should also be taken into consideration. In comparison with the typological approach, the diachronic approach demonstrates three explicit advantages. Firstly, a diachronic perspective allows a revelation of the dynamic evolution process of conceptual boundary variation. As found in this study, the conceptual boundaries between *pò*, *qiē* and *kāi* keep changing all through the four chronological stages. In contrast, the typological approach takes a snapshot of a certain synchronic period for cross-linguistic comparison. This results in a static view on the conceptual boundary of these semantically related lexical items. Secondly, a diachronic approach affords a systematic study on the linguistic representation and categorization of events of separation state change within one language. Through observing the representation and categorization changes, it is possible to understand how languages evolve in their characterization of the external world. Thirdly, cross-stage comparison indicates how human cognition develops in their categorization of the same event category. Such cognitive development is grounded in the advancement of social-culture and the progress of science and technology.

The second implication consists in the integration of extensional and intensional levels in semantic analysis. It is revealed that both extensional usages and intensional readings should be taken into consideration for two reasons. In the first place, intensional readings originate from extensional usages. Intensional readings are parallel with specific extensional usages. For instance, this study shows that intensional readings like "to explain" and "to reveal" are semantic extensions from extensional usages that denote separating objects so as to reveal their interior. Secondly, the integration of extensional and intensional levels contributes to a whole-trajectory investigation of lexical semantic change. The emergence and appearance of both extensional usages and intensional readings are explicitly displayed along this trajectory. The exact chronological time at which different intensional readings come into being is also demonstrated. Moreover, as noted above, semantic change feeds grammaticalization. A whole-trajectory exploration of semantic change indicates the direction of grammaticalization on the one hand and reveals the pathway and regularity of grammaticalization on the other hand.

Thirdly, although this study only centers on Chinese, a detailed analysis of semantic change across four chronological stages, in fact, constitutes an intra-typological study. Since Chinese has a long developing history, a comparison of the linguistic categorization of events of separation state change across its four chronological stages inherently forms a typological exploration. A typological analysis of the linguistic categorization of the four time periods reveals that categorization is neither universally determined nor varying unpredictably. Moreover, it is found that linguistic categorization is social-culturally grounded. Social development and cultural context greatly influence the human categorization of events of separation state change. The diachronic variation involved in linguistic categorization is predictable when all possible underlying variables are brought to view. For instance, by taking into account numerous variables like <material composition>, <functional change>, <endstate>, <mode of change>, it is found that <functional change> is the variable that assumes a high weight in driving the diachronic variation of *pò*.

In addition, the fourth implication resides in the combination of statistical methods and the theoretical framework of prototype theory. For one thing, the statistical methods make for the subjective investigation of semantic change and allows a relatively objective way of data analysis. MCA shows the association between individual usages and between numerous variable levels. Ctree and random forest uncover the weight assumed by different variables in determining the extensional usages of lexical items. For another, the incorporation of prototype theory offers an analytical prototypical structure for concept representation and concept analysis. Both extensional usages and intensional readings are viewed in terms of a prototypically-based conceptual structure. In this way, the prototypical status of different usages and readings is explicitly demonstrated by means of the prototypical structure. More importantly, the statistical method of MCA and prototype theory finely match with each other. Prototype theory argues for a prototypical structure. MCA correspondingly maps the individual usages into a prototypical structure with a centroid and a boundary. Meanwhile, prototype theory affords a cognitively efficient rationale for explicating such prototypical structures.

7.4 Limitations

The first limitation of this study we have to admit is our intentional underestimation of syntactic change. We constrain our research scope within diachronic conceptual variation and leave in-depth analysis on syntactic variation for future study. The major reason is that previous studies (Xu 2001, 2005; Hu 2005) have done far more work on syntactic variation than on conceptual variation. Although we to some extent have explored the chronological distribution of four syntactic structures of *pò* in 6.2.2, major parts of this book are on conceptual structures. In the same vein, in plotting the prototypical conceptual structure of the three targeted lexical items, only conceptual variables but no syntactic variables have been taken into consideration.

Secondly, Chapter 5 has addressed the conceptual boundary variations of three semantically similar lexical items, namely *pò*, *qiē*, and *kāi*. These three lexical items were chosen because their conceptual boundaries constitute a controversial issue in linguistics. They are all monomorphemic verbs and behaved similarly in ancient Chinese, thus are regarded as break verbs. But they are different in their syntactic collocation in Mandarin. *Pò and kāi* are more similar to each other. They both relegate to the slot subsequent to the main verb and function as verb complements. Nonetheless, *qiē* still keeps its main verb status. In this sense, their syntactic pattern should also be taken into consideration in our future study.

The third limitation is that diachronic variation at the intensional level is not processed with statistical algorithms. The diachronic trajectory of those multiple intensional readings is manually depicted based on related conceptual variables. Although our proposed multivariate model is twin-track, only the extensional track is statistically analyzed while the intensional track calls for further statistical devotion.

Another limitation is the limited range of break verbs that have been attended to. This study only deals with three break verbs. To systematically explore the categorization of events of separation state change, more break verbs should be taken into consideration in future studies.

7.5 Future directions

To make up for the above-mentioned research limitations, future studies will take the following measures.

Firstly, future diachronic studies on events of separation state change will attend to both conceptual variation and syntactic variation. The syntactic distribution of break verbs across different time periods will be summarized. The syntactic status of break verbs will also be kept track of. Semantic change at the semantic-syntactic interface will also be explored. In this way, the internal relation between conceptual change and syntactic change is expected to be revealed.

Secondly, syntactic variables like syntactic pattern, transitivity of the verb as well as the syntactic slot will also be incorporated into multivariate data analysis together with conceptual variables. In this sense, a complete behavioral profile (BP) (Gries 2006; Divjak and Gries 2006) of the targeted lexical items will be yielded. As demonstrated in Table 7.1, semantic variables include those variables that have been considered in this study, and more relevant variables like with or without agent, animacy, and volition will also be taken into account. Syntactic variables include both the argument structure and the transitivity of the verbs. With this BP, a more comprehensive analysis of break verbs is expected to be conducted. Not only MCA but also MDS algorithms can be freely made use of for mapping spatial distribution of lexical items.

Table 7.1 BP vectors and levels

General level	Type of ID tag	ID tag	ID tag levels
Semantic	Agent	agent	with, without
		animacy	animate, inanimate
		volition	volitional, nonvolitional
		functional change	affected, new, noimped, neutral
		initiation of force	onset, extended
	Figure	material composition	fragile, fleshy, flexible, stiff
	Change	locus predictability	predictable, unpredictable
		change pattern	incremental, nonincremental
	Transition type + Ground	endstate	partial, pieces, surface
		separation mode	clean, messy
		reversibility	reversible, irreversible
Syntactic	Argument structure	construction	simple, causative, serial, resultative
	verb	transitivity	transitive, intransitive

Thirdly, the MCA algorithm will be attempted to deal with diachronic variations at the intensional level. The intensional level is concerned with the intensional readings of lexical items. These intensional readings cluster together in a prototypically structured set. With the MCA algorithm, we hope to show such a prototypical structure on the one hand and demonstrate the historical trajectory of these intensional readings on the other hand. Moreover, the corresponding relationship between extensional usages and intensional readings is expected to be uncovered in an objective fashion.

In addition, more break verbs like *duàn*, *suì*, *shé*, *liè* as well as *làn* will also be addressed in future studies. In this way, the lexical field of break verbs is expected to be constructed. And how this lexical field segments and categorizes the conceptual field of events of separation state change is expected to be revealed in a more systematic way. Moreover, principles that are involved in the labor division among these verbs in their categorization of events of separation state change will also be demonstrated.

REFERENCES

Ameka, Felix K. and James Essegbey. 2007. Cut and break verbs in Ewe and the causative alternation construction. *Cognitive Linguistics* 18(2): 241-250.

Aristotle. 1933. *Metaphysics*. trans. H. Tredennick. London: Heinemann.

Beavers, John and Andrew Koontz-Garboden. 2012. Manner and result in the roots of verbal meaning. *Linguistic Inquiry* (43): 331-369.

Berlin, Brent and Paul Kay. 1969. *Basic Color Terms: Their Universality and Evolution*. Berkeley: University of California Press.

Bohnemeyer, Juergen. 2007. Morpholexical relatedness and the argument structure of verbs of cutting and breaking. *Cognitive Linguistics* 18(2): 153-177.

Bohnemeyer, Juergen, Melissa Bowerman and Penelope Brown. 2001. Cut and break clips. In Stephen C. Levinson, and Nick J. Enfield (eds.), *Language and Cognition Group, Max Plank Institute for Psycholinguistics* (pp. 90-96). Nijmegen: MPI.

Bolinger, Dwight. 1968. Entailment and the meaning of structures. *Glossa* 2: 119-127.

Borer, Hagit. 1994. The projection of arguments. In Elena Benedicto and Jeffrey Runner (eds.), *Functional Projections. University of Massachusetts Occasional Papers in Linguistics 17*, pp. 19-47. University of Massachusetts, GLSA.

Bouveret, Myriam. 2009. Mapping between frames and constructions: French and English verbs of breaking. Paper presented at the Third International

Conference of AFLiCo (the French Cognitive Linguistics Association), Universite Paris-X.

Bouveret, Myriam and Eve Sweetser. 2009. Multi-frame semantics, metaphoric extensions and grammar. Proceedings of the Thirty-Fifth Annual Meeting of the Berkeley Linguistics Society.

Bowerman, Melissa. 1978. The acquisition of word meaning: An investigation into some current conflicts. In Natalie Waterson and Catherine E. Snow (eds.), *The Development of Communication*, pp. 263-287. New York: Wiely.

Bowerman, Melissa. 2005. Why can't you "open" a nut or "break" a cooked noodle? Learning covert object categories in action word meanings. In Lisa Gershkoff-Stowe and David Raikson (eds.), *Building Object Categories in Developmental Time: 32nd Carnegie Symposium on Cognition*, pp. 33-62. Mahwah, NJ: Lawrence Erlbaum.

Bowerman, Melissa. 2012. *Ten Lectures on Language, Cognition, and Language Acquisition*. Beijing: Foreign Language Teaching and Research Press.

Bowerman, Melissa and Asifa Majid. 2003. Kids' cut and break. In Nick J. Enfield (ed.), *Field Research Manual, Part I: Multimodal Interaction, Space, Event Representation,* pp. 70-71. Nijmegen: Max Planck Institute for Psycholinguistics.

Bowerman, Melissa and Soonja Choir. 2001. Shaping meanings from language: Universals and language-specific in the acquisition of spatial semantic categories. In Melissa Bowerman and Stephen C. Levinson (eds.), *Language Acquisition and Conceptual Development*, pp. 475-511. Cambridge: Cambridge University Press.

Bowerman, Melissa and Soonja Choir. 2003. Space under construction: Language-specific spatial categorization in first language acquisition. In Dedre Gentner and Susan Goldin-Meadow (eds.), *Language in Mind: Advances in the Study of Language and Thought,* pp. 387-427. Cambridge, MA: MIT Press.

Bowerman, Melissa, Majid Asifa, Erkelens M., Narasimhan Bhuvana, and Chen Jidong. 2004. Learning how to encode events of "cutting and breaking":

A crosslinguistic study of semantic development. Poster presented at the 2004 Child Language Research Forum "Constructions and Acquisition", Stanford, CA: Stanford University.

Brown, Penelope. 2007. 'She had just cut/broken off her head': Cutting and breaking verbs in Tzeltal. *Cognitive Linguistics* 18(2): 329-330.

Bybee, Joan. 2010. *Language, Usage and Cognition*. Cambridge: Cambridge University Press.

Carey, Susan. 2009. *On Origins of Concepts*. Oxford: Oxford University Press.

Chen, Jidong. 2007. 'He cut-break the rope': Encoding and categorizing cutting and breaking events in Mandarin. *Cognitive Linguistics* 18(2): 273-285.

Clark, Eve. 1978. Discovering what words can do. In Donka Farkas, Wesley M. Jacobsen and Karol W. Todrys (eds.), *Papers from the Parasession on the Lexicon*. Chicago: Chicago Linguistic Society.

Clark, Eve. 1979. Building a vocabulary: Words for objects, actions and relations. In Paul Fletcher and Michael Garman (eds.), *Language Acquisition*. Cambridge, MA: Cambridge University Press.

Clark, Eve., Kathie L. Carpenter and Werner Deutsch. 1995. Reference states and reversals: Undoing actions with verbs. *Journal of Child Language* (2): 633-662.

Colleman, Timothy and Bernard de Clerk. 2011. Constructional semantics on the move: On semantic specialization in the English double object construction. *Cognitive Linguistics* 22(1): 183-209.

Croft, William. 1999. Domains and image-schemas. *Cognitive Linguistics* (10): 1-31.

Croft, William. 2006. The relevance of an evolutionary model to historical linguistics. In Ole Nedergard Thomsen (ed.), *Competing Models of Linguistic Change: Evolution and Beyond*, pp. 91-132. Amsterdam and Philadelphia: John Benjamins.

Croft, William. 2009. Aspectual and causal structure in event representation. In Virginia Gathercole and Mueller Gathercole (eds.), *Routes to Language Development: In Honor of Melissa Bowerman*, pp. 139-166. Mahwah:

Lawrence Erlbaum Associates.

Croft, William. 2010. The origins of grammaticalization in the verbalization of experience. *Linguistics* 48(1): 1-48.

Croft, William. 2012. *Verbs: Aspect and Causal Structure*. Oxford: Oxford University Press.

Croft, William. 2015. Force dynamics and directed change in event lexicalization and argument realization. In Roberto G. de Almeida and Christina Manouilidou (eds.), *Cognitive Science Perspectives on Verb Representation and Processing*, pp. 103-129. Berlin: Springer.

Croft, William and Alan Cruse. 2004. *Cognitive Linguistics*. Cambridge: Cambridge University Press.

Cui, Zairong. 2001. *Historical Evolution of Chinese DRINK and EAT Conceptual Field*. Beijing: The Commercial Press. [崔宰荣, 2001. 汉语 "吃喝" 语义场的历史演变. 北京: 商务印书馆.]

Denny, Peter J. 1986. The semantic role of noun classifiers. In Colette Craig (eds.), *Noun Classes and Categorization*, pp. 297-308. Amsterdam: John Benjamins.

Divjak, Dagmar and Stefan Th. Gries. 2006. Ways of trying in Russian: Clustering behavioral profiles. *Corpus Linguistics and Linguistic Theory* 2(1): 23-60.

Divjak, Divjak and Antti Arppe. 2013. Extracting prototypes from exemplars: What can corpus tell us about concept representation? *Cognitive Linguistics* 24(2): 221-274.

Dong, Zhengcun. 2009. How does the verb "Ti" get the meaning of speaking? *Chinese Linguistics* (2): 41-46. [董正存, 2009. 动词 "提" 产生言说义的 过程及动因. 汉语学报(2): 41-46.]

Du, Xiang. 2002. Action Semantic Field and Its Evolution in Vernacular Translation of Zhi Jian. Peiking University, Unpublished doctoral dissertation. [杜翔, 2002. 支谦译经动作语义场及其演变研究. 北京大学 博士学位论文.]

Enfield, Nick J. 2007. Lao separation verbs and the logic of linguistic event categorization. *Cognitive Linguistics* 18(2): 287-296.

Essegbey, James. 2007. Cut and break verbs in Sranan. *Cognitive Linguistics* 18(2): 231-239.

Evans, Nikolas. 2010. Semantic typology. In Jae Jung Song (ed.), *The Oxford Handbook of Linguistic Typology*, pp.504-533. Oxford: Oxford University Press.

Evans, Vyvyan and Melanie Green. 2006. *Cognitive Linguistics: An Introduction*. Edinburgh: Edinburgh University Press.

Fillmore, Charles J. 1967. The grammar of hitting and breaking. *Working Papers in Linguistics* (1): 9-29.

Fillmore, Charles J. 1982. Frame semantics. In Linguistic Society of Korea (eds). *Linguistics in the Morning Calm*, pp.111-138. Seoul: Hanshin.

Fillmore, Charles J. 1985. Frames and the semantics of understanding. *Quaderni di Semantica* 6(2): 222-253.

Fillmore, Charles J. and Beryl T. Atkins. 1992. Towards a frame-based lexicon: The semantics of RISK and its neighbors. In Adrien Lehrer and Eva F. Kittay (eds.), *Frame, Fields and Contrasts: New Essays in Semantic and Lexical Organization*, pp.75-103. Hillsdale, New Jersey: Lawrence Erlbaum Associates.

Firth, John. 1957. *Papers in Linguistics*. London: Oxford University Press.

Fujii, Yoko. 1999. The story of "break": Cognitive categories of objects and the system of verbs. In Masako K. Hiraga, Chris Sinha and Sherman Wilcox (eds.), *Cultural, Psychological and Typological Issues in Cognitive Linguistics*, pp. 313-332. Amsterdam: John Benjamins.

Fujii, Seiko, Paula Radetzky, and Eve Sweetser. 2013a. Splitting, cutting and breaking talk in Japanese. Paper presented at the 12th International Cognitive Linguistics Conference, University of Alberta, Edmonton, Alberta.

Fujii, Seiko, Paula Radetzky and Eve Sweetser. 2013b. A multi-frame analysis of separation verbs. In Mike Borkent, Barbara Dancygier and Jennifer Hinnell (eds.), *Language and the Creative Mind*, pp. 137-154. Stanford: CSLI

Publications.

Gaby, Alice. 2007. Describing cutting and breaking events in Kuuk Thaayorre. *Cognitive Linguistics* 18(2): 263-272.

Garib, Hiba. 2012. A semantic analysis of "cut" and "break" verbs in Sorani Kurdish. Unpublished Doctoral Dissertation. University of Kansas.

Geeraerts, Dirk. 1983. Prototype theory and diachronic semantics: A case study. *Indognermanische Forschungen* (88): 1-32.

Geeraerts, Dirk. 1988. Where does prototypicality come from? In Brygida Rudzka-Ostyn (ed.), *Topics in Cognitive Linguistics,* pp. 207-229. Amsterdam/Philadelphia: John Benjamins.

Geeraerts, Dirk. 1997. *Diachronic Prototype Semantics: A Contribution to Historical Lexicology*. Oxford: Clarendon Press.

Geeraerts, Dirk. 1998. Neologism at short range. In Rainer Schulze (ed.), *Making Meaningful Choices in English: On Dimensions, Perspectives, Methodology and Evidence*, pp.77-88. Tubingen: Günter Narr Verlag.

Geeraerts, Dirk. 2002. The interaction of metaphor and metonymy in composite expressions. In René Dirven and Ralf Pörings (eds.), *Metaphor and Metonymy in Comparison and Contrast,* pp. 435-465. Berlin: Mouton de Gruyter.

Geeraerts, Dirk. 2006. The semantic structure of Dutch over. In Dirk Geeraerts (ed.), *Words and Other Wonders: Papers on Lexical and Semantic Topics*, pp.48-73. Berlin: Mouton de Gruyter.

Geeraerts, Dirk. 2007. Family resemblances, radial networks, and multidimensional models of meaning. In Maria Losada Friend, Pilar Ron Vaz, Sonia Hernández Santano and Jorge Casanova (eds.), *Proceedings of the XXX AEDEAN Conference*. Huelva: Servicio de Publicaciones de la Universidad de Huelva.

Geeraerts, Dirk. 2010. *Theories of Lexical Semantics*. Oxford: Oxford University Press.

Geeraerts, Dirk. 2018. *Ten Lectures on Cognitive Sociolinguistics*. Leiden: Brill.

Gibson, Kathleen R. and Tim Ingold. 1993. *Tools, Language and Cognition in*

Human Evolution. Cambridge: Cambridge University Press.

Glynn, Dylan. 2010. Introduction to the field. In Dylan Glynn and Kerstin Fischer (eds.), *Quantitative Methods in Cognitive Semantics: Corpus-Driven Approaches*, pp.1-42. Berlin: Mouton de Gruyter.

Glynn, Dylan. 2014. Polysemy and synonymy: Cognitive theory and corpus method. In Dylan Glynn and Justyna A. Robinson (eds.), *Corpus Methods for Semantics: Quantitative Studies in Polysemy and Synonymy*, pp. 7-38. John Benjamins.

Goddard, Cliff. 1998. *Semantic Analysis: A Practical Introduction*. Oxford: Oxford University Press.

Goddard, Cliff. 2005. Natural semantic metalanguage. In Keith Brown (eds.), *Encyclopedia of Language and Linguistics* (2nd ed), pp. 544-551. Amsterdam: Elsevier.

Goddard, Cliff and Anna Wierzbicka. 1994. *Semantic and Lexical Universals: Theory and Empirical Findings.* Amsterdam: John Benjamins.

Goddard, Cliff and Anna Wierzbicka. 2002. *Meaning and Universal Grammar: Theory and Empirical Findings*, vol. I and II. Amsterdam: John Benjamins.

Goddard, Cliff and Anna Wierzbicka. 2009. Contrastive semantics of physical activity verbs: "Cutting" and "chopping" in English, Polish, and Japanese. *Language Sciences* (31): 60-96.

Goldberg, Adele. 2010. Verbs, constructions, and semantic frames. In Malka Rappaport Hovav, Edit Doron and Ivy Sichel (eds.), *Lexical Semantics, Syntax, and Event Structure*, pp.39-58. Oxford: Oxford University Press.

Goossens, Louis. 1990. Metaphtonymy: The interaction of metaphor and metonymy in expressions for linguistic action. *Cognitive Linguistics* 1: 323-340.

Greenacre, Michael J. 1984. *Theory and Applications of Correspondence Analysis*. London: Academic Press.

Greenacre, Michael J. 2007. *Correspondence Analysis in Practice* (2nd ed). London: Taylor and Francis Group.

Gries, Stefan. 2006. Corpus-based methods and cognitive semantics: The many senses of *to run*. In Stefan Th. Gries and Stefanowitsch Anatol (eds.). *Corpora in Cognitive Linguistics: Corpus-Based Approaches to Syntax and Lexis,* pp. 57-100. Berlin: Mouton de Gruyter.

Guerssel, Mohamed, Kenneth Hale, Mary Laughren, Beth Levin, and Josie White Eagle. 1985. A crosslinguistic study of transitivity alternations. In Willimam H. Eilfort, Paul D. Kroeber and Karen L. Peterson (eds.), *Papers from the Parasession on Causatives and Agentivity at the 21st Regional Meeting*, pp. 48-63. Chicago: Chicago Linguistic Society.

Györi, Gábor. 1996. Historical aspects of grammaticalization. In Eugene H Casad (eds.) *Cognitive Linguistics in the Redwood: The Expansion of a New Paradigm in Linguistics*, pp. 175-206. Berlin: Mouton de Gruyter.

Györi, Gábor. 2002. Semantic change and cognition. *Cognitive Linguistics* 13(2): 123-166.

Hale, Kenneth L. and Samuel J. Keyser. 1987. *A View from the Middle: Lexicon Project Working Papers 10*. Cambridge, MA: Center for Cognitive Science, MIT Press.

Harmon, Zara and Vsevolod Kapatsinski. 2017. Putting old tools to novel uses: The role of form accessibility in semantic extension. *Cognitive Psychology* 98: 22-44.

Harris, Zellig S. 1954. Distributional structure. *Word* 10: 146–162.

Haspelmath, Martin. 1993. More on the typology of inchoative/causative verb Alternations. In Bernard Comrie and Maria Polinsky (eds.), *Causatives and Transitivity*, pp. 87-120. Amsterdam: John Benjamins.

Heine, Bernd, Ulrike Claudi and Friederike Hunnemeyer. 1991. From cognition to grammar: Evidence from African languages. In Elizabeth Closs Traugott and Bernd Heine (eds.), *Approaches to Grammaticalization* (Vol.1), pp. 149-187. Amsterdam: John Benjamins.

Hilpert, Martin. 2013. Corpus-based approaches to constructional change. In Thomas Hoffman and Graeme Trousdale (eds.), *The Oxford Handbook of Construction Grammar*. Oxford: Oxford University Press.

Hopper, Paul J. 1991. On some principles of grammaticalization. In Elizabeth

Closs Traugott and Bernd Heine (eds.), *Approaches to Grammaticalization* (Vol.1), pp. 17-35. Amsterdam: John Benjamins.

Hopper, Paul J., and Elizabeth Closs Traugott. 2003(1993). *Grammaticalization.* Cambridge: Cambridge University Press.

Hu Chirui. 2005. The early forms of resultative construction and the relevant criterion. *Studies of the Chinese Language* (3): 214-225. [胡敕瑞, 2005. 动结式的早期形式及判定标准. 中国语文(3): 214-225.]

Huang, C.-T. James. 2015. On syntactic analyticity and parametric theory. In Audrey Li, Andrew Simpson, and Wei-Tien Dylan Tsai (eds.), *Chinese Syntax in a Cross-Linguistic Perspective,* pp.1-48. Oxford: Oxford University Press.

Huttenlocher, Janellen and Lui Felicia. 1979. The semantic organization of some simple nouns and verbs. *Journal of Verbal Learning and Verbal Behavior* (18): 141-162.

Jackendoff, Ray. 1990. *Semantic Structures*. Cambridge, MA: MIT Press.

Jansegers, Marlies, and Stefan Th. Gries. 2020. Towards a dynamic behavioral profile: A diachronic study of polysemous *sentir* in Spanish. *Corpus Linguistics and Linguistic Theory* 16(1): 145-187.

Jespersen, Otto. 1928 (1927). *A Modern English Grammar on Historical Principles: Part 3 Syntax, Vol. 2.* Carl Winter: Heidelberg.

Jia, Yanzi and Fuxiang, Wu. 2017. A lexical typological approach to Chinese Eat and Drink verbs. *Chinese Teaching in the World* 31(3): 361-381. [贾燕子, 吴福祥, 2017. 词汇类型学视角的汉语 "吃" "喝" 类动词研究. 世界汉语教学, 31(3): 361-381.]

Jiang, Shaoyu. 1985. Lexical semantic development and change. *Linguistic Researches* (2): 7-12. [蒋绍愚, 1985. 词义的发展和变化. 语文研究(2), 7-12.]

Jiang, Shaoyu. 1999. *The emerging period of Chinese resultative constructions.* Beijing: Peking University Press. [蒋绍愚, 1999. 汉语动结式产生时代. 北京：北京大学出版社.]

Jiang, Shaoyu. 2005. Historical change from *zou* to *pao*. Proceedings in memory of Mr Li Fanggui's Centennial Birth. Institute of Language in China Research Academy/Washington University.

Jiang, Shaoyu, 2006. Preliminary exploration of the historical development of the meaning and vocabulary system of Chinese language: Taking "throw" as an example. *Journal of Peking University* (philosophy and social sciences) 43(4): 84-105. [蒋绍愚, 2006. 汉语词义和词汇系统的历时演变初探——以"投"为例. 北京大学学报, 43(4): 84-105.]

Jiang, Shaoyu. 2011. Lexicon, syntax and the expression of cognition. *Language Teaching and Linguistic Studies* (4): 20-27. [蒋绍愚, 2011. 词汇、语法和认知的表达. 语言教学与研究(4): 20-27.]

Jiang, Shaoyu. 2016. *A Summary on Chinese Diachronic Lexicology,* 2nd. Beijing: The Commercial Press. [蒋绍愚, 2016. 汉语历时词汇学概要. 第2版. 北京: 商务印书馆.]

Kay, Paul and Chad, K. McDaniel. 1978. The linguistic significance of the meanings of basic color terms. *Language* 54: 610-646.

Keil, Frank. C. 1979. *Semantic and Conceptual Development*. Harvard: Harvard University Press.

Kemmerer, David. 2003. Why can you hit someone on the arm but not break someone on the arm? — A neurological investigation of the English body-part possessor ascension construction. *Journal of Neurolinguistics* (16):13-36.

Kraska-Szlenk, Iwona. 2014. Semantic extensions of body part terms: Common patterns and their interpretation. *Language Sciences* 44: 15-39.

Kronenfeld, David and Gabriella Rundblad. 2003. The semantic structure of lexical fields: variation and change. In Regine Eckardt, Klaus von Heusinger, Christoph Schwarze (eds.), *Words in Time: Diachronic Semantics from Different Points of View*, pp. 67-114. Berlin: Mounton de Gruyter.

Kwon, Iksoo. 2016. How do Koreans break and cut things?: A cognitive-semantics approach to BREAK predicates and CUT predicates in Korean. *Linguistic Research* 33(1): 65-94.

Labov, William. 1973. The boundaries of words and their meanings. In Charles-James N. Bailey and Roger W. Shuy (eds.), *New Ways of Analyzing Variation in English*, pp.340-373. Washington: Georgetown University Press.

Labov, William. 1978. Denotational structure. In Donka Farkas, Wesley M. Jacobsen and Karol W. Todrys (eds.), *Papers from the Parasession on the Lexicon*. Chicago: Chicago Linguistic Society.

Lakoff, George. 1987. *Women, Fire and Dangerous Things: What Categories Reveal about the Mind*. Chicago: University of Chicago Press.

Langacker, Ronald. 1987. *Foundations of Cognitive Grammar, Volume I: Theoretical Prerequisites*. Stanford: Stanford University Press.

Langacker, Ronald. 1999. Assessing the cognitive linguistic enterprise. In Theo Janssen and Gisela Redeker (eds), pp.13-60. *Cognitive Linguistics: Foundations, Scope, and Methodology*. Berlin: Mouton de Gruyter.

Langacker, Ronald. 2008. *Cognitive Grammar: A Basic Introduction*. Oxford: Oxford University Press.

Levin, Beth. 1993. *English Verb Classes and Alternations*. Chicago: University of Chicago Press.

Levin, Beth and Steven Pinker. 1991. Introduction to special issues of cognition on lexical and conceptual semantics. *Cognition* (41): 1-7.

Levin, Beth and Malka Rappaport Hovav. 1995. *Unaccusativity: At the Syntax-Lexical Semantics Interface*. Cambridge: MA: MIT Press.

Levin, Beth and Malka Rappaport Hovav. 2008. Lexicalized manner and result are in complementary distribution. Paper presented at the Twenty-fourth Annual Conference of the Israel Association for Theoretical Linguistics, Jerusalem: The Hebrew University of Jerusalem.

Levinson, Stephen C. 2007. Cut and break verbs in Yélî Dnye, the Papuan language of Rossel Island. *Cognitive Linguistics* 18(2): 207-218.

Levshina, Natalia. 2015. *How to Do Linguistics with R: Data Exploration and Statistical Analysis*. Amsterdam: John Benjamins.

Li, Fuyin. 2008. *An Overview on Cognitive Linguistics*. Beijing: Peking

University Press. [李福印, 2008. 认知语言学概论. 北京：北京大学出版社.]

Li, Ming. 2004. Delocutive verbs in Chinese. *Studies of the Chinese Language* (5): 401-411. [李明, 2004. 从言语到言说行为. 中国语文(5): 401-411.]

Li, Zuofeng. 1994. Intransitive and transitive verbs in Pre-Qin dynasty. *Studies of the Chinese Language* (4): 287-296. [李佐丰, 1994. 先秦的不及物动词和及物动词. 中国语文(4): 287-296.]

Lüpke, Friederike. 2007. Smash it again, Sam: Verbs of cutting and breaking in Jalonke. *Cognitive Linguistics,* 18(2): 251-261.

Majid, Asifa, Miriam van Staden, and James S. Boster. 2004. Event categorization: A cross-linguistic perspective. In Kenneth Forbus, Dedre Gentner, and Terry Regier (eds.), pp. 885-890. *Proceedings of the 26th annual meeting of the Cognitive Science Society*. Mahwah, NJ: Lawrence Erlbaum.

Majid, Asifa, Mellisa Bowerman, Miriam van Staden, and James S. Boster. 2007a. The semantic categories of breaking and cutting events: A crosslinguistic perspective. *Cognitive Linguistics* 18(2): 133-152.

Majid, Asifa, Maruabbe Gullberg, Miriam van Staden and Melissa Bowerman. 2007b. How similar are semantic categories in closely related languages? A comparison of cutting and breaking in four Germanic languages. *Cognitive Linguistics* 18(2): 179-194.

Mckoon, Gail and Jessica Love. 2011. Verbs in the lexicon: Why is hitting easier than breaking? *Language Cognition* 3(2): 313-330.

Mel'čuk, Igor. 1981. Meaning-text models: A recent trend in soviet linguistics. *Annual Review of Anthropology* (10): 27-62.

Mervis, Carolyn. B and Eleanor Rosch. 1981. Categorization of natural objects. *Annual Review of Psychology* (32): 89-115.

Mohanan, Tara and Lionel Wee. 1999. *External Possession*. Amsterdam: John Benjamins.

Moore, Randi, Katherine Donelson, Alyson Eggleston and Juergen Bohnemeyer. 2015. Semantic typology: New approaches to crosslinguistic variation in language and cognition. *Linguistics Vanguard* 1 (1): 189-200.

Næss, Åshild. 2012. Cutting and breaking in Äiwoo: Event integration and the complexity of lexical expressions. *Cognitive Linguistics* 23(2): 395-420.

Narasimhan, Bhuvana. 2007. Cutting, breaking, and tearing verbs in Hindi and Tamil. *Cognitive Linguistics* 18(2): 195-205.

Norrick, Neal. R. 1981. *Semiotic Principles in Semantic Theory. Amsterdam Studies in the Theory and History of Linguistic Science IV*. Amsterdam/ Philadelphia: John Benjamins.

Nosofsky, Robert M. 1988. Similarity, frequency, and category representations. *Journal of Experimental Psychology: Learning, Memory, and Cognition* 14: 54-65.

O'Connor, Loretta. 2007. 'Chop, shred, snap apart': Verbs of cutting and breaking in Lowland Chontal. *Cognitive Linguistics* 18(2): 219-230.

Otomo, Asako and Akiko Torii. 2005. An NSM approach to the meaning of tear and its Japanese equivalents. *Paper presented at the Annual Conference of the Australian Linguistic Society.*

Palancar, Enrique L. 2007. Cutting and breaking verbs in Otomi: An example of lexical specification. *Cognitive Linguistics* 18(2): 307-317.

Piersman, Yves and Geeraerts, Dirk. 2006. Metonymy as a prototypical category. *Cognitive Linguistics* 17(3): 269-316.

Pinker, Steve. 1989. *Learnability and Cognition: The Acquisition of Argument Structure*. Cambridge, MA: MIT Press.

Pullman, S. G. 1983. *Word Meaning and Belief*. London, Canberra: Croom Helm.

Pye, Clifton. 1996. K'iche' Maya verbs of breaking and cutting. In Melissa Goodel and Dong Ik Choi (eds.), pp. 87-98. *Kansas Working Papers in Linguistics 21*. Lawrence, KS: University of Kansas.

Pye, Clifton, Diane Frome Loeb and Yin-yin Piao. 1995. The acquisition of breaking and cutting. In Eve V. Clark (eds.), *The Proceeding of the Twenty-seventh Annual Child Language Research Forum*, pp. 227-236. Stanford: Center for the Study of Language and Information.

Rappaport Hovav, Malka and Beth Levin. 1998. Building verb meanings. In Miriam Butt and Wilhelm Geuder (eds.) *The Projection of Arguments: Lexical and Compositional Factors*, pp. 97-133. CSLI Publications.

Rappaport Hovav, Malka and Beth Levin. 2001. An event structure account of English resultatives. *Language* (77): 766-797.

Rappaport Hovav, Malka and Beth Levin. 2005. Change of state verbs: Implications for theories of argument projection. In Erteschik-Shir, Nomi and Rapoport Tova (eds.), *The Syntax of Aspect: Deriving Thematic and Aspectual Interpretation,* pp.274-287. Oxford: Oxford University Press.

Rappaport Hovav, Malka and Beth Levin. 2010. Reflections on manner/result complementarity. In Malka Rappaport Hovav, Edit Doron and Ivy Sichel (eds.). *Lexical Semantics, Syntax, and Event Structure*, pp. 21-38. Oxford: Oxford University Press.

Robert, Stéphane. 2008. Words and their meanings: Principles of variation and stabilization. In Martine Vanhove (eds.), *From Polysemy to Semantic Change*, pp. 55-93. Amsterdam: John Benjamins.

Rosch, Eleanor. 1973. On the internal structure of perceptual and semantic categories. In T. E. Moore (ed.), *Cognitive Development and the Acquisition of Language*, pp.111-144. Academic.

Rosch, Eleanor. 1975. Cognitive representation of semantic categories. *Journal of Experimental Psychology* 104 (3): 192-233.

Rosch, Eleanor. 1977. Human categorization. In Neil Warrant (eds.), *Studies in Cross-Cultural Psychology,* pp. 3-49. London: Academic.

Rosch, Eleanor. 1978. Principles of categorization. In Eleanor Rosch and BB Lloyd (eds.), *Cognition and Categorization*, pp. 27-48. Hillsdale, NJ: Lawrence Erlbaum.

Rosch, Eleanor and Carolyn. B. Mervis. 1975. Family resemblance: Studies in the internal structure of categories, *Cognitive Psychology* (7): 573-605.

Sapir, Edward. 1921. *Language: An Introduction to the Study of Speech*. New York: Harcourt Brace Jovanovich.

Saussure, Ferdinand, de. 1983 (1916). *Cours de linguistique generale*. Paris:

PAYOT.

Shaefer, Ronald P. 1979. Child and adult categories. *Kansas Working Papers in Linguistics* (4): 61-76.

Shaefer, Ronald P. 1980. An Experimental Assessment of the Boundaries Demarcating Three Basic Semantic Categories in the Domain of Separation. Unpublished doctoral dissertation, University of Kansas.

Shi Yuzhi, 2003. The change of conceptualization of verbs in the history of Chinese and its effect on grammar. *Chinese Language Teaching* (4): 1-8. [石毓智, 2003. 古今汉语动词概念化方式的变化及其对语法的影响. 汉语学习(4): 1-8.]

Slobin, Dan I. 1996. From thought and language to thinking for speaking. In John J. Gumperz and Stephen C. Levinson (eds.), *Rethinking Linguistic Relativity*, pp.70-96. Cambridge: Cambridge University Press.

Spalek, Alexandra Anna. 2012. Putting order into literal and figurative uses of verbs: romper as a case study. *An International Journal of Hispanic Linguistics* 1(2): 140-167.

Spalek, Alexandra Anna. 2015. Spanish change of state verbs in composition with atypical theme arguments: Clarifying the meaning shifts. *Lingua* (157): 36-53.

Strobl, Carolin, Malley, James, and Tutz, Gerhard. 2009. An introduction to recursive partitioning: Rationale, application, and characteristics of classification and regression trees, bagging, and random forests. *Psychological Methods* 14(4): 323–348.

Sun, Chaofen. 1999. The origin of the Chinese verbal suffixes. In Alain Peyraube and Sun Chaofen (eds.), *Studies on Chinese Historical Syntax and Morphology: In Honor of Mei Tsu-Lin*, pp.183-202, Paris: EHESS, CRLAO.

Sweetser, Eve. 1988. Grammaticalization and semantic bleaching. In Berkeley Linguistics Society(ed.), *Proceedings of the Fourteenth Annual Meeting*, 389-405.

Sweetser, Eve. 1990. *From Etymology to Pragmatics*. Cambridge: Cambridge University Press.

Tagliamonte, Sali A. and Baayen, R. Harald. 2012. Models, forests, and trees of York English: Was/were variation as a case study for statistical practice. *Language Variation and Change* 24: 135-178.

Talmy, Leonard. 1991. Path to realization: A typology of event conflation. *Proceedings of the 17th Annual Meeting of the Berkeley Linguistics Society.* Berkeley, California: Berkeley Linguistics Society.

Talmy, Leonard. 2000a. *Towards A Cognitive Semantics, vol. I: Concept Structuring Systems.* Cambridge, MA: MIT Press.

Talmy, Leonard. 2000b. *Towards A Cognitive Semantics, vol. II: Typology and Process in Concept Structuring.* Cambridge, MA: MIT Press.

Taylor, John R. 2002. Near synonyms as co-extensive categories: "High" and "tall" revisited. *Language Sciences* 25: 263-284.

Taylor, John. 2003. *Linguistic Categorization* (3rd edition). Oxford: Oxford University Press.

Taylor, John. 2007. Semantic categories of cutting and breaking: Some final thoughts. *Cognitive Linguistics* 18(2): 331-337.

Thomason, Richmond. H. 1972. A Semantic theory of sortal incorrectness. *Journal of Philosophical Logic* 1: 209-258.

Toth, Nicholas and Kathy Schick. 1993. Early stone industries and inferences regarding language and cognition. In Kathleen R. Gibson and Tim Ingold (eds.), *Tools, Language and Cognition in Human Evolution*, pp. 346-362. Cambridge: Cambridge University Press.

Traugott, Elizabeth C. 1982. From propositional to textual and expressive meaning: Some semantic-pragmatic aspects of grammaticalization. In Winfred P. Lehmann and Yakov Malkiel (eds.), *Perspectives on Historical Linguistics*, pp. 245-271. Amsterdam: John Benjamins.

Traugott, Elizabeth C. 1985. Conventional and dead metaphors revisited. In Wolf Paprotte and Rene Dirven (eds.), *The Ubiquity of Metaphor: Metaphor in Language and Thought,* pp.17-56. Amsterdam: John Benjamins.

Traugott, Elizabeth C. 1988. Pragmatic strengthening and grammaticalization. In Shelley Axmaker, Annie Jaisser, and Helen Singmaster (eds.), *Proceedings of the Fourteenth Annual Meeting of the Berkeley Linguistic Society*, pp. 406-416. Berkeley, CA: Berkeley Linguistics Society.

Traugott, Elizabeth C. 1989. On the rise of epistemic meanings in English: An example of subjectification in semantic change. *Language* 65: 31-55.

Traugott, Elizabeth C and Ekkehard König. 1991. The semantic-pragmatics of grammaticalization revisited. In Elizabeth Closs Traugott and Bernd Heine (eds.), *Approaches to Grammaticalization* (Vol.1), pp. 189-219. Amsterdam: John Benjamins.

Traugott, Elizabeth C and Richard B. Dasher. 2002. *Regularity in Semantic Change*. Cambridge: Cambridge University Press.

van Staden, Miriam. 2007. 'Please open the fish': Verbs of separation in Tidore, a Papuan language of Eastern Indonesia. *Cognitive Linguistics* 18(2): 297-306.

Vendryes, Joseph. 1925. *Language: A Linguistic Introduction to History*. Translated by Pual, Radin. New York: Alfred A. Knopf.

Wang, Li. 2013(1957–1958). *Outline of the History of Chinese*. Beijing: Zhong Hua Book Company. [王力, 2013(1957–1958). 汉语史稿. 北京：中华书局.]

Wang, Liling, 2012. Revisiting the Delocutive origin of the verb *ti*. *Studies of the Chinese Language* (6):514-518. [王丽玲, 2012. 也谈动词"提"言说义的来源. 中国语文(6): 514-518.]

Wei, Peiquan. 2000. A study on causative structures in Middle Chinese. *Collected Papers on Diachronic Semantics* 71(4): 807-947. [魏培泉, 2000. 说中古汉语的使成结构.历时语言研究所集刊, 71(4): 807-947.]

Weinreich, Uriel, William Labov and Marvin I. Herzog. 1968. Empirical foundations for a theory of language Change. In Winfred P. Lehmann and Yakov Makliel (eds.), pp. 95-195. *Directions for Historical Linguistics*. Austin: University of Texas Press.

Werner, Heinz and Kaplan Bernard. 1963. *Symbol Formation: An Organismic Developmental Approach to Language and the Expression of Thought*. New York: Wiley.

Wierzbicka, Anna. 1985. *Lexicography and Conceptual Analysis*. Ann Arbor: Karoma Publishers.

Wierzbicka, Anna. 1996. *Semantics: Primes and Universals*. Oxford: Oxford University Press.

Wierzbicka, Anna. 2006. *English: Meaning and Culture*. New York: Oxford University Press.

Winters, Margret E. 1987. Syntactic and semantic space: The development of the French subjunctive. In Giacalone-Ramat Anna, Onofrio Carruba and Giuliano Bernini (eds), pp.607-618. Papers from 7th International Conference on Historical Linguistics. Amsterdam: John Benjamins.

Wittgenstein, Ludwig. 1953/2001. *Philosophical Investigations*. New York: Blackwell Publishing.

Wong, Andrew D. 2008. On the actuation of semantic change: The case of *tongzhi. Language Sciences* 30: 423-449.

Wu, Fuxiang. 1999. A tentative study on the origin of resultative constructions in Modern Chinese. In Lansheng Jiang and Jingyi Hou (eds.), *Studies on Chinese Present and History*—Collected Papers from First Chinese Linguistic International Seminar. Beijing: Chinese Academy of Social Sciences Press. [吴福祥. 1999. 试讨论现代汉语动补结构的来源. 汉语现状与历史的研究//江蓝生，侯精一. 首届汉语语言学国际研讨会论文集. 北京: 中国社会科学出版社.]

Wu, Fuxiang, 2007. The semantic changes of the Chinese locative term *hou. Studies of the Chinese Language* (6): 494-506. [吴福祥, 2007. 汉语方所词语"后"的语义演变. 中国语文(6): 494-506.]

Wu, Fuxiang. 2015. Studies on semantic changes in Chinese: Retrospection and prospection. *Research in Ancient Chinese Language* 4: 2-13. [吴福祥, 2015. 汉语语义演变研究的回顾与前瞻. 古汉语研究(4): 2-13]

Wu, Tieping. 1984. Contagiousness of lexical meanings. *Linguistic Researches* (4): 57-59. [伍铁平, 1984. 词义的感染. 语文研究(4): 57-59.]

Xu, Dan. 2001. Investigating semantic influence on syntactic structure from the emergence of resultative constructions—a study on the divergence of the semantic and function of Chinese verbs. *Linguistic Researches* (2): 5-12.[徐丹, 2001. 从动补结构的形成看语义对句法结构的影响——兼谈汉语动词语义及功能的分化. 语文研究(2): 5-12.]

Xu, Dan. 2005. Typological changes of some verbs in Chinese: The case of po (to break > broken). *Studies of the Chinese Language* (4): 333-339. [徐丹, 2005. 谈 "破" —汉语某些动词的类型转变. 中国语文(4): 333-339.]

Xu, Dan. 2006. *Typological Change in Chinese Syntax*. Oxford: Oxford University Press.

Yang, Daran. 2015. A study on the causative alternation from a non-derivational perspective. In Xinchun Su and Tingting He (eds.) *Chinese Lexical Semantics* (pp.161-169), *Springer.*

Zhang Weiwei and Nian Liu. 2016. Advanced quantitative methods in cognitive linguistics research. *Journal of Foreign Languages* (1): 71-79. [张炜炜, 刘念, 2016. 认知语言学定量研究的几种新方法. 外国语(1): 71-79.]

Appendixes

APPENDIX 1:

Frequency of the 34 usages of *pò* across the four chronological stages

Usages	EMC		LMC		EMand		MdMand		Total
	AF[①]	RF	AF	RF	AF	RF	AF	RF	
fles_affsur	18	9.3	43	6.2	329	21.8	157	12.7	547
fles_affpar	5	2.6	110	15.9	255	16.9	273	22	643
sti_noipar	7	3.6	110	15.9	170	11.2	123	9.9	410
sti_affpar	21	10.9	126	18.2	142	9.5	116	9.4	405
flex_affpar	2	1	90	13	156	10.3	103	8.3	351
fles_noipar	12	6.2	21	3	138	9.1	51	4.1	222
fra_affpie	22	11.4	48	6.9	45	3	54	4.4	169
flex_noipar	2	1	1	0.1	106	7	10	0.8	119
fra_affpar	2	1	33	4.7	28	1.9	47	3.8	110
ten_newpar	11	5.7	11	1.6	11	0.7	62	5	95
sti_noisur	14	7.3	8	1.2	14	0.9	30	2.4	66
fra_neupie	8	4.1	8	1.2	4	0.3	45	3.6	65
fra_noipie	9	4.7	6	0.9	39	2.6	9	0.7	63
fra_noipar	1	0.5	16	2.3	13	0.9	31	2.5	61
fles_newpar	12	6.2	4	0.6	4	0.3	24	1.9	44
fra_noisur	7	3.6	5	0.7	4	0.3	27	2.2	43
sti_newpar	7	3.6	13	1.9	5	0.3	6	0.5	31
fles_affpie	5	2.6	1	0.1	0	0	16	1.3	22
flex_affpie	0	0	0	0	6	0.4	12	1	18

① Note: AF stands for absolute frequency, and RF represents relative frequency.

Continued

Usages	EMC		LMC		EMand		MdMand		Total
	AF	RF	AF	RF	AF	RF	AF	RF	
fra_neupar	1	0.5	6	0.9	7	0.5	3	0.2	17
fra_newpie	2	1	1	0.1	0	0	12	1	15
ten_noipar	6	3.1	0	0	1	0.1	8	0.6	15
sti_affpie	1	0.5	4	0.6	1	0.1	8	0.6	14
sti_neupar	0	0	13	1.9	0	0	1	0.1	14
ten_affpar	1	0.5	2	0.2	10	0.7	8	0.7	21
ten_neupar	0	0	11	1.6	11	0.7	0	0	22
ten_newpie	13	6.7	0	0	0	0	0	0	13
sti_newpie	2	1	1	0.1	6	0.4	3	0.2	12
fles_newpie	2	1	1	0.1	0	0	0	0	3
fra_newpar	0	0	0	0	0	0	1	0.1	1
sti_noipie	0	0	0	0	1	0.1	0	0	1
ten_affpie	0	0	0	0	1	0.1	0	0	1
ten_neusur	0	0	0	0	1	0.1	0	0	1
ten_noisur	0	0	0	0	0	0	1	0.1	1
Total 34	193	100	693	100	1,508	100	1,241	100	3,635

APPENDIX 2

Examples and translations for the first 22 usages

Usages	Examples	Translations
fles_affsur	头被打破了。	"His head was broken."
fles_affpar	挖眼睛，破肚子。	"Dig his eyes and break his belly."
sti_noipar	杨生破门而入。	"Yang Sheng opened the door forcibly and came in."
sti_affpar	木鱼子敲破了。	"The wooden box is knocked broken."
flex_affpar	衣服破了。	"The clothes worn out."
fles_noipar	破腹出脏。	"Open the belly and take out the gut."
fra_affpie	既讫，掷破瓯走去。	"After then, he threw and broke the cup and left."
flex_noipar	撕破窗纸一看。	"Tear the window paper and look through."
fra_affpar	三尺杖子破瓦盆。	"He smashed the earthen basin with a three-feet stick."
ten_newpar	破石榴以献。	"Separate the pomegranate and offer it."
sti_noisur	破其外青皮，得白心。	"Break its exterior skin and get the inner white core."
fra_neupie	温差风化隧使表层岩石破裂。	"Temperature difference and efflorescence break the surface of the rock."
fra_noipie	凿山破石，勿使阻碍。	"Dig the hill and break the stone, so that they are no longer barriers."
fra_noipar	此古器，当是破冢得之。	"These ancient utensils were gained when we opened the grave."
fles_newpar	破雁，炙而分食之。	"Separate the wild goose, then roast it and eat it."

Continued

Usages	Examples	Translations
fra_noisur	卵破，有婴儿出焉。	"The egg broke and a baby came out."
sti_newpar	逃者隧取竹一竿，破以为蔑。	"The escapers made sawali with a long bamboo. "
fles_affpie	扑的一声，把头颅轰破。	"With a sound, his head was bombed broken. "
flex_affpie	衣服破碎。	"The clothes became tattered."
fra_neupar	风鸣条，雨破块。	"The wind blows branches with a sound and the rain broke the soil blocks. "
fra_newpie	碾破青山作路。	"Broke the mountain and turn it into a road."
ten_noipar	青椒破口去籽切粗丝。	"Open the pepper and take out the seed and slice."

APPENDIX 3

Example of dataset①

Number	Concordances	source
EMC1	凡种麻，用白麻子。白麻子为雄麻。颜色虽白，啮[破]枯燥无膏润者，秕子也，亦不中种。市★者，口含少时	【文件名:\06六朝\齐民要术·贾思勰.txt
EMC2	摘瓜法在步道上引手而取，勿听浪人踏瓜蔓，及翻覆之。踏则茎[破]，翻则成细，皆令瓜不茂而蔓早死。若无	【文件名:\06六朝\齐民要术·贾思勰.txt
EMC3	...置孔中，令底下向。瓠一行，覆上土，厚三尺。二十日出，黄色好，[破]以为瓢。其中白肤，以养★致肥；	【文件名:\06六朝\齐民要术·贾思勰.txt
EMC4	....先燥晒，欲种时，布子於坚地，一升子与一掬湿土和之，以脚蹉令[破]作两段。多种者，以★瓦蹉之亦得	【文件名:\06六朝\齐民要术·贾思勰.txt
EMC5	...一转，令好调熟，调熟如麻地。即於六月中旱时，耧耩作垅，蹉子令[破]，手散，还劳令平，一同春法。但	【文件名:\06六朝\齐民要术·贾思勰.txt
EMC6	...种小小供食者，自可畦种。畦种者一如葵法。若种者，★生子，令中[破]，笼盛，一日再度以水沃之，令生	【文件名:\06六朝\齐民要术·贾思勰.txt
EMC7	《三秦记》曰"汉武果园，一名'御宿'，有大梨如五升，落地即[破]。取者以布囊盛之，名曰'含消梨'。"	【文件名:\06六朝\齐民要术·贾思勰.txt
EMC8	作林檎★法林檎赤熟时，擘[破]，去子、心、★，日晒令乾。或磨或捣，下细绢筛；★者更磨捣，以细...	【文件名:\06六朝\齐民要术·贾思勰.txt
EMC9	作柰脯法柰熟时，中[破]，曝乾，即成矣。	【文件名:\06六朝\齐民要术·贾思勰.txt
EMC10	...势尽乃止。布袋绞取滓汁，著瓷碗中。取醋石榴两三个，擘取子，捣[破]，少著粟饭浆水酸者和之，布绞取	【文件名:\06六朝\齐民要术·贾思勰.txt
EMC11	其冒霜雪远行者，常啮蒜令[破]，以揩唇，既不劈裂，又令辟恶。小儿面患皴者，夜烧梨令熟，以糠汤...	【文件名:\06六朝\齐民要术·贾思勰.txt
EMC12	...亦有全掷一团著汤中，尝有酪味，还漉取曝乾。一团则得五遍煮，不[破]。看热两渐薄，乃削研，用倍省矣	【文件名:\06六朝\齐民要术·贾思勰.txt
EMC13	治羊疥方取藜芦根，★咀令[破]，以泔浸之，以瓶盛，塞口，於灶边常令暖，数日醋香，便中用。以★...	【文件名:\06六朝\齐民要术·贾思勰.txt
EMC14	...芡子"是也。由子形上花似鸡冠，故名曰"鸡头"。八月中收取，擘[破]，取子，散著池中，自生也。	【文件名:\06六朝\齐民要术·贾思勰.txt
EMC15	神★酒方净扫刷★令净，有土处，刀削去，必使极净。反斧背椎[破]，令大小如枣、栗；斧刃则杀小。用故纸	【文件名:\06六朝\齐民要术·贾思勰.txt
EMC16	...刚、生灭也。於席上摊黍饭令极冷，贮出★汁，於盆中调和，以手搦[破]之，无块，然後内瓮中。春以两重	【文件名:\06六朝\齐民要术·贾思勰.txt
EMC17	...米者，初下以炊米两石为再馏黍，黍熟，以净席薄摊令冷，块大者擘[破]，然後下之。没水而已，勿更找劳	【文件名:\06六朝\齐民要术·贾思勰.txt
EMC18	...摊，令极冷。於黍饭初熟时浸★，向晓昧旦日未出时，下酿，以手搦[破]块，仰置勿盖。日西更淘三斗米浸	【文件名:\06六朝\齐民要术·贾思勰.txt
EMC19	...久水尽，★熟极软，泻著席上，摊之令冷。挹取★汁，於瓮中搦黍令[破]，泻瓮中，复以酒杷搅之。每★酘	【文件名:\06六朝\齐民要术·贾思勰.txt
EMC20	...治★，曝令燥。渍★必须累饼置水中，以水没饼为候。七日许，搦令[破]，漉去滓。炊糯米为黍，摊令极冷	【文件名:\06六朝\齐民要术·贾思勰.txt
EMC21	...体时，於瓮中和粉，痛抨使均柔，令相著；亦可椎打，如椎★法。擘[破]块，内著瓮中。盆合，泥封。裂则	【文件名:\06六朝\齐民要术·贾思勰.txt
EMC22	...月三十日停，是以不须咸，咸则不美。盘上调和令均，捣使熟，还擘[破]如枣大。作浪中坑，火烧令赤，去	【文件名:\06六朝\齐民要术·贾思勰.txt
EMC23	...为限。先量水，浸麦★讫；然後净淘米，炊为再馏，摊令冷，细擘★[破]，勿令有块子，一顿下酿，更不重	【文件名:\06六朝\齐民要术·贾思勰.txt
EMC24	...泔汁尽，重装作再馏饭。下，摔去热气，令如人体，於盆中和之，擘[破]饭块，以★拌之，必令均调。下酿	【文件名:\06六朝\齐民要术·贾思勰.txt
EMC25	...欲作酢者，糟常湿下；压糟极燥者，酢味薄。作法用石磑子辣谷令[破]，以水拌而蒸之。熟便下，摔去热气	【文件名:\06六朝\齐民要术·贾思勰.txt
EMC26	...水者，宜以鱼眼汤★银洽反半许半生用。朝歌大蒜，辛辣异常，宜分[破]去心——全心——用之，不然辣则	【文件名:\06六朝\齐民要术·贾思勰.txt
EMC27	...土，蒸令气馏，下著屋北阴乾之。当时随食者，取即汤★去腥气，擘[破]。先细切葱白，和麻油，苏亦好。	【文件名:\06六朝\齐民要术·贾思勰.txt
EMC28	★茄子法用子未成者，子成则不好也。以竹刀骨刀四[破]之，用铁则渝黑。汤★去腥气。细切葱白，熬油令香	【文件名:\06六朝\齐民要术·贾思勰.txt
EMC29	...蜜涂瓮。此蜀人方，美好。又法取小瓜百枚，豉五升，盐三程式。[破]，去瓜子，以盐布瓜片中，次著瓮中	【文件名:\06六朝\齐民要术·贾思勰.txt
EMC30	....令有盐味，不须多，合藏之，密泥★口。软而黄，便可食，大者六[破]，小者四[破]，五寸断之，广狭尽	【文件名:\06六朝\齐民要术·贾思勰.txt
EMC31	...紧线以割之。其近盆底土恶之处，不中用者，割却少许。然後十字坼[破]之，又中断为段，较薄割为饼。唯	【文件名:\06六朝\齐民要术·贾思勰.txt
EMC32	...十七、八子。十一月、十二月熟，其树黄实，俗名之为'丹'了。横[破]之，可作★或微长如★蒌子，从[破]之	【文件名:\06六朝\齐民要术·贾思勰.txt
EMC33	...子，著，而腹内空含汁，大者含各馀。实形团团然，工如瓜蒌，横[破]之，可作爵形，并应器用，太人珍贵	【文件名:\06六朝\齐民要术·贾思勰.txt
EMC34	...智，叶如★荷，茎如竹箭。子从心中出，一枚有十子，子内白滑，四[破]去之，了外皮，蜜煮为糁，味辛。	【文件名:\06六朝\齐民要术·贾思勰.txt
EMC35	种茄子法茄子，九月熟时摘取，擘[破]，水淘子，取沈者，速曝乾裹置。至二月畦种。治畦下水，一如葵法。	【文件名:\06六朝\齐民要术·贾思勰.txt
EMC36	颜□辞去曰"夫玉生于山，制则[破]焉，非弗宝贵矣，然夫璞不完。	【文件名:\04西汉\刘向 战国策.TXT
EMC37	...埴也，其取之地而已为盆盎也，与其未离于地也无以异。其已成器而[破]碎漫澜而复归其故故与其为盆盎，	【文件名:\04西汉\刘安 淮南子.TXT
EMC38	...者不与焉。夫舟浮于水，车转于陆，此势之自然也。木击折□，水戾[破]舟，不怨木石而罪巧拙者，知故不载	【文件名:\04西汉\刘安 淮南子.TXT
EMC39	...人哉？"处十月，知伯围襄子于晋阳，襄子疏队而击之，大败知伯，[破]其首以为饮器。故《老子》曰"知其	【文件名:\04西汉\刘安 淮南子.TXT
EMC40	...百姓暴骸。粟得水湿而热，甑得火而液。水中有火，火中有水；疾雷[破]石，阴阳相薄。汤沐之于河，有益	【文件名:\04西汉\刘安 淮南子.TXT
EMC41	...以定文圆；无准绳，虽鲁般不能以定曲直。是故钟子期死而伯牙绝弦[破]琴，知世莫赏也；惠施死而庄子寝	【文件名:\04西汉\刘安 淮南子.TXT
EMC42	阖闾伐楚，五战入郢，烧高府之粟，[破]九龙之钟，鞭平王之墓，舍昭王之宫；昭王奔随，百姓父兄，携幼扶	【文件名:\04西汉\刘安 淮南子.TXT
EMC43	...通，天地所以隔外内也。其入中国，必下领水，领水之山峭峻，漂石[破]舟，不可以大船载食粮下也。越人	【文件名:\05东汉\全汉文.txt
EMC44	...上，雨则凝结成雹焉。太平之世，则风不鸣条，开甲散萌而已。雨不[破]块，润叶津茎而已。雷不惊人，号	【文件名:\05东汉\全汉文.txt
EMC45	...骏等四十馀人群党盛兵弩，白昼入乐府攻射官寺，缚束长吏子弟，斫[破]器物，宫中皆奔走伏匿。莽自冕钳	【文件名:\05东汉\全汉文.txt
EMC46	...渭，云合电发，腾波流，机骇蜂轶，疾如奔星，击如震霆，砰贲せ，[破]穹庐，脑沙幕，髓余吾。遂猎乎王	【文件名:\05东汉\全汉文.txt
EMC47	昔大禹治水，山陵当路者毁之，故凿龙门，辟伊阙，析底柱，[破]碣石，堕断天地之性。此乃人功所造，	【文件名:\05东汉\全汉文.txt
EMC48	...莫不计度，以为汤功累世不可及，而汤过人情所有。汤尚如此，虽复[破]绝筋骨，暴露形骸，犹复制于脣舌	【文件名:\05东汉\全汉文.txt
EMC49	...昭宁堂池东南榆树大十围，东僵，击东阁，阁即东永巷之西垣也。皆[破]折瓦坏，发屋拔木，予甚惊焉。又	【文件名:\05东汉\全汉文.txt
EMC50	...发狂兴，悲毒俱行伤人，大谏横加绝理，瓦石飞起，地土上柱皇天，[破]室屋，动山阜，谏而不从，因而消	【文件名:\05东汉\史论\太平经.TXT
EMC51	...?泉者，地之血；石者，地之骨也；良土，地之肉也。洞泉为得血，[破]石为[破]骨，良土深凿之，投瓦石坚	【文件名:\05东汉\史论\太平经.TXT
EMC52	...神人，示其文章。得戒止恶神不上白，尚可须臾饮食诸谷，慎无烧山[破]石，延及草木，折华伤枝，实于市	【文件名:\05东汉\史论\太平经.TXT
EMC53	...安能为悲哭感动而崩？使至诚之声能动城土，则其对林木哭，能折草[破]木乎？向水火而泣，能涌水灭火乎	【文件名:\05东汉\史论\王充 论衡.TXT
EMC54	...碎，不足怪也；仆头碎首，力不能自将也。有扣头而死者，未有使头[破]首碎者也。此时或扣头荐百里奚，	【文件名:\05东汉\史论\王充 论衡.TXT
EMC55	...□者，竹木之类也。夫竹生於山，木长於林，未知所入。截竹为筒，[破]以为牒，加笔墨之迹，乃成文字，	【文件名:\05东汉\史论\王充 论衡.TXT
EMC56	...括口喉之中，动摇其舌，张歙其口，故能成言。譬犹吹箫笙，箫笙折[破]，气越不括，手无所弄，则不成音	【文件名:\05东汉\史论\王充 论衡.TXT
EMC57	...尺一寸，四十五弦。黄帝书"泰帝使素女鼓瑟而悲，帝禁不止，故[破]其瑟为二十五弦。"春秋，师旷为晋平	【文件名:\05东汉\史论\风俗通义.TXT
EMC58	楚王佩□而逐菟，为走而[破]其□也。因佩两□以为之豫。两□相触，[破]乃逾疾，乱国之治，有似于此。	【文件名:\04西汉\刘安 淮南子.TXT
EMC59	...高者木修，广其地而薄其德。譬犹陶人为器也。□□其土而不益厚，[破]乃愈疾。圣人不先风吹，不先雷毁，	【文件名:\04西汉\刘安 淮南子.TXT
EMC60	...从横兮，扬波怒而澎湃。正（一作"云"）惟布而雷动兮，相击冲而[破]碎，或窈窕而四塞兮，诚若雨而不坠	【文件名:\05东汉\全汉文.txt
EMC61	人君不行仁恩，[破]胎伤孕，春杀无辜，则岁星失度。（《御览》五）	【文件名:\05东汉\全汉文.txt
EMC62	...经之训所不解。尝闻先代轩之使，奏籍之书，皆藏於周秦之室。及其[破]也，遗弃无见之者，独蜀人有严君	【文件名:\05东汉\全汉文.txt

① Since the dataset in this study contains more than 18,000 concordance lines, we only put some data here to give an impression on how our dataset looks like.

APPENDIX 4

R code for MCA

```
install.packages(c("FactoMineR", "factoextra"))
library("FactoMineR")
library("factoextra")
library(ca)
setwd ("E:/Phd/KULeuven/Speelman/mcl")
breakcut <- read.csv("breaktest000.csv", sep="", row.names = 1)
data(breakcut)
head(breakcut[, 1:7], 3)
breakcut.active <- breakcut[1:3626, 1:4]
head(breakcut.active[,1:6])
MCA(breakcut.active, ncp = 5, graph = TRUE)
res.mca <- MCA(breakcut.active, graph = FALSE)
print(res.mca)
get_eigenvalue(res.mca)
fviz_eig(res.mca)
get_mca_ind(res.mca)
get_mca_var(res.mca)
fviz_mca_ind(res.mca)
fviz_mca_var(res.mca)
fviz_mca_biplot(res.mca,col.ind="grey",col.var="black")
library("factoextra")
```

```
eig.val <- get_eigenvalue(res.mca)
fviz_screeplot(res.mca, addlabels = TRUE, ylim = c(0, 45))
fviz_mca_biplot(res.mca,
        repel = TRUE, # Avoid text overlapping (slow if many point)
        ggtheme = theme_minimal())
var <- get_mca_var(res.mca)
var
fviz_mca_var(res.mca, choice = "mca.cor",
        repel = TRUE, # Avoid text overlapping (slow)
        ggtheme = theme_minimal())
fviz_mca_var(res.mca,
        repel = TRUE, # Avoid text overlapping (slow)
        ggtheme = theme_minimal())
fviz_mca_var(res.mca, col.var="black", shape.var = 15,
        repel = TRUE)
fviz_mca_var(res.mca, col.var = "cos2",
        gradient.cols = c("#00AFBB", "#E7B800", "#FC4E07"),
        repel = TRUE, # Avoid text overlapping
        ggtheme = theme_minimal())
fviz_mca_var(res.mca, col.var = "cos2",
        gradient.cols = c("#00AFBB", "#E7B800", "#FC4E07"),
        repel = TRUE, # Avoid text overlapping
        ggtheme = theme_minimal())
keynote<- as.factor(breakcut$ct)
keynote
head(keynote)
fviz_mca_ind(res.mca, habillage = keynote, addEllipses = TRUE)
fviz_mca_ind(res.mca, label="none", habillage = keynote,
        addEllipses = TRUE, ellipse.level = 0.05)
fviz_mca_biplot(res.mca, axe=c(1,2),
        habillage = keynote, addEllipses = TRUE,
```

```
        label = "var", shape.var = 15,ellipse.level=0.95,col.var="black") +
scale_color_brewer(palette="Dark2")+
theme_minimal()
data2<- mjca(breakcut.active)  # ajusted mca for a higher proportion
```

APPENDIX 5

R code for Ctree

```
setwd ("E:/Phd/KULeuven/Speelman/mcl")
library(mclm)
install.packages(c("lmerTest", "car", "effects", "party"))
library(lmerTest)  # for summary(glmer()) with p-values
library(car)       # for Anova()
library(effects)   # for plot(allEffects())
library(party)     # for ctree()
cd <- read_conc("PO2ctree.csv")
str(cd)
cd            # example kwic lines and list of columns
print_kwic(cd) # see ?print_kwic for more details
cd_ctree <- ctree(semantic_type ~ material_composition + spatial_
configuration + functional_change +
            degree_of_effect + transitivity + text_type + chronological_
time,
            data = cd, control=ctree_control(maxdepth=4))
plot(cd_ctree)
```

APPENDIX 6

R code for random forest

```
Library (Rling)
library (party)
cd <- read_conc("PO1lmctree.csv")
setwd ("E:/Phd/KULeuven/Speelman/mcl")
library(mclm)
install.packages(c("lmerTest", "car", "effects", "party"))
library(lmerTest)  # for summary(glmer()) with p-values
library(car)      # for Anova()
library(effects)   # for plot(allEffects())
library(party)    # for ctree()
cd <- read_conc("pomaterialmeaningctree.csv")
set.seed(129)
mhc.ctree <- ctree(CT~ Usage + FC + MC + ES + SC + TT,
           data = cd,control=ctree_control(maxdepth=4))
plot(mhc.ctree)
set.seed(35)
mhc.rf <- cforest(CT ~ FC + MC + ES + SC,
           data = cd, controls = cforest_unbiased(ntree = 1000, mtry = 2))
mhc.varimp <- varimp(mhc.rf, conditional = TRUE)
round(mhc.varimp, 3)
dotchart(sort(mhc.varimp), main = "Conditional importance of variables")
```

ACKNOWLEDGEMENTS

In retrospect of my three-year doctoral training and my one-year dissertation writing, I would like to express my thanks, gratitude and appreciation to my supervisor, teachers, committee members, group members and family members. Without their help, encouragement, tolerance and consolation, I cannot bring this dissertation into shape so smooth and steady.

I first owe a special debt of gratitude to my supervisor Professor Li (prefers to be called Thomas), for his strictness and rigorousness, for his assistance and encouragement, and for his patience and tolerance. As my MA and PhD supervisor, Thomas trained me as a doctoral student the very first day I started my MA study. He advised me to read classic works and journal articles when I had no idea what cognitive linguistics is. He advises me to always follow the deadline and exhorts me to think innovatively and behave internationally.

My appreciation also goes to teachers at Beihang University for their academic insight in class, particularly to Professor Wei and Professor Lin. Professor Wei led me into the field of corpus linguistics and made me realize the importance of citing linguistic facts as evidence. Professor Lin opened my mind in the great work of Wittgenstein and taught me how to think as rigorous as a philosopher.

I would also like to thank my proposal defending committee, including Professor Wei Naixing, Professor Lin Yunqing, Professor Sun Ya, Professor Ren Wei, and Professor Yuan Ye, who provided insightful questions, comments, criticisms and suggestions.

My thanks also go to my dissertation defending committee, including Professor Shen Jianxuan, Professor Wei Naixing, Professor Lin Yunqing, Professor Wang Yina, late Professor Liu Shisheng and Professor Gao Mingle. They put forward great questions, comments and suggestions. I benefited a lot from their strict academic attitude and prudent academic style.

Supported by the CSC scholarship and Beihang short-term visiting scholarship, I have been fortunate to further my doctoral study at Leuven University and University of New Mexico where I learned a lot from Professor Dirk Geeraerts, Professor Sherman Wilcox and Professor William Croft. Professor Geeraerts instructed me on how to code data closely and thoroughly and told me to understand every line of my data as if they are my family. Professor Wilcox initiated my understanding of how to write and publish English papers. Professor Croft generously shared with me his work on multidimensional scaling and guided me to practice his method with my data.

Thanks also go to my group members at Beihang University. They offered me great assistance all through my proposal defense and dissertation defense. I learned a lot from their discussion during our Reading Club in the past seven years. They are Longbo Ren, Yu Deng, Yu Shen, Lin Yu, Zhiyong Hu, Hongxia Jia, Jinmei Li, Mengmin Xu, Yiyun Liao, Chenxi Niu, Junjie Jin, Na Liu, Cuiying Zhang, Shu Qi, Ning Guo, Shan Zuo, Guannan Zhao, Junjie Lu, Wenjing Du, Siqing Ma, Mengxue Duan and Wei Guo etc. Appreciation is also due to my friends Weiwei Zhang, Tianyu Li, Sai Ma, Qingnan Meng, Danqing Huang, Shuang Li, Lin Li, Song Yu, Yingying, Weidong, Lijie Si and Huiwen Chang who gave me different kinds of help in my writing. Thanks also go to my classmates and friends in my doctoral class, including Yuesen Yang (also my MA classmate), Mengjie Zhang, Guangfa Zhang, Lei Zhang, Qiang Fang, Xiuling Shang, Meng Liu and Ruiqi Luan. Special thanks to Yuesen Yang, who is my mealmate and who celebrates every birthday (both hers and mine) with me all through our doctoral years.

This book is supported by Academic Excellence Scholarship of Beihang

University. I would like to thank Professor Dong Min for her great help in my application for this scholarship.

This book could not be completed without the love and care from my family. My parents are great supporters for my long-term education. They gave me immeasurable love all through my school years. I thank them for their perseverance with all my heart. Special thanks also go to my parents-in-law, who are always proud of having a doctoral daughter-in-law.

Finally, I am immensely grateful to my husband, Sun Hao, for always being there since I was 19, for marrying me when I started my doctoral study in 2016 and for accompanying me until my defending day.